"The chief glory of every
people arises from its Au-
thors."—Dr. Johnson.

THE UNIVERSAL LIBRARY.

LONDON:
INGRAM, COOKE & CO

POETRY.—Vol. I., Part 2.

LA FONTAINE'S FABLES.

THE THIEVES AND THE ASS.

THE

FABLES OF LA FONTAINE.

TRANSLATED FROM THE FRENCH

BY E. WRIGHT.

The Dairy Woman.

LONDON:

INGRAM, COOKE, AND CO. 227, STRAND.

1853.

THE FABLES

OF

LA FONTAINE.

TRANSLATED FROM THE FRENCH,

By ELIZUR WRIGHT, Junr.

INTRODUCTION.

THIS elegant translation of the most famous fabulist of modern times (if we may be allowed to call the seventeenth century *modern*), is the work of an American author, who has admirably succeeded in embodying both the spirit, the grace, and the vivacity of the original in the translation.

As Fables have interested and instructed mankind in every age, and as the Fables of La Fontaine may be said to be the standard collection of modern times, this translation has been considered as a most appropriate addition to the UNIVERSAL LIBRARY.

LONDON, *February,* 1853.

A PREFACE

FABLE, THE FABULISTS, AND LA FONTAINE.

BY THE TRANSLATOR.

HUMAN nature, when fresh from the hand of God, was full of poetry. Its sociality could not be pent within the bounds of the actual. To the lower inhabitants of air, earth, and water,—and even to those elements themselves, in all their parts and forms,—it gave speech and reason. The skies it peopled with beings, on the noblest model of which it could have any conception—to wit, its own. The intercourse of these beings, thus created and endowed,—from the deity kindled into immortality by the imagination, to the clod personified for the moment,—gratified one of its strongest propensities ; for man may well enough be defined as the historical animal. The faculty which, in after ages, was to chronicle the realities developed by time, had at first no employment but to place on record the productions of the imagination. Hence, fable blossomed and ripened in the remotest antiquity. We see it mingling itself with the primeval history of all nations. It is not improbable that many of the narratives which have been preserved for us, by the bark or parchment of the first rude histories, as serious matters of fact, were originally apologues, or parables, invented to give power and wings to moral lessons, and afterwards modified, in their passage from mouth to mouth; by the well-known magic of credulity. The most ancient poets graced their productions with apologues. Hesiod's fable of the Hawk and the Nightingale is an instance. The fable or parable was anciently, as it is even now, a favourite weapon of the most successful orators. When Jotham would show the Shechemites the folly of their ingratitude, he uttered the fable of the Fig-Tree, the Olive, the Vine, and the Bramble. When the prophet Nathan would oblige David to pass a sentence of condemnation upon himself in the matter of Uriah, he brought before him the apologue of the rich man who, having many sheep, took away that of the poor man who had but one. When Joash, the king of Israel, would rebuke the vanity of Amaziah, the king of Judah, he referred him to the fable of the Thistle and the Cedar. Our blessed Saviour, the best of all teachers, was remarkable for his constant use of parables, which are but fables— we speak it with reverence—adapted to the gravity of the subjects on which he discoursed. And, in profane history, we read that Stesichorus put the Himerians on their guard against the tyranny of Phalaris by the fable of the Horse and the Stag. Cyrus, for the instruction of kings, told the story of the fisher obliged to use his nets to take the fish that turned a deaf ear to the sound of his flute. Menenius Agrippa, wishing to bring back the mutinous Roman people from Mount Sacer, ended his harangue with the fable of the Belly and the Members. A Ligurian, in order to dissuade King Comanus from yielding to the Phocians a portion of his territory as the site of Marseilles, introduced into his discourse the story of the bitch that borrowed a kennel in which to bring forth her young, but, when they were sufficiently grown, refused to give it up.

In all these instances, we see that fable was a mere auxiliary of discourse—an implement of the orator. Such, probably, was the origin of the apologues which now form the bulk of the most popular collections. Æsop, who lived about six hundred years before Christ, so far as we can reach the reality of his life, was an orator who wielded the apologue with remarkable skill. From a servile condition, he rose, by the force of his genius, to be the counsellor of kings and states. His wisdom was in demand far and wide, and on the most important occasions. The pithy apologues which fell from his lips, which, like the rules of arithmetic, solved the difficult problems of human conduct constantly presented to him, were remembered when the speeches that contained them were forgotten. He seems to have written nothing himself ; but it was not long before the gems which he scattered began to be gathered up in collections, as a distinct species of literature. The great and good Socrates employed himself, while in prison, in turning the fables of Æsop into verse. Though but a few fragments of his composition have come down to us, he may, perhaps, be regarded as the father of fable, considered as a distinct art. Induced by his example, many Greek poets and philosophers tried their hands in it. Archilocus, Alcæus, Aristotle, Plato, Diodorus, Plutarch, and Lucian, have left us specimens. Collections of fables bearing the name of Æsop became current in the Greek language. It was not, however, till the year 1447, that the large collection which now bears his name was put forth in Greek prose by

L 2

Planudes, a monk of Constantinople. This man turned the life of Æsop itself into a fable; and La Fontaine did it the honour to translate it as a preface to his own collection. Though burdened with insufferable puerilities, it is not without the moral that a rude and deformed exterior may conceal both wit and worth.

The collection of fables in Greek verse by Babrias was exceedingly popular among the Romans. It was the favourite book of the Emperor Julian. Only six of these fables, and a few fragments, remain; but they are sufficient to show that their author possessed all the graces of style which befit the apologue. Some critics place him in the Augustan age; others make him contemporary with Moschus. His work was versified in Latin, at the instance of Seneca; and Quinctilian refers to it as a reading-book for boys. Thus, at all times, these playful fictions have been considered fit lessons for children, as well as for men, who are often but grown-up children. So popular were the fables of Babrias and their Latin translation, during the Roman empire, that the work of Phædrus was hardly noticed. The latter was a freedman of Augustus, and wrote in the reign of Tiberius. His verse stands almost unrivalled for its exquisite elegance and compactness; and posterity has abundantly avenged him for the neglect of contemporaries. La Fontaine is perhaps more indebted to Phædrus than to any other of his predecessors; and, especially in the first six books, his style has much of the same curious condensation. When the seat of the empire was transferred to Byzantium, the Greek language took precedence of the Latin; and the rhetorician Aphtonius wrote forty fables in Greek prose, which became popular. Besides these collections among the Romans, we find apologues scattered through the writings of their best poets and historians, and embalmed in those specimens of their oratory which have come down to us.

The apologues of the Greeks and Romans were brief, pithy, and epigrammatic, and their collections were without any principle of connexion. But, at the same time, though probably unknown to them, the same species of literature was flourishing elsewhere under a somewhat different form. It is made a question, whether Æsop, through the Assyrians, with whom the Phrygians had commercial relations, did not either borrow his art from the Orientals, or lend it to them. This disputed subject must be left to those who have a taste for such inquiries. Certain it is, however, that fable flourished very anciently with the people whose faith embraces the doctrine of metempsychosis. Among the Hindoos, there are two very ancient collections of fables, which differ from those which we have already mentioned, in having a principle of connexion throughout. They are, in fact, extended romances, or dramas, in which all sorts of creatures are introduced as actors, and in which there is a development of sentiment and passion as well as of moral truth, the whole being wrought into a system of morals particularly adapted to the use of those called to govern. One of these works is called the *Pantcha Tantra*, which signifies "Five Books," or Pentateuch. It is written in prose. The other is called the *Hitopadesa*, or "Friendly Instruction," and is written in verse. Both are in the ancient Sanscrit language,

and bear the name of a Brahmin, Vishnoo Sarmah, as the author. Sir William Jones, who is inclined to make this author the true Æsop of the world, and to doubt the existence of the Phrygian, gives him the preference to all other fabulists, both in regard to matter and manner. He has left a prose translation of the *Hitopadesa*, which, though it may not fully sustain his enthusiastic preference, shows it not to be entirely groundless. We give a sample of it, and select a fable which La Fontaine has served up as the twenty-seventh of his eighth book. It should be understood that the fable, with the moral reflections which accompany it, is taken from the speech of one animal to another.

"Frugality should ever be practised, but not excessive parsimony; for see how a miser was killed by a bow drawn by himself!"

"How was that?" said Hiranyaca.

"In the county of Calyanacataca," said Menthara, "lived a mighty hunter, named Bhairaza, or Terrible. One day he went, in search of game, into a forest on the mountains Vindhya; when, having slain a fawn, and taken it up, he perceived a boar of tremendous size; he therefore threw the fawn on the ground, and wounded the boar with an arrow; the beast, horribly roaring, rushed upon him, and wounded him desperately, so that he fell, like a tree stricken with an axe.

*   *   *   *   *

"In the meanwhile, a jackal, named Lougery, was roving in search of food; and, having perceived the fawn, the hunter, and the boar, all three dead, he said to himself, 'What a noble provision is here made for me!'

"As the pains of men assail them unexpectedly, so their pleasures come in the same manner; a divine power strongly operates in both.

"'Be it so; the flesh of these three animals will sustain me a whole month, or longer.

"'A man suffices for one month; a fawn and a boar, for two; a snake, for a whole day; and then I will devour the bowstring.' When the first impulse of his hunger was allayed, he said, 'This flesh is not yet tender; let me taste the twisted string, with which the horns of this bow are joined.' So saying, he began to gnaw it; but, in the instant when he had cut the string, the severed bow leaped forcibly up, and wou··· him in the breast, so that he departed in the agonie.. death. This I meant, when I cited the verse, Frugality should ever be practised, &c."

*   *   *   *   *

"What thou givest to distinguished men, and what thou eatest every day—that, in my opinion, is thine own wealth: whose is the remainder which thou hoardest?"

Works of Sir William Jones, vol. vi. p. 36.

It was one of these books which Chosroës, the king of Persia, caused to be translated from the Sanscrit into the ancient language of his country, in the sixth century of the Christian era, sending an embassy into Hindostan expressly for that purpose. Of the Persian book a translation was made, in the time of the Calif Mansour, in the eighth century, into Arabic. This Arabic translation it is which became famous under the title of "The Book of Calila and Dimna, or the Fable·· 'Bidpaï.'" Calila and Dimna are the names of two ···· ···· their figure in the history, and Bidpaï is ··· ·· ··· principal human interlocutors, who ··· ·· ·· mistaken for the author. This remar···· ·· book was turned into verse by several of the Arabic poets, was translated into Greek, Hebrew, La·· ·, modern Persian, and, in the course ·f ·· few centuries, either directly or indirectly, into most of the languages of modern Europe.

Forty-one of the unadorned and disconnected fables of Æsop were also translated into Arabic at a period somewhat more recent than the Hegira, and passed by the name of the "Fables of Lokman." Their want of poetical ornament prevented them from acquiring much popularity with the Arabians; but they became well known in Europe, as furnishing a convenient text-book in the study of Arabic.

The *Hitopadesa*, the fountain of poetic fables, with its innumerable translations and modifications, seems to have had the greatest charms for the Orientals. As it passed down the stream of time, version after version, the ornament and machinery outgrew the moral instruction, till it gave birth, at last, to such works of mere amusement as the "Thousand and One Nights."

Fable slept, with other things, in the dark ages of Europe. Abridgments took the place of the large collections, and probably occasioned the entire loss of some of them. As literature revived, fable was resuscitated. The crusades had brought European mind in contact with the Indian works which we have already described, in their Arabic dress. Translations and imitations in the European tongues were speedily multiplied. The " Romance of the Fox," the work of Perrot de Saint Cloud, one of the most successful of these imitations, dates back to the thirteenth century. It found its way into most of the northern languages, and became a household book. It undoubtedly had great influence over the taste of succeeding ages, shedding upon the severe and satirical wit of the Greek and Roman literature the rich, mellow light of Asiatic poetry. The poets of that age were not confined, however, to fables from the Hindoo source. Marie de France, also, in the thirteenth century, versified one hundred of the fables of Æsop, translating from an English collection, which does not now appear to be extant. Her work is entitled the *Ysopet*, or " Little Æsop." Other versions, with the same title, were subsequently wr¹ᵗten. It was in 1447 that Planudes, already refe. ⬛o, wrote in Greek prose a collection of fables, prefacing it with a life of Æsop, which, for a long time, passed for the veritable work of that ancient. In the next century, Abstemius wrote two hundred fables in Latin prose, partly of modern, but chiefly of ancient invention. At this time, the vulgar languages had undergone so great changes, that works in them of two or three centuries old could not be understood, and, consequently, the Latin became the favourite language of authors. Many collections of fables were written in it, both in prose and verse. By the art of printing, these works were greatly multiplied; and again the poets undertook the task of translating them into the language of the people. The French led the way in this species of literature, their language seeming to present some great advantages for it. One hundred years before La Fontaine, Corrozet, Guillaume Gueroult, and Philibert Hegemon, had written beautiful fables in verse, which it is supposed La Fontaine must have read and profited by, although they have become nearly obsolete in his time. It is a remarkable fact, that these poetical fables should so soon have been forgotten. It was soon after their appearance that the lan-

guages of Europe attained their full development; and, at this epoch, prose seems to have been universally preferred to poetry. So strong was this preference, that Ogilby, the Scotch fabulist, who had written a collection of fables in English verse, reduced them to prose on the occasion of publishing a more splendid edition in 1668. It seems to have been the settled opinion of the critics of that age, as it has, indeed, been stoutly maintained since, that the ornaments of poetry only impair the force of the fable—that the Muses, by becoming the handmaids of old Æsop, part with their own dignity without conferring any on him. La Fontaine has made such an opinion almost heretical. In his manner there is a perfect originality, and an immortality every way equal to that of the matter which he gathered up from all parts of the great storehouse of human experience. His fables are like pure gold enveloped in solid rock-crystal. In English, a few of the fables of Gay, of Moore, and of Cowper, may be compared with them in some respects, but we have nothing resembling them as a whole. Gay, who has done more than any other, though he has displayed great power of invention, and has given his verse a flow worthy of his master, Pope, has yet fallen far behind La Fontaine in the general management of his materials. His fables are all beautiful poems, but few of them are beautiful fables. His animal speakers do not sufficiently preserve their animal characters. It is quite otherwise with La Fontaine. His beasts are made most nicely to observe all the proprieties not only of the scene in which they are called to speak, but of the great drama into which they are from time to time introduced. His work constitutes an harmonious whole. To those who read it in the original, it is one of the few which never cloy the appetite. As in the poetry of Burns, you are apt to think the last verse you read of him the best.

But the main object of this Preface was to give a few traces of the life and literary career of our poet. A remarkable poet cannot but have been a remarkable man. Suppose we take a man with native benevolence amounting almost to folly; but little cunning, caution, or veneration; good perceptive, but better reflective faculties; and a dominant love of the beautiful;—and toss him into the focus of civilisation in the age of Louis XIV. It is an interesting problem to find out what will become of him. Such is the problem worked out in the life of JEAN DE LA FONTAINE, born on the eighth of July, 1621, at Château-Thierry. His father, a man of some substance and station, committed two blunders in disposing of his son. First, he encouraged him to seek an education for ecclesiastical life, which was evidently unsuited to his dispositions. Second, he brought about his marriage with a woman who was unfitted to secure his affections, or to manage his domestic affairs. In one other point, he was not so much mistaken : he laboured unremittingly to make his son a poet. Jean was a backward boy, and showed not the least spark of poetical genius till his twenty-second year. His poetical faculties did not ripen till long after that time. But his father lived to see him all, and more than all, that he had ever hoped.

But we will first, in few words, despatch the worst—for there is a very bad part—of his life. It was not specially *his* life; it was the life of the age in which he lived. The man of strong amorous propensities, in that age and country, who was, nevertheless, faithful to vows of either marriage or celibacy,—the latter vows then proved sadly dangerous to the former,—may be regarded as a miracle. La Fontaine, without any agency of his own affections, found himself married at the age of twenty-six, while yet as immature as most men are at sixteen. The upshot is, that his patrimony dwindled; and, though he lived many years with his wife, and had a son, he neglected her more and more, till at last he forgot that he had been married, though he unfortunately did not forget that there were other women in the world besides his wife. His genius and benevolence gained him friends everywhere with both sexes, who never suffered him to want, and who had never cause to complain of his ingratitude. But he was always the special-favourite of the Aspasias who ruled France and her kings. To please them, he wrote a great deal of fine poetry, much of which deserves to be ever-lastingly forgotten. It must be said for him, that his vice became conspicuous only in the light of one of his virtues. His frankness would never allow concealment. He scandalised his friends Boileau and Racine; still, it is matter of doubt whether they did not excel him rather in prudence than in purity. But, whatever may be said in palliation, it is lamentable to think that a heaven-lighted genius should have been made in any way to minister to a hell-envenomed vice, which has caused unutterable woes to France and the world. Some time before he died, he repented bitterly of this part of his course, and laboured, no doubt sincerely, to repair the mischiefs he had done.

As we have already said, Jean was a backward boy. But, under a dull exterior, the mental machinery was working splendidly within. He lacked all that outside care and prudence,—that constant looking out for breakers,—which obstruct the growth and ripening of the reflective faculties. The vulgar, by a queer mistake, call a man *absent-minded*, when his mind shuts the door, pulls in the latch-string, and is wholly at home. La Fontaine's mind was exceedingly domestic. It was nowhere but at home when, riding from Paris to Château-Thierry, a bundle of papers fell from his saddle-bow without his perceiving it. The mail-carrier, coming behind him, picked it up, and overtaking La Fontaine, asked him if he had lost anything. "Certainly not," he replied, looking about him with great surprise. "Well, I have just picked up these papers," rejoined the other. "Ah! they are mine," cried La Fontaine; "they involve my whole estate." And he eagerly reached to take them. On another occasion he was equally at home. Stopping on a journey, he ordered dinner at an hotel, and then took a ramble about the town. On his return, he entered another hotel, and, passing through into the garden, took from his pocket a copy of Livy, in which he quietly set himself to read till his dinner should be ready. The book made him forget his appetite, till a servant informed him of his mistake, and he returned to his hotel just in time to pay his bill and proceed on his journey.

It will be perceived that he took the world quietly, and his doing so undoubtedly had important bearings on the style in which he wrote. But we will give another anecdote, which is still more characteristic of his peculiar mental structure. Not long after his marriage, with all his indifference to his wife, he was persuaded into a fit of singular jealousy. He was intimate with an ex-captain of dragoons, by the name of Poignant, who had retired to Château-Thierry; a frank, open-hearted man, but of extremely little gallantry. Whenever Poignant was not at his inn, he was at La Fontaine's, and consequently with his wife, when he himself was not at home. Some person took it in his head to ask La Fontaine why he suffered these constant visits. "And why," said La Fontaine, "should I not? He is my best friend." "The public think otherwise," was the reply; "they say that he comes for the sake of Madame La Fontaine." "The public is mistaken; but what must I do in the case?" said the poet. "You must demand satisfaction, sword in hand, of one who has dishonoured you." "Very well," said La Fontaine, "I will demand it." The next day he called on Poignant, at four o'clock in the morning, and found him in bed. "Rise," said he, "and come out with me!" His friend asked him what was the matter, and what pressing business had brought him so early in the morning. "I shall let you know," replied La Fontaine, "when we get abroad." Poignant, in great astonishment, rose, followed him out, and asked whither he was leading. "You shall know by and by," replied La Fontaine; and at last, when they had reached a retired place, he said, "My friend, we must fight." Poignant, still more surprised, sought to know in what he had offended him, and moreover, represented to him that they were not on equal terms. "I am a man of war," said he, "while, as for you, you have never drawn a sword." "No matter," said La Fontaine; "the public requires that I should fight you." Poignant, after having resisted in vain, at last drew his sword, and, having easily made himself master of La Fontaine's, demanded the cause of the quarrel. "The public maintains," said La Fontaine, "that you come to my house daily, not for my sake, but my wife's." "Ah! my friend," replied the other, "I should never have suspected that was the cause of your displeasure, and I protest I will never again put a foot within your doors." "On the contrary," replied La Fontaine, seizing him by the hand, "I have satisfied the public, and now you must come to my house, every day, or I will fight you again." The two antagonists returned, and breakfasted together in good-humour.

It was not, as we have said, till his twenty-second year, that La Fontaine showed any taste for poetry. The occasion was this:—An officer, in winter-quarters at Château-Thierry, one day read to him, with great spirit, an ode of Malherbe, beginning thus—

> Que direz-vous, races futures,
> Si quelquefois un vrai discours
> Vous récite les aventures
> De nos abominables jours?

Or, as we might paraphrase it,—

> What will ye say, ye future days,
> If I, for once, in honest rhymes,
> Recount to you the deeds and ways
> Of our abominable times?

La Fontaine listened with mechanical transports

of joy, admiration, and astonishment, as if a man born with a genius for music, but brought up in a desert, had for the first time heard a well-played instrument. He set himself immediately to reading Malherbe, passed his nights in learning his verses by heart, and his days in declaiming them in solitary places. He also read Voiture, and began to write verses in imitation. Happily, at this period, a relative named Pintrel, directed his attention to ancient literature, and advised him to make himself familiar with Horace, Homer, Virgil, Terence, and Quinctilian. He accepted this counsel. M. de Maucroix, another of his friends, who cultivated poetry with success, also contributed to confirm his taste for the ancient models. His great delight, however, was to read Plato and Plutarch, which he did only through translations. The copies which he used are said to bear his manuscript notes on almost every page, and these notes are the maxims which are to be found in his fables. Returning from this study of the ancients, he read the moderns with more discrimination. His favourites, besides Malherbe, were Corneille, Rabelais, and Marot. In Italian, he read Ariosto, Boccaccio, and Machiavel. In 1654, he published his first work, a translation of the *Eunuch* of Terence. It met with no success. But this does not seem at all to have disturbed its author. He cultivated verse-making with as much ardour and good-humour as ever ; and his verses soon began to be admired in the circle of his friends. No man had ever more devoted friends. Verses that have cost thought are not relished without thought. When a genius appears, it takes some little time for the world to educate itself to a knowledge of the fact. By one of his friends, La Fontaine was introduced to Fouquet, the minister of finance, a man of great power, and who rivalled his sovereign in wealth and luxury. It was his pride to be the patron of literary men, and he was pleased to make La Fontaine his poet, settling on him a pension of one thousand francs per annum, on condition that he should produce a piece in verse each quarter,—a condition which was exactly complied with till the fall of the minister.

Fouquet was a most splendid villain, and positively, though perhaps not comparatively, deserved to fall. But it was enough for La Fontaine that Fouquet had done him a kindness. He took the part of the disgraced minister, without counting the cost. His " Elegy to the Nymphs of Vaux" was a shield to the fallen man, and turned popular hatred into sympathy. The good-hearted poet rejoiced exceedingly in its success. *Bon-homme* was the appellation which his friends pleasantly gave him, and by which he became known everywhere ;—and never did a man better deserve it in its best sense. He was good by nature—not by the calculation of consequences. Indeed it does not seem ever to have occurred to him that kindness, gratitude, and truth, could have any other than good consequences. He was truly a Frenchman without guile, and possessed to perfection that comfortable trait,—in which French character is commonly allowed to excel the English,—*good-humour* with the whole world.

La Fontaine was the intimate friend of Molière, Boileau, and Racine. Molière had already established · a reputation ; but the others became known to the world at the same time. Boileau hired a small chamber in the Faubourg Saint Germain, where they all met several times a week; for La Fontaine, at the age of forty-four, had left Château-Thierry, and become a citizen of Paris. Here they discussed all sorts of topics, admitting to their society Chapelle, a man of less genius, but of greater conversational powers, than either of them—a sort of connecting link between them and the world. Four poets, or four men, could hardly have been more unlike. Boileau was blustering, blunt, peremptory, but honest and frank ; Racine, 'of a pleasant and tranquil gaiety, but mischievous and sarcastic ; Molière was naturally considerate, pensive, and melancholy ; La Fontaine was often absent-minded, but sometimes exceedingly jovial, delighting with his sallies, his witty *naïvetés*, and his arch simplicity. These meetings, which no doubt had a great influence upon French literature, La Fontaine, in one of his prefaces, thus describes :—" Four friends, whose acquaintance had begun at the foot of Parnassus, held a sort of society, which I should call an Academy, if their number had been sufficiently great, and if they had had as much regard for the Muses as for pleasure. The first thing which they did was to banish from among them all rules of conversation, and everything which savours of the academic conference. When they met, and had sufficiently discussed their amusements, if chance threw them upon any point of science or belles-lettres, they profited by the occasion ; it was, however, without dwelling too long on the same subject, flitting from one thing to another like the bees that meet divers sorts of flowers on their way. Neither envy, malice, nor cabal, had any voice among them. They adored the works of the ancients, never refused due praise to those of the moderns, spoke modestly of their own, and gave each other sincere counsel, when any one of them—which rarely happened—fell into the malady of the age, and published a book."

The absent-mindedness of our fabulist not unfrequently created much amusement on these occasions, and made him the object of mirthful conspiracies. So keen'y was the game pursued by Boileau and Racine, that the more considerate Molière felt obliged sometimes to expose and rebuke them. Once, after having done so, he privately told a stranger, who was present with them, the wits would have worried themselves in vain ; they could not have obliterated the *bonhomme.*

La Fontaine, as we have said, was an admirer of Rabelais ;—to what a pitch, the following anecdote may show. At one of the meetings at Boileau's were present Racine, Valincourt, and a brother of Boileau's, a doctor of the Sorbonne. The latter took it upon him to set forth the merits of St. Augustin in a pompous eulogium. La Fontaine, plunged in one of his habitual reveries, listened without hearing. At last, rousing himself as if from a profound sleep, to prove that the conversation had not been lost upon him, he asked the doctor, with a very serious air, whether he thought St. Augustin had as much wit as Rabelais. The divine, surprised, looked at him from head to foot, and only replied, " Take care, Monsieur La Fontaine ;—you have put one of your stockings on wrong side outwards"—which was the fact.

It was in 1668 that La Fontaine published his first collection of fables, under the modest title *Fables Choisies, mises en Vers*, in a quarto volume, with figures designed and engraved by Chauveau. It contained six books, and was dedicated to the Dauphin. Many of the fables had already been published in a separate form. The success of this collection was so great, that it was reprinted the same year in a smaller size. Fables had come to be regarded as beneath poetry; La Fontaine established them at once on the top of Parnassus. The ablest poets of his age did not think it beneath them to enter the lists with him; and it is needless to say they came off second best.

One of the fables of the first book is addressed to the Duke de la Rochefoucauld, and was the consequence of a friendship between La Fontaine and the author of the celebrated "Maxims." Connected with the duke was Madame La Fayette, one of the most learned and ingenious women of her age, who consequently became the admirer and friend of the fabulist. To her he wrote verses abundantly, as he did to all who made him the object of their kind regard. Indeed, notwithstanding his avowed indolence, or rather passion for quiet and sleep, his pen was very productive. In 1669, he published "Psyché," a romance in prose and verse, which he dedicated to the Duchess de Bouillon, in gratitude for many kindnesses. The prose is said to be better than the verse; but this can hardly be true in respect to the following lines, in which the poet under the apt name of Polyphile, in a hymn addressed to Pleasure, undoubtedly sketches himself :—

> Volupté, Volupté, qui fus jadis maltresse
>   Du plus bel esprit de la Grèce,
> Ne me dédaigne pas ; viens-t'en loger chez moi :
>   Tu n'y seras pas sans emploi :
> J'aime le jeu, l'amour, les livres, la musique,
> La ville et la campagne, enfin tout ; il n'est rien
>   Qui ne me soit souverain bien,
> Jusqu'au sombre plaisir d'un cœur mélancolique.
> Viens donc . . . .

The characteristic grace and playfulness of this seem to defy translation. To the mere English reader, the sense may be roughly given thus :—

> Delight, Delight, who didst as mistress hold
>   The finest wit of Grecian mould,
>   Disdain not me ; but come,
>   And make my house thy home.
>   Thou shalt not be without employ :
> In play, love, music, books, I joy,
> In town and country ; and, indeed, there's nought,
> E'en to the luxury of sober thought,—
>   The sombre, melancholy mood,—
>   But brings to me the sovereign good.
>   Come, then, &c.

The same Polyphile, in recounting his adventures on a visit to the infernal regions, tells us that he saw, in the hands of the cruel Eumenides,

> ————Les auteurs de maint hymen forcé,
> L'amant chiche, et la dame au cœur intéressé ;
> La troupe des censeurs, peuple à l'Amour rebelle ;
> Ceux enfin dont les vers ont noirci quelque belle.

> ————Artificers of many a loveless match,
> And lovers who but sought the pence to catch ;
> The crew censorious, rebels against Love ;
> And those whose verses soiled the fair above.

To be "rebels against Love" was quite unpardonable with La Fontaine ; and to bring about a "*hymen forcé*" was a crime, of which he probably spoke with some personal feeling. The great popularity of "Psyché" encouraged the author to publish two volumes of poems and tales in 1671, in which were contained several new fables. The celebrated Madame de Sévigné thus speaks of these fables, in one of her letters to her daughter :— "But have you not admired the beauty of the five or six fables of La Fontaine, contained in one of the volumes which I sent you ? We were charmed with them the other day at M. de la Rochefoucauld's : we got by heart that of the Monkey and the Cat." Then, quoting some lines, she adds,— "This is painting ! And the Pumpkin—and the Nightingale—they are worthy of the first volume !" It was in his Stories that La Fontaine excelled ; and Madame de Sévigné expresses a wish to invent a fable which would impress upon him the folly of leaving his peculiar province. He seemed himself not insensible where his strength lay, and seldom ventured upon any other ground, except at the instance of his friends. With all his lightness, he felt a deep veneration for religion—the most spiritual and rigid which came within the circle of his immediate acquaintance. He admired Jansenius and the Port Royalists, and heartily loved Racine, who was of their faith. Count Henri-Louis de Loménie, of Brienne,—who, after being secretary of state, had retired to the Oratoire, —was engaged in bringing out a better collection of Christian lyrics. To this work he pressed La Fontaine, whom he called his particular friend, to lend his name and contributions. Thus the author of "Psyché," "Adonis," and "Joconde," was led to the composition of pious hymns, and versifications of the Psalms of David. Gifted by nature with the utmost frankness of disposition, he sympathised fully with Arnauld and Pascal in the war against the Jesuits ; and it would seem, from his *Ballade sur Escobar*, that he had read and relished the "Provincial Letters." This ballad, as it may be a curiosity to many, shall be given entire :—

Ballade

SUR ESCOBAR.

> C'est à bon droit que l'on condamne à Rome
> L'évêque d'Ypré.* auteur de vains débats;
> Ses sectateurs nous défendent en somme
> Tous les plaisirs que l'on goûte ici-bas.
> En paradis allant au petit pas,
> On y parvient, quoi qu'ARNAULD nous en die :
> La volupté sans cause il a bannie,
>   Veut-on monter sur les célestes tours,,
> Chemin pierreux est grande rêverie,
>   ESCOBAR sait un chemin de velours.

> Il ne dit pas qu'on peut tuer un homme
>   Qui sans raison nous tient en altercas
> Pour un fétu ou bien pour une pomme ;
>   Mais qu'on le peut pour quatre ou cinq ducats.
> Même il soutient qu'on peut en certains cas
> Faire un serment plein de supercherie,
> S'abandonner aux douceurs de la vie,
>   S'il est besoin conserver ses amours.
> Ne faut-il pas après cela qu'on crie :
>   ESCOBAR sait un chemin de velours ?

* Corneille Jansenius.

Au nom de Dieu, lisez-moi quelque somme
De ces écrits dont chez lui l'on fait cas.
Qu'est-il besoin qu'à présent je les nomme ?
Il en est tant qu'on ne les connoît pas !
De leurs avis servez-vous pour compas :
N'admettez qu'eux en votre librairie ;
Brûlez ARNAULD avec sa coterie,
  Près d'ESCOBAR ce ne sont qu'esprits lourds.
Je vous le dis : ce n'est point raillerie,
  ESCOBAR sait un chemin de velours.

ENVOI.

Toi, que l'orgueil poussa dans la voirie,
Qui tiens là-bas noire concièrgerie,
Lucifer, chef des infernales cours,
Pour éviter les traits de ta furie,
  ESCOBAR sait un chemin de velours.

Thus does the *Bon-homme* treat the subtle Escobar, the prince and prototype of the moralists of *expediency.* To translate his artless and delicate irony is hardly possible. The writer of this hasty Preface offers the following only as an attempted imitation :—

Ballad

UPON ESCOBAR.

GOOD cause has Rome to reprobate
 The bishop who disputes her so ;
His followers reject and hate
 All pleasures that we taste below.
To heaven an easy pace may go,
Whatever crazy ARNAULD saith,
Who aims at pleasure causeless wrath.
 Seek we the better world afar ?
We're fools to choose the rugged path :
 A velvet road hath ESCOBAR.

Although he does not say you can,
 Should one with you for nothing strive,
Or for a trifle, kill the man—
 You can for ducats four or five.
Indeed, if circumstances drive,
Defraud, or take false oaths you may,
Or to the charms of life give way,
 When Love must needs the door unbar.
Henceforth must not the pilgrim say,
 A velvet road hath ESCOBAR ?

Now, would to God that one would state
 The pith of all his works to me.
What boots it to enumerate ?
 As well attempt to drain the sen !—
Your chart and compass let them be ;
All other books put under ban ;
Burn ARNAULD and his rigid clan—
 They're blockheads if we but compare ;—
It is no joke,—I tell you, man,
 A velvet road hath ESCOBAR.

ADDRESS.

Thou warden of the prison black,
 Who didst on heaven turn thy back,
 The chieftain of th' infernal war !
To shun thy arrows and thy rack,
 A velvet road hath ESCOBAR.

The verses of La Fontaine did more for his reputation than for his purse. His paternal estate wasted away under his carelessness ; for, when the ends of the year refused to meet, he sold a piece of land sufficient to make them do so. His wife, no better qualified to manage worldly gear than himself, probably lived on her family friends, who were able to support her, and who seem to have done so without blaming him. She had lived with him in Paris for some time after that city became his abode ; but, tiring at length of the city life, she had returned to Château-Thierry, and occupied the family mansion. At the earnest expostulation of Boileau and Racine, who wished to make him a better husband, he returned to Château-Thierry himself, in 1666, for the purpose of becoming reconciled to his wife. But his purpose strangely vanished. He called at his own house, learned from the domestic, who did not know him, that Madame La Fontaine was in good health, and passed on to the house of a friend, where he tarried two days, and then returned to Paris without having seen his wife. When his friends inquired of him his success, with some confusion he replied, " I have been to see her, but I did not find her : she was well." Twenty years after that, Racine prevailed on him to visit his patrimonial estate, to take some care of what remained. Racine, not hearing from him, sent to know what he was about, when La Fontaine wrote as follows :—" Poignant, on his return from Paris, told me that you took my silence in very bad part; the worse, because you had been told that I have been incessantly at work since my arrival at Château-Thierry, and that, instead of applying myself to my affairs, I have had nothing in my head but verses. All this is no more than half true : my affairs occupy me as much as they deserve to—that is to say not at all ; but the leisure which they leave me—it is not poetry, but idleness, which makes away with it." On a certain occasion, in the earlier part of his life, when pressed in regard to his improvidence, he gaily produced the following epigram, which has commonly been appended to his fables as "The Epitaph of La Fontaine, written by Himself" :—

JEAN s'en alla comme il étoit venu,
Mangea le fonds avec le revenu,
Tint les trésors chose peu nécessaire.
 Quant à son temps, bien sut le dispenser :
 Deux parts en fit, dont il souloit passer
L'une à dormir, et l'autre à ne rien faire.

This confession, the immortality of which was so little foreseen by its author, liberally rendered, amounts to the following :—

JOHN went as he came—ate his farm with its fruits,
Held treasure to be but the cause of disputes ;
And, as to his time, be it frankly confessed,
Divided it daily as suited him best,—
Gave a part to his sleep, and to nothing the rest.

It is clear that a man who provided so little for himself needed good friends to do it ; and Heaven kindly furnished them. When his affairs began to be straitened, he was invited by the celebrated Madame de la Sablière to make her house his home; and there, in fact, he was thoroughly domiciliated for twenty years. " I have sent away all my domestics," said that lady, one day ; " I have kept only my dog, my cat, and La Fontaine." She was, perhaps, the best-educated woman in France, was the mistress of several languages, knew Horace and Virgil by heart, and had been thoroughly indoctrinated in all the sciences by the ablest masters. Her husband, M. Rambouillet de la Sablière, was secretary to the king, and register of domains, and to immense wealth united considerable poetical talents, with a thorough knowledge of the world. It was the will of Madame de la Sablière, that her favourite poet should have no further care for his external wants; and never was a mortal more perfectly resigned. He did all honour to the sincerity of his amiable hostess; and, if he ever showed a want of independence, he certainly did not of gratitude. Compliments of more touching tenderness we nowhere meet than those which La Fontaine has paid to his benefactress. He published nothing which was not first submitted to her eye, and entered into her affairs and friendships with all her heart. Her unbounded confidence in his integrity she expressed by saying, " La Fontaine never lies in prose." By her death, in 1693, our fabulist was left without a home; but his many friends vied with each other which should next furnish one. He was then seventy-two years of age, had turned his attention to personal religion, and received the seal of conversion at the hands of the Roman Catholic church. In his conversion, as in the rest of his life, his frankness left no room to doubt his sincerity. The writings which had justly given offence to the good were made the subject of a public confession, and everything in his power was done to prevent their circulation. The death of one who had done so much for him, and whose last days, devoted with the most self-denying benevolence to the welfare of her species, had taught him a most salutary lesson, could not but be deeply felt. He had just left the house of his deceased benefactress, never again to enter it, when he met M. d'Hervart in the street, who eagerly said to him, " My dear La Fontaine, I was looking for you, to beg you to come and take lodgings in my house." " I was going thither," replied La Fontaine. A reply could not have been more characteristic. The fabulist had not in him sufficient hypocrisy of which to manufacture the commonplace politeness of society. His was the politeness of a warm and unsuspecting heart. He never concealed his confidence, in the fear that it might turn out to be misplaced.

His second collection of fables, containing five books, La Fontaine published in 1678-9, with a dedication to Madame de Montespan ; the previous six books were republished at the same time, revised and enlarged. The twelfth book was not added till many years after, and proved, in fact, the song of the dying swan. It was written for the special use of the young Duke de Bourgogne, the royal pupil of Fénélon, to whom it contains frequent allusions. The eleven books now published sealed the reputation of La Fontaine, and were received with distinguished regard by the king, who appended to the ordinary protocol or imprimatur for publication the following reasons : " In order to testify to the author the esteem we have for his person and his merit, and because youth have received great advantage in their education from the fables selected and put in verse, which he has heretofore published." The author was, moreover, permitted to present his book in person to the sovereign. For this purpose he repaired to Versailles, and after having well delivered himself of his compliment to royalty,

perceived that he had forgotten to bring the book which he was to present ; he was, nevertheless, favourably received, and loaded with presents. But it is added, that, on his return, he also lost, by his absence of mind, the purse full of gold which the king had given him, which was happily found under a cushion of the carriage in which he rode.

In his advertisement to the second part of his Fables, La Fontaine informs the reader that he had treated his subjects in a somewhat different style. In fact, in his first collection, he had timidly confined himself to the brevity of Æsop and Phædrus ; but, having observed that those fables were most popular in which he had given most scope to his own genius, he threw off the trammels in the second collection, and, in the opinion of the writer, much for the better. His subjects, too, in the second part, are frequently derived from the Indian fabulists, and bring with them the richness and dramatic interest of the *Hitopadesa.*

Of all his fables, the Oak and the Reed is said to have been the favourite of La Fontaine. But his critics have almost unanimously given the palm of excellence to the Animals sick of the Plague, the first of the seventh book. Its exquisite poetry, the perfection of its dialogue, and the weight of its moral, well entitle it to the place. That must have been a soul replete with honesty, which could read such a lesson in the ears of a proud and oppressive court. Indeed, we may look in vain through this encyclopædia of fable for a sentiment which goes to justify the strong in their oppression of the weak. Even in the midst of the fulsome compliments which it was the fashion of his age to pay to royalty, La Fontaine maintains a reserve and decency peculiar to himself. By an examination of his fables, we think, we might fairly establish for him the character of an honest and disinterested lover and respecter of his species. In his fable entitled Death and the Dying, he unites the genius of Pascal and Molière ; in that of the Two Doves is a tenderness quite peculiar to himself, and an insight into the heart worthy of Shakspeare. In his Mogul's Dream are sentiments worthy of the very high-priest of nature, and expressed in his own native tongue with a felicity which makes the translator feel that all his labours are but vanity and vexation of spirit. But it is not the purpose of this brief Preface to criticise the Fables. It is sufficient to say, that the work occupies a position in French literature, which, after all has been said that can be for Gay, Moore, and others,—English versifiers of fables,—is left quite vacant in ours.

Our author was elected a member of the French Academy in 1684, and received with the honour of a public session. He read on this occasion a poem of exquisite beauty, addressed to his benefactress, Madame de la Sablière. In that distinguished body of men he was a universal favourite ; and none, perhaps, did more to promote its prime object—the improvement of the French language. We have already seen how he was regarded by some of the greatest minds of his age. Voltaire, who never did more than justice to merit other than his own, said of the Fables, " I hardly know a book which more abounds with charms adapted to the people, and at the same time to persons of refined taste. I believe that, of all authors, La Fontaine is the most universally read. He is for all minds and all ages." La Bruyère, when admitted to the Academy, in 1693, was warmly applauded for his *éloge* upon La Fontaine, which contained the following words :—" More equal than Marot, and more poetical than Voiture, La Fontaine has the playfulness, felicity, and artlessness of both. He instructs while he sports, persuades men to virtue by means of beasts, and exalts trifling subjects to the sublime ; a man unique in his species of composition, always original, whether he invents or translates,—who has gone beyond his models, himself a model hard to imitate."

La Fontaine, as we have said, devoted his latter days to religion. In this he was sustained and cheered by his old friends Racine and De Maucroix. Death overtook him while applying his poetical powers to the hymns of the church. To De Maucroix he wrote, a little before his death,—" I assure you that the best of your friends cannot count upon, more than fifteen days of life. For these two months I have not gone abroad, except occasionally to attend the Academy, for a little amusement. Yesterday, as I was returning from it, in the middle of the Rue du Chantre, I was taken with such a faintness that I really thought myself dying. O, my friend, to die is nothing ; but think you how I am going to appear before God ! You know how I have lived. Before you receive this billet, the gates of eternity will perhaps have been opened upon me ! " To this, a few days after, his friend replied,—" If God, in his kindness, restores you to health, I hope you will come and spend the rest of your life with me, and we shall often talk together of the mercies of God. If, however, you have not strength to write, beg M. Racine to do me that kindness, the greatest he can ever do for me. Adieu, my good, my old, and my true friend. May God, in his infinite goodness, take care of the health of your body, and that of your soul." He died the 13th of April, 1695, at the age of seventy-three, and was buried in the cemetery of the Saints-Innocents.

When Fénélon heard of his death, he wrote a Latin eulogium, which he gave to his royal pupil to translate. " La Fontaine is no more ! " said Fenelon, in this composition ; " he is no more ! and with him have gone the playful jokes, the merry laugh, the artless graces, and the sweet Muses."

FABLES OF LA FONTAINE.

TO MONSEIGNEUR THE DAUPHIN.

I SING the heroes of old Æsop's line,
Whose tale, though false when strictly we define,
Containeth truths it were not ill to teach.
With me all natures use the gift of speech ;
Yea, in my work, the very fishes preach,
And to our human selves their sermons suit.
'Tis thus to come at man I use the brute.

SON OF A PRINCE the favourite of the skies,
On whom the world entire hath fix'd its eyes,
Who hence shall count his conquests by his days,
And gather from the proudest lips his praise,
A louder voice than mine must tell in song
What virtues to thy kingly line belong.
I seek thine ear to gain by lighter themes,
Slight pictures, deck'd in magic nature's beams ;
And if to please thee shall not be my pride,
I'll gain at least the praise of having tried.

BOOK I.

I.—THE GRASSHOPPER AND THE ANT.

A GRASSHOPPER gay
Sang the summer away,
And found herself poor
By the winter's first roar.
Of meat or of bread,
Not a morsel she had !
So a begging she went,
To her neighbour the ant,
For the loan of some wheat,
Which would serve her to eat
Till the season came round.
I will pay you, she saith,
On an animal's faith,
Double weight in the pound
Ere the harvest be bound.
The ant is a friend
(And here she might mend)
Little given to lend.
How spent you the summer ?
Quoth she, looking shame
At the borrowing dame.
Night and day to each comer
I sang, if you please.
You sang ! I'm at ease ;
For 'tis plain at a glance,
Now, ma'am, you must dance.

II.—THE RAVEN AND THE FOX.

PERCH'D on a lofty oak,
Sir Raven held a lunch of cheese ;
Sir Fox, who smelt it in the breeze,
Thus to the holder spoke :—
Ha ! how do you do, Sir Raven ?
Well, your coat, sir, is a brave one !
So black and glossy, on my word, sir,
With voice to match, you were a bird, sir,
Well fit to be the Phœnix of these days.
Sir Raven, overset with praise,
Must snow how musical his croak.
Down fell the luncheon from the oak ;
Which snatching up, Sir Fox thus spoke :—
The flatterer, my good sir,
Aye liveth on his listener ;
Which lesson, if you please,
Is doubtless worth the cheese.
A bit too late, Sir Raven swore
The rogue should never cheat him more

III.—THE FROG THAT WISHED TO BE AS BIG AS THE OX.

THE tenant of a bog,
An envious little frog,
Not bigger than an egg,
A stately bullock spies,
And, smitten with his size,
Attempts to be as big.
With earnestness and pains,
She stretches, swells, and strains,
And says, Sis Frog, look here ! see me !
Is this enough ? No, no.
Well, then, is this ? Poh ! poh !
Enough ! you don't begin to be.
And thus the reptile sits,
Enlarging till she splits.
The world is full of folks
Of just such wisdom ;—
The lordly dome provokes
The cit to build his dome ;
And, really, there is no telling
How much great men set little ones a swelling.

IV.—THE TWO MULES.

Two mules were bearing on their backs,
One, oats ; the other, silver of the tax.
The latter, glorying in his load,
March'd proudly forward on the road ;
And, from the jingle of his bell,
'Twas plain he liked his burden well.
    But in a wild-wood glen
    A band of robber men
Rush'd forth upon the twain.
    Well with the silver pleased,
    They by the bridle seized
The treasure-mule so vain.
Poor mule ! in struggling to repel
His ruthless foes, he fell
Stabb'd through ; and with a bitter sighing,
He cried, Is this the lot they promised me ?
My humble friend from danger free,
While, weltering in my gore, I'm dying ?
    My friend, his fellow-mule replied,
It is not well to have one's work too high.
If thou hadst been a miller's drudge, as I,
    Thou wouldst not thus have died.

V.—THE WOLF AND THE DOG.

A prowling wolf, whose shaggy skin
(So strict the watch of dogs had been)
    Hid little but his bones,
Once met a mastiff dog astray.
A prouder, fatter, sleeker Tray,
    No human mortal owns.
Sir Wolf in famish'd plight,
    Would fain have made a ration
    Upon his fat relation ;
But then he first must fight ;
    And well the dog seem'd able
    To save from wolfish table
His carcass snug and tight.
So, then, in civil conversation
    The wolf express'd his admiration
Of Tray's fine case. Said Tray, politely,
Yourself, good sir, may be as sightly,
    Quit but the woods, advised by me.
    For all your fellows here, I see,
Are shabby wretches, lean and gaunt,
Belike to die of haggard want.
With such a pack, of course it follows,
One fights for every bit he swallows.
    Come, then, with me, and share
    On equal terms our princely fare.
      But what with you
      Has one to do ?
Inquires the wolf. Light work indeed}
Replies the dog ; you only need
    To bark a little now and then,
    To chase off duns and beggar men,
To fawn on friends that come or go forth,
Your master please, and so forth ;
    For which you have to eat
    All sorts of well-cook'd meat—
Cold pullets, pigeons, savoury messes—
Besides unnumber'd fond caresses.
    The wolf, by force of appetite,
    Accepts the terms outright,

Tears glistening in his eyes,
But faring on, he spies
    A gall'd spot on the mastiff's neck.
What's that ? he cries. O, nothing but a speck.
A speck ? Ay, ay ; 'tis not enough to pain me ;
Perhaps the collar's mark by which they chain me.
    Chain ! chain you ! What ! run you not, then,
    Just where you please, and when ?
      Not always, sir ; but what of that ?
      Enough for me, to spoil your fat !
      It ought to be a precious piece
      Which could to servile chains entice ;
    For me, I'll shun them while I've wit.
      So ran Sir Wolf, and runneth yet.

VI.—THE HEIFER, THE GOAT, AND THE SHEEP, IN COMPANY WITH THE LION.

The heifer, the goat, and their sister the sheep,
Compacted their earnings in common to keep,
'Tis said, in time past, with a lion, who sway'd
Full lordship o'er neighbours, of whatever grade.
The goat, as it happen'd, a stag having snared,
Sent off to the rest, that the beast might be shared.
All gather'd ; the lion first counts on his claws,
And says, We'll proceed to divide with our paws
The stag into pieces, as fix'd by our laws.
    This done, he announces part first as his own ;
    'Tis mine, he says, truly, as lion alone.
To such a decision there's nought to be said,
As he who has made it is doubtless the head.
Well, also, the second to me should belong ;
'Tis mine, be it known, by the right of the strong.
Again, as the bravest, the third must be mine.
To touch but the fourth whoso maketh a sign,
    I'll choke him to death
    In the space of a breath !

VII.—THE WALLET.

From heaven, one day, did Jupiter proclaim,
Let all that live before my throne appear,
And there if any one hath aught to blame,
In matter, form, or texture of his frame,
He may bring forth his grievance without fear.
Redress shall instantly be given to each.
Come, monkey, now, first let us have your speech.
    You see these quadrupeds your brothers ;
    Comparing, then, yourself with others,
    Are you well satisfied ? And wherefore not ?
Said Jock. Haven't I four trotters with the rest ?
Is not my visage comely as the best ?
    But this my brother Bruin, is a blot
    On thy creation fair ;
And sooner than be painted I'd be shot,
    Were I, great sire, a bear.
The bear approaching, doth he make complaint ?
Not he ;—himself he lauds without restraint.
The elephant he needs must criticise ;
    To crop his ears and stretch his tail were wise ;
    A creature he of huge, misshapen size.
The elephant though famed as beast judicious,
While on his own account he had no wishes,
Pronounced dame whale too big to suit his taste ;
Of flesh and fat she was a perfect waste.
The little ant, again, pronounced the gnat too wee ;
To such a speck, a vast colossus she.

Each censured by the rest, himself content,
Back to their homes all living things were sent.
Such folly liveth yet with human fools.
For others lynxes, for ourselves but moles,
Great blemishes in other men we spy,
Which in ourselves we pass most kindly by.
As in this world we're but way-farers,
Kind Heaven has made us wallet-bearers.
The pouch behind our own defects must store,
The faults of others lodge in that before.

VIII.—THE SWALLOW AND THE LITTLE BIRDS.

    By voyages in air,
    With constant thought and care,
Much knowledge had a swallow gain'd,
Which she for public use retain'd.
The slightest storms she well foreknew,
And told the sailors ere they blew.
A farmer sowing hemp once having found,
She gather'd all the little birds around,
And said, My friends, the freedom let me take
To prophesy a little, for your sake,
    Against this dangerous seed.
    Though such a bird as I
    Knows how to hide or fly,
    You birds a caution need.
    See you that waving hand?
    It scatters on the land
What well may cause alarm.
    'Twill grow to nets and snares,
    To catch you unawares,
    And work you fatal harm!
    Great multitudes I fear,
    Of you, my birdies dear,
    That falling seed, so little,
    Will bring to cage or kettle!
But though so perilous the plot,
You now may easily defeat it:
All lighting on the seeded spot,
Just scratch up every seed and eat it.
    The little birds took little heed,
    So fed were they with other seed.
    Anon the field was seen
    Bedeck'd in tender green.
The swallow's warning voice was heard again:
My friends, the product of that deadly grain,
    Seize now, and pull it root by root,
    Or surely you'll repent its fruit.
False, babbling prophetess, says one,
You'd set us at some pretty fun!
To pull this field a thousand birds are needed,
While thousands more with hemp are seeded.
    The crop now quite mature,
The swallow adds, Thus far I've fail'd of cure;
    I've prophesied in vain
    Against this fatal grain:
It's grown. And now, my bonny birds,
Though you have disbelieved my words
    Thus far, take heed at last,—
When you shall see the seed time past,
And men, no crops to labour for,
On birds shall wage their cruel war,
    With deadly net and noose;
    Of flying then beware,
    Unless you take the air,
Like woodcock, crane, or goose.
But stop; you're not in plight
For such adventurous flight,

O'er desert waves and sands,
In search of other lands.
Hence, then, to save your precious souls,
    Remaineth but to say,
    'Twill be the safest way
To chuck yourselves in holes.
    Before she had thus far gone,
    The birdlings, tired of hearing,
    And laughing more than fearing,
    Set up a greater jargon
Than did, before the Trojan slaughter,
The Trojans round old Priam's daughter.
    And many a bird, in prison grate,
    Lamented soon a Trojan fate.

'Tis thus we heed no instincts but our own;
Believe no evil till the evil's done.

IX.—THE CITY RAT AND THE COUNTRY RAT.

    A CITY rat, one night,
    Did with a civil stoop
    A country rat invite
    To end a turtle soup.

    Upon a Turkey carpet
    They found the table spread,
    And sure I need not harp it
    How well the fellows fed.

    The entertainment was
    A truly noble one;
    But some unlucky cause
    Disturb'd it when begun.

    It was a slight rat-tat,
    That put their joys to rout;
    Out ran the city rat;
    His guest, too, scamper'd out.

    Our rats but fairly quit,
    The fearful knocking ceased.
    Return we, cried the cit,
    To finish there our feast.

    No, said the rustic rat;
    To-morrow dine with me.
    I'm not offended at
    Your feast so grand and free,—

    For I've no fare resembling;
    But then I eat at leisure,
    And would not swap for pleasure
    So mix'd with fear and trembling.

X.—THE WOLF AND THE LAMB.

    THAT innocence is not a shield,
    A story teaches, not the longest.
    The strongest reasons always yield
    To reasons of the strongest.

    A lamb her thirst was slaking
    Once at a mountain rill.
    A hungry wolf was taking
    His hunt for sheep to kill,
When, spying on the streamlet's brink
This sheep of tender age,
He howl'd in tones of rage,
How dare you roil my drink!

133

Your impudence I shall chastise !
Let not your majesty, the lamb replies,
  Decide in haste or passion !
For sure 'tis difficult to think
    In what respect or fashion
My drinking here could roil your drink,
Since on the stream your majesty now faces
I'm lower down full twenty paces.
    You roil it, said the wolf ; and, more, I know
    You cursed and slander'd me a year ago.
O no ! how could I such a thing have done !
    A lamb that has not seen a year,
    A suckling of its mother dear ?
Your brother then.   But brother I have none.
    Well, well, what's all the same,
    'Twas some one of your name.
Sheep, men, and dogs of every nation,
Are wont to stab my reputation,
      As I have truly heard.
      Without another word,
He made his vengeance good,—
Bore off the lambkin to the wood,
And there without a jury,
Judged, slew, and ate her in his fury.

XI. — THE MAN AND HIS IMAGE.
TO M. THE DUKE DE LA ROCHEFOUCAULD.

A MAN, who had no rivals in the love
    Which to himself he bore,
Esteem'd his own dear beauty far above
    What earth had seen before.
More than contented in his error,
He lived the foe of every mirror.
Officious fate, resolved our lover
From such an illness should recover,
Presented always to his eyes
The mute advisers which the ladies prize ;—
Mirrors in parlours, inns, and shops,—
Mirrors the pocket furniture of fops,—
Mirrors on every lady's zone,
From which his face reflected shone.
What could our dear Narcissus do ?
From haunts of men he now withdrew,
On purpose that his precious shape
From every mirror might escape.
    But in his forest glen alone,
      Apart from human trace,
      A watercourse,
      Of purest source,
While with unconscious gaze
He pierced its waveless face,
    Reflected back his own.
Incensed with mingled rage and fright,
He seeks to shun the odious sight ;
But yet that mirror sheet, so clear and still,
He cannot leave, do what he will.

Ere this, my story's drift you plainly see.
From such mistake there is no mortal free.
    That obstinate self-lover
    The human soul doth cover ;
The mirrors follies are of others,
In which, as all are genuine brothers,
Each soul may see to life depicted
Itself with just such faults afflicted ;
And by that charming placid brook,
Needless to say, I mean your Maxim Book.

XII.—THE DRAGON WITH MANY HEADS, AND THE DRAGON WITH MANY TAILS.

AN envoy of the Porte Sublime,
As history says, once on a time,
Before th' imperial German court
    Did rather boastfully report
The troops commanded by his master's firman,
As being a stronger army than the German :
    To which replied a Dutch attendant,
    Our prince has more than one dependant
Who keeps an army at his own expense.
    The Turk, a man of sense,
    Rejoin'd, I am aware
What power your emperor's servants share.
It brings to mind a tale both strange and true,
A thing which once, myself, I chanced to view.
    I saw come darting through a hedge,
    Which fortified a rocky ledge,
    A hydra's hundred heads ; and in a trice
    My blood was turning into ice.
    But less the harm than terror,—
    The body came no nearer ;
    Nor could unless it had been sunder'd
    To parts at least a hundred.
    While musing deeply on this sight,
    Another dragon came to light,
    Whose single head avails
    To lead a hundred tails :
And, seized with juster fright,
    I saw him pass the hedge,—
    Head, body, tails,—a wedge
Of living and resistless powers.—
The other was your emperor's force ; this ours.

XIII.—THE THIEVES AND THE ASS.

Two thieves, pursuing their profession,
Had of a donkey got possession,
    Whereon a strife arose,
    Which went from words to blows.
The question was to sell, or not to sell ;
But while our sturdy champions fought it well,
    Another thief, who chanced to pass,
    With ready wit rode off the ass.

    This ass is, by interpretation,
    Some province poor, or prostrate nation.
    The thieves are princes this and that,
    On spoils and plunder prone to fat,—
    As those of Austria, Turkey, Hungary.
    (Instead of two, I've quoted three—
    Enough of such commodity.)
    These powers engaged in war all,
    Some fourth thief stops the quarrel,
      According all to one key
      By riding off the donkey.

XIV.—SIMONIDES PRESERVED BY THE GODS

    THREE sorts there are, as Malherbe says,
    Which one can never overpraise—
    The gods, the ladies, and the king ;
    And I, for one, endorse the thing.

The heart, praise tickles and entices ;
Of fair one's smile, it oft the price is.
See how the gods sometimes repay it.
Simonides—the ancients say it—
Once undertook, in poem lyric,
To write a wrestler's panegyric ;
Which ere he had proceeded far in, ·
He found his subject somewhat barren.
No ancestors of great renown,
His sire of some unnoted town,
Himself as little known to fame,
The wrestler's praise was rather tame.
The poet, having made the most of
Whate'er his hero had to boast of,
Digress'd, by choice that was not all luck's,
To Castor and his brother Pollux ;
Whose bright career was subject ample,
For wrestlers, sure, a good example.
Our poet fatten'd on their story,
Gave every fight its place and glory,
   Till of his panegyric words
   These deities had got two thirds.
     All done, the poet's fee
     A talent was to be.
But when he comes his bill to settle,
The wrestler, with a spice of mettle,
Pays down a third, and tells the poet,
The balance they may pay who owe it.
The gods than I are rather debtors
To such a pious man of letters.
But still I shall be greatly pleased
To have your presence at my feast,
Among a knot of guests select,
My kin, and friends I most respect.
More fond of character than coffer,
Simonides accepts the offer.
While at the feast the party sit,
And wine provokes the flow of wit,
It is announced that at the gate
Two men, in haste that cannot wait,
Would see the bard. He leaves the table,
No loss at all to'ts noisy gabble.
The men were Leda's twins, who knew
What to a poet's praise was due,
And, thanking, paid him by foretelling
The downfall of the wrestler's dwelling.
From which ill-fated pile, indeed,
No sooner was the poet freed,
Than, props and pillars failing,
Which held aloft the ceiling
     So splendid o'er them,
     It downward loudly crash'd,
     The plates and flagons dash'd,
       And men who bore them ;
       And, what was worse,
     Full vengeance for the man of verse,
     A timber broke the wrestler's thighs,
     And wounded many otherwise.
The gossip Fame, of course, took care
Abroad to publish this affair.
A miracle ! the public cried, delighted.
No more could god-beloved bard be slighted.
His verse now brought him more than double,
With neither duns, nor care, nor trouble.
   Whoe'er laid claim to noble birth
     Must buy his ancestors a slice,
   Resolved no nobleman on earth
     Should overgo him in the price.
   From which these serious lessons flow :—
   Fail not your praises to bestow

On gods and godlike men. Again,
To sell the product of her pain
Is not degrading to the muse.
Indeed, her art they do abuse,
Who think her wares to use,
And yet a liberal pay refuse.
Whate'er the great confer upon her,
They're honour'd by it while they honour.
Of old, Olympus and Parnassus
In friendship heaved their sky-crown'd masses.

XV.—DEATH AND THE UNFORTUNATE.

A POOR unfortunate, from day to day,
Call'd Death to take him from this world away.
O Death, he said, to me how fair thy form !
Come quick, and end for me life's cruel storm.
Death heard, and, with a ghastly grin,
Knock'd at his door, and enter'd in.
With horror shivering, and affright,
Take out this object from my sight,
   The poor man loudly cried ;
Its dreadful looks I can't abide ;
O stay him, stay him ; let him come no nigher ;
O Death ! O Death ! I pray thee to retire.

     A gentleman of note
   In Rome, Mæcenas, somewhere wrote :—
   Make me the poorest wretch that begs,
   Sore, hungry, crippled, clothed in rags,
   In hopeless impotence of arms and legs ;
     Provided, after all, you give
     The one sweet liberty to live,
   I'll ask of Death no greater favour
   Than just to stay away for ever.

XVI.—DEATH AND THE WOODMAN.

A POOR wood-chopper, with his fagot load,
Whom weight of years, as well as load, oppress'd,
Sore groaning in his smoky hut to rest,
Trudged wearily along his homeward road.
At last his wood upon the ground he throws,
And sits him down to think o'er all his woes.
To joy a stranger, since his hapless birth,
What poorer wretch upon this rolling earth ?
No bread sometimes, and ne'er a moment's rest ;
Wife, children, soldiers, landlords, public tax,
All wait the swinging of his old, worn axe,
And paint the veriest picture of a man unblest.
On Death he calls. Forthwith that monarch grim
Appears, and asks what he should do for him.
Not much, indeed ; a little help I lack
To put these fagots on my back.

   Death ready stands all ills to cure,
     But let us not his cure invite.
   Than die, 'tis better to endure,—
     Is both a manly maxim and a right.

XVII.—THE MAN BETWEEN TWO AGES, AND HIS TWO MISTRESSES.

   A MAN of middle age, whose hair
   'Was bordering on the gray,
   Began to turn his thoughts and care
   The matrimonial way.

By virtue of his ready,
     A store of choices had he
Of ladies bent to suit his taste ;
On which account he made no haste.
To court well was no trifling art.
Two widows chiefly gain'd his heart;
The one yet green, the other more mature,
Who found for nature's wane in art a cure.
These dames, amidst their joking and caressing
     The man they long'd to wed,
Would sometimes set themselves to dressing
     His party-colour'd head.
       Each aiming to assimilate
       Her lover to her own estate,
       The older piecemeal stole
       The black hair from his poll,
       While eke, with fingers light,
       The young one stole the white.
Between them both, as if by scald,
His head was changed from gray to bald.
For these, he said, your gentle pranks,
I owe you, ladies, many thanks.
       By being thus well shaved,
       I less have lost than saved.
     Of Hymen, yet, no news at hand,
       I do assure ye.
     By what I've lost, I understand
       It is in your way,
Not mine, that I must pass on.
Thanks, ladies, for the lesson.

XVIII.—THE FOX AND THE STORK.

OLD Mister Fox was at expense, one day,
     To dine old Mistress Stork.
The fare was light, was nothing, sooth to say,
     Requiring knife and fork.
That sly old gentleman, the dinner-giver,
Was, you must understand, a frugal liver.
     This once, at least, the total matter
     Was thinnish soup served on a platter,
For madam's slender beak a fruitless puzzle
Till all had pass'd the fox's lapping muzzle.
     But little relishing his laughter,
     Old gossip Stork, some few days after,
     Return'd his Foxship's invitation.
     Without a moment's hesitation,
     He said he'd go, for he must own he
     Ne'er stood with friends for ceremony.
       And so, precisely at the hour,
       He hied him to the lady's bower,
     Where, praising her politeness,
     He finds her dinner right nice.
     Its punctuality and plenty,
     Its viands, cut in mouthfuls dainty,
     Its fragrant smell, were powerful to excite,
     Had there been need, his foxish appetite.
     But now the dame, to torture him,
       Such wit was in her,
       Served up her dinner
     In vases made so tall and slim,
     They let their owner's beak pass in and out,
     But not, by any means, the fox's snout !
       All arts without avail,
       With drooping head and tail,
     As ought a fox a fowl had cheated,
     The hungry guest at last retreated.

Ye knaves, for you is this recital,
You'll often meet Dame Stork's requital.

XIX.—THE BOY AND THE SCHOOLMASTER.

       WISE counsel is not always wise,
       As this my tale exemplifies.
A boy, that frolick'd on the banks of Seine,
Fell in, and would have found a watery grave,
Had not that hand that planteth ne'er in vain
A willow planted there, his life to save.
While hanging by its branches as he might,
A certain sage preceptor came in sight ;
To whom the urchin cried, Save, or I'm drown'd.
The master, turning gravely at the sound,
Thought proper for a while to stand aloof,
And give the boy some seasonable reproof.
     You little wretch ! this comes of foolish playing,
     Commands and precepts disobeying.
     A naughty rogue, no doubt, you are,
     Who thus requite your parents' care.
     Alas ! their lot I pity much,
     Whom fate condemns to watch o'er such.
     This having coolly said, and more,
     He pull'd the drowning lad ashore.

This story hits more marks than you suppose.
All critics, pedants, men of endless prose,—
     Three sorts so richly bless'd with progeny,
     The house is bless'd that doth not lodge any,—
May in it see themselves from head to toes.
       No matter what the task,
       Their precious tongues must teach ;
       Their help in need you ask,
       You first must hear them preach.

XX.—THE COCK AND THE PEARL.

       A COCK scratch'd up, one day,
       A pearl of purest ray,
     Which to a jeweller he bore.
     I think it fine, he said,
     But yet a crumb of bread
     To me were worth a great deal more.

       So did a dunce inherit
       A manuscript of merit,
     Which to a publisher he bore.
     'Tis good, said he, I'm told,
     Yet any coin of gold
     To me were worth a great deal more.

XXI.—THE HORNETS AND THE BEES.

THE artist by his work is known.

A piece of honey-comb one day,
Discover'd as a waif and stray,
The hornets treated as their own.
Their title did the bees dispute,
And brought before a wasp the suit.
The judge was puzzled to decide,
For nothing could be testified
Save that around this honey-comb
There had been seen, as if at home,
Some longish, brownish, buzzing creatures,
Much like the bees in wings and features.
But what of that ? for marks the same,
The hornets, too, could truly claim.

Between assertion, and denial,
The wasp, in doubt, proclaim'd new trial ;
And, hearing what an ant-hill swore,
Could see no clearer than before.
What use, I pray, of this expense ?
At last exclaim'd a bee of sense.
We've labour'd months in this affair,
And now are only where we were.
Meanwhile the honey runs to waste :
'Tis time the judge should show some haste.
The parties, sure, have had sufficient bleeding,
Without more fuss of scrawls and pleading.
Let's set ourselves at work, these drones and we,
And then all eyes the truth may plainly see,
Whose art it is that can produce
The magic cells, the nectar juice.
  The hornets, flinching on their part,
  Show that the work transcends their art.
  The wasp at length their title sees,
  And gives the honey to the bees.

  Would God that suits at law with us
  Might all be managed thus !
  That we might, in the Turkish mode,
  Have simple common sense for code !
  They then were short and cheap affairs,
  Instead of stretching on like ditches,
  Ingulfing in their course all riches,—
The parties leaving for their shares,
The shells (and shells there might be moister)
From which the court has suck'd the oyster.

XXII.—THE OAK AND THE REED.

THE oak one day address'd the reed :—
To you ungenerous indeed
Has nature been, my humble friend,
With weakness aye obliged to bend.
The smallest bird that flits in air
Is quite too much for you to bear ;
The slightest wind that wreathes the lake
Your ever-trembling head doth shake.
  The while, my towering form
  Dares with the mountain top
  The solar blaze to stop,
  And wrestle with the storm.
What seems to you the blast of death,
To me is but a zephyr's breath.
Beneath my branches had you grown,
  That spread far round their friendly bower,
Less suffering would your life have known,
  Defended from the tempest's power.
Unhappily you oftenest show
  In open air your slender form,
Along the marshes wet and low,
  That fringe the kingdom of the storm.
  To you declare I must,
  Dame Nature seems unjust.
Then modestly replied the reed :
Your pity, sir, is kind indeed,
But wholly needless for my sake.
The wildest wind that ever blew
Is safe to me compared with you.
I bend, indeed, but never break.
Thus far, I own, the hurricane
Has beat your sturdy back in vain ;
But wait the end. Just at the word,
The tempest's hollow voice was heard.

The North sent forth her fiercest child,
Dark, jagged, pitiless, and wild.
The oak, erect, endured the blow ;
The reed bow'd gracefully and low.
But, gathering up its strength once more,
In greater fury than before,
  The savage blast
  O'erthrew, at last,
That proud, old, sky-encircled head,
Whose feet entwined the empire of the dead !

BOOK II.

I.—AGAINST THE HARD TO SUIT.

WERE I a pet of fair Calliope,
I would devote the gifts conferr'd on me
To dress in verse old Æsop's lies divine ;
For verse, and they, and truth, do well combine.
But, not a favourite on the Muses' hill,
I dare not arrogate the magic skill
To ornament these charming stories.
A bard might brighten up their glories,
No doubt. I try,—what one more wise must do.
Thus much I have accomplish'd hitherto ;—
  By help of my translation,
  The beasts hold conversation
In French, as ne'er they did before.
Indeed, to claim a little more,
The plants and trees, with smiling features,
Are turn'd by me to talking creatures.
Who says that this is not enchanting ?
Ah, say the critics, hear what vaunting
From one whose work, all told, no more is
Than half-a-dozen baby stories.
Would you a theme more credible, my censors,
In graver tone, and style which now and then soars ?
Then list ! For ten long years the men of Troy,
By means that only heroes can employ,
Had held the allied hosts of Greece at bay,—
Their minings, batterings, stormings day by day,
Their hundred battles on the crimson plain,
Their blood of thousand heroes, all in vain,—
When, by Minerva's art, a horse of wood,
Of lofty size before their city stood,
Whose flanks immense the sage Ulysses hold,
Brave Diomed, and Ajax fierce and bold,
Whom, with their myrmidons, the huge machine
Would bear within the fated town unseen,
To wreak upon its very gods their rage—
Unheard-of stratagem, in any age.
Which well its crafty authors did repay . . . .
  Enough, enough, our critic folks will say ;
  Your period excites alarm,
  Lest you should do your lungs some harm ;
  And then your monstrous wooden horse,
  With squadrons in it at their ease,
  Is even harder to endorse
Than Renard cheating Raven of his cheese.
  And, more than that, it fits you ill
  To wield the old heroic quill.
Well, then, a humbler tone, if such your will is :—
Long sigh'd and pined the jealous Amaryllis
For her Alcippus, in the sad belief,
None, save her sheep and dog, would know her grief

Thyrsis, who knows, among the willows slips,
And héars the gentle shepherdess's lips
  Beseech the kind and gentle zephyr
  To bear these accents to her lover . . . . .
      Stop, says my censor:
To laws of rhyme quite irreducible,
That couplet needs again the crucible ;
      Poetic men, sir,
      Must nicely shun the shocks
      Of rhymes unorthodox.
A curse on critics ! hold your tongue !
Know I not how to end my song !
Of time and strength what greater waste
Than my attempt to suit your taste !

      Some men, more nice than wise,
      There's nought that satisfies.

II.—THE COUNCIL HELD BY THE RATS.

      Old Rodilard, a certain cat,
      Such havoc of the rats had made,
      'Twas difficult to find a rat
        With nature's debt unpaid.
      The few that did remain,
        To leave their holes afraid,
      From usual food abstain,
        Not eating half their fill.
      And wonder no one will
That one who made of rats his revel,
With rats pass'd not for cat, but devil.
Now, on a day, this dread rat-eater,
Who had a wife, went out to meet her ;
And while he held his caterwauling,
The unkill'd rats, their chapter calling,
Discuss'd the point, in grave debate,
How they might shun impending fate.
      Their dean, a prudent rat,
Thought best, and better soon than late,
      To bell the fatal cat ;
That, when he took his hunting round,
The rats, well caution'd by the sound,
Might hide in safety under ground;
      Indeed he knew no other means.
        And all the rest
        At once confess'd
      Their minds were with the dean's.
No better plan, they all believed,
Could possibly have been conceived,
No doubt the thing would work right well,
If any one would hang the bell.
      But, one by one, said every rat,
      I'm not so big a fool as that.
The plan, knock'd up in this respect,
The council closed without effect.
And many a council I have seen,
Or reverend chapter with its dean,
      That, thus resolving wisely,
      Fell through like this precisely.

        To argue or refute
          Wise counsellors abound ;
        The man to execute
          Is harder to be found.

III.—THE WOLF ACCUSING THE FOX BEFORE THE MONKEY.

      A wolf, affirming his belief
      That he had suffer'd by a thief,
        Brought up his neighbour fox—
      Of whom it was by all confess'd,
      His character was not the best—
        To fill the prisoner's box.
      As judge between these vermin,
      A monkey graced the ermine ;
      And truly other gifts of Themis
      Did scarcely seem his ;
      For while each party plead his cause,
      Appealing boldly to the laws,
      And much the question vex'd,
      Our monkey sat perplex'd.
        Their words and wrath expended,
        Their strife at length was ended;
        When, by their malice taught,
        The judge this judgment brought :
Your characters, my friends, I long have known,
        As on this trial clearly shown ;
And hence I fine you both—the grounds at large
        To state would little profit—
You wolf, in short, as bringing groundless charge,
        You fox, as guilty of it.

  Come at it right or wrong, the judge opined
  No other than a villain could be fined.

IV.—THE TWO BULLS AND THE FROG.

      Two bulls engaged in shocking battle,
      Both for a certain heifer's sake,
      And lordship over certain cattle ;
      A frog began to groan and quake.
        But what is this to you !
      Inquired another of the croaking crew.
        Why, sister, don't you see,
        The end of this will be,
      That one of these big brutes will yield,
      And then be exiled from the field !
      No more permitted on the grass to feed,
    He'll forage, through our marsh, on rush and reed ;
      And while he eats or chews the cud,
      Will trample on us in the mud.
      Alas ! to think how frogs must suffer
      By means of this proud lady heifer !
    This fear was not without good sense.
    One bull was beat, and much to their expense
    For, quick retreating to their reedy bower,
    He trod on twenty of them in an hour.

      Of little folks it oft has been the fate
      To suffer for the follies of the great.

V.—THE BAT AND THE TWO WEASELS.

      A blundering bat once stuck her head
      Into a wakeful weasel's bed ;
      Whereat the mistress of the house,
        A deadly foe of rats and mice,
        Was making ready in a trice
      To eat the stranger as a mouse.
        What ! do you dare, she said, to creep in
        The very bed I sometimes sleep in,

Now, after all the provocation
I've suffer'd from your thievish nation !
Are you not really a mouse,
That gnawing pest of every house,
Your special aim to do the cheese ill!
Ay, that you are, or I'm no weasel.
I beg your pardon, said the bat ;
My kind is very far from that.
What! I a mouse ! Who told you such a lie?
Why, ma'am, I am a bird ;
And, if you doubt my word,
Just see the wings with which I fly.
Long live the mice that cleave the sky !
These reasons had so fair a show,
The weasel let the creature go.
By some strange fancy led
The same wise blunderhead,
But two or three days later,
Had chosen for her rest
Another weasel's nest,
This last, of birds a special hater.
New peril brought this step absurd:
Without a moment's thought or puzzle,
Dame weasel oped her peaked muzzle
To eat th' intruder as a bird.
Hold ! do not wrong me, cried the bat;
I'm truly no such thing as that.
Your eyesight strange conclusions gathers.
What makes a bird, I pray ? Its feathers.
I'm cousin of the mice and rats.
Great Jupiter confound the cats !
The bat, by such adroit replying,
Twice saved herself from dying.

And many a human stranger
Thus turns his coat in danger ;
And sings, as suits where'er he goes,
God save the king !—or save his foes !

VI.—THE BIRD WOUNDED BY AN ARROW.

A BIRD, with plumèd arrow shot,
In dying case deplored her lot:
Alas ! she cried, the anguish of the thought !
This ruin partly by myself was brought !
Hard-hearted men ! from us to borrow
What wings to us the fatal arrow !
But mock us not, ye cruel race,
For you must often take our place.

The work of half the human brothers
Is making arms against the others.

VII.—THE BITCH AND HER FRIEND.

A BITCH, that felt her time approaching,
And had no place for parturition,
Went to a female friend, and, broaching
Her delicate condition,
Got leave herself to shut
Within the other's hut.
At proper time the lender came
Her little premises to claim.
The bitch crawl'd meekly to the door,
And humbly begg'd a fortnight more.
Her little pups, she said, could hardly walk.
In short, the lender yielded to her talk.

The second term expired, the friend had come
To take possession of her house and home.
The bitch, this time, as if she would have bit her,
Replied, I'm ready, madam, with my litter,
To go when you can turn me out.
Her pups, you see, were fierce and stout.

The creditor, from whom a villain borrows,
Will fewer shillings get again than sorrows.
If you have trusted people of this sort,
You'll have to plead, and dun, and fight ; in short,
If in your house you let one step a foot,
He'll surely step the other in to boot.

VIII.—THE EAGLE AND THE BEETLE.

JOHN RABBIT, by Dame Eagle chased,
Was making for his hole in haste,
When, on his way, he met a beetle's burrow.
I leave you all to think
If such a little chink
Could to a rabbit give protection thorough.
But, since no better could be got,
John Rabbit there was fain to squat.
Of course, in an asylum so absurd,
John felt ere long the talons of the bird.
But first, the beetle, interceding, cried,
Great queen of birds, it cannot be denied,
That, maugre my protection, you can bear
My trembling guest, John Rabbit, through the air.
But do not give me such affront, I pray ;
And since he craves your grace,
In pity of his case,
Grant him his life, or take us both away ;
For he's my gossip, friend, and neighbour.
In vain the beetle's friendly labour ;
The eagle clutch'd her prey without reply,
And as she flapp'd her vasty wings to fly,
Struck down our orator and still'd him ;
The wonder is she hadn't kill'd him.
The beetle soon, of sweet revenge in quest,
Flew to the old, gnarl'd mountain oak
Which proudly bore that haughty eagle's nest.
And while the bird was gone,
Her eggs, her cherish'd eggs, he broke,
Not sparing one.
Returning from her flight, the eagle's cry,
Of rage and bitter anguish, fill'd the sky.
But, by excess of passion blind,
Her enemy she fail'd to find.
Her wrath in vain, that year it was her fate
To live a mourning mother, desolate.
The next, she built a loftier nest ; 'twas vain ;
The beetle found and dash'd her eggs again.
John Rabbit's death was thus revenged anew.
The second mourning for her murder'd brood
Was such, that through the giant mountain wood,
For six long months, the sleepless echo flew.
The bird, once Ganymede, now made
Her prayer to Jupiter for aid ;
And, laying them within his godship's lap,
She thought her eggs now safe from all mishap ;
The god his own could not but make them—
No wretch would venture there to break them.
And no one did. Their enemy, this time,
Upsoaring to a place sublime,
Let fall upon his royal robes some dirt,
Which Jove just shaking, with a sudden flirt,

Threw out the eggs, no one knows whither.
When Jupiter inform'd her how th' event
Occurr'd by purest accident,
The eagle raved; there was no reasoning with her;
She gave out threats of leaving court,
To make the desert her resort,
And other braveries of this sort.
Poor Jupiter in silence heard
The uproar of his favourite bird.
Before his throne the beetle now appear'd,
And by a clear complaint the mystery clear'd.
The god pronounced the eagle in the wrong.
But still, their hatred was so old and strong,
These enemies could not be reconciled ;
And, that the general peace might not be spoil'd,—
The best that he could do,—the god arranged,
That thence the eagle's pairing should be changed,
To come when beetle folks are only found
Conceal'd and dormant under ground.

IX.—THE LION AND THE GNAT.

Go, paltry insect, nature's meanest brat !
Thus said the royal lion to the gnat.
The gnat declared immediate war.
Think you, said he, your royal name
To me worth caring for ?
Think you I tremble at your power or fame !
The ox is bigger far than you ;
Yet him I drive, and all his crew.
This said, as one that did no fear owe,
Himself he blew the battle charge,
Himself both trumpeter and hero.
At first he play'd about at large,
Then on the lion's neck, at leisure, settled,
And there the royal beast full sorely nettled.
With foaming mouth, and flashing eye,
He roars. All creatures hide or fly,—
Such mortal terror at
The work of one poor gnat !
With constant change of his attack,
The snout now stinging, now the back,
And now the chambers of the nose;
The pigmy fly no mercy shows.
The lion's rage was at its height ;
His viewless foe now laugh'd outright,
When on his battle-ground he saw,
That every savage tooth and claw
Had got its proper beauty
By doing bloody duty ;
Himself, the hapless lion, tore his hide,
And lash'd with sounding tail from side to side.
Ah ! bootless blow, and bite, and curse !
He beat the harmless air, and worse ;
For, though so fierce and stout,
By effort wearied out,
He fainted, fell, gave up the quarrel.
The gnat retires with verdant laurel.
Now rings his trumpet clang
As at the charge it rang.
But while his triumph note he blows,
Straight on our valiant conqueror goes
A spider's ambuscade to meet,
And make its web his winding-sheet.

We often have the most to fear
From those we most despise ;
Again, great risks a man may clear,
Who by the smallest dies.

X.—THE ASS LOADED WITH SPONGES, AND THE ASS LOADED WITH SALT.

A MAN, whom I shall call an ass-eteer,
His sceptre like some Roman emperor bearing,
Drove on two coursers of protracted ear,
The one, with sponges laden, briskly faring ;
The other lifting legs
As if he trod on eggs,
With constant need of goading,
And bags of salt for loading.
O'er hill and dale our merry pilgrims pass'd,
Till, coming to a river's ford at last,
They stopp'd quite puzzled on the shore.
Our asseteer had cross'd the stream before ;
So, on the lighter beast astride,
He drives the other, spite of dread,
Which, loath indeed to go ahead,
Into a deep hole turns aside,
And, facing right about,
Where he went in, comes out ;
For duckings two or three
Had power the salt to melt,
So that the creature felt
His burden'd shoulders free.
The sponger, like a sequent sheep,
Pursuing through the water deep,
Into the same hole plunges
Himself, his rider, and the sponges.
All three drank deeply : asseteer and ass
For boon companions of their load might pass ;
Which last became so sore a weight,
The ass fell down,
Belike to drown,
His rider risking equal fate.
A helper came, no matter who.
The moral needs no more ado—
That all can't act alike,—
The point I wish'd to strike.

XI.—THE LION AND THE RAT.

To show to all your kindness, it behoves :
There's none so small but you his aid may need.
I quote two fables for this weighty creed,
Which either of them fully proves.
From underneath the sward
A rat, quite off his guard,
Popp'd out between a lion's paws.
The beast of royal bearing
Show'd what a lion was
The creature's life by sparing—
A kindness well repaid ;
For, little as you would have thought
His majesty would ever need his aid,
It proved full soon
A precious boon.
Forth issuing from his forest glen,
T' explore the haunts of men,
In lion net his majesty was caught,
From which his strength and rage
Served not to disengage.
The rat ran up, with grateful glee,
Gnaw'd off a rope, and set him free.

By time and toil we sever
What strength and rage could never.

XII.—THE DOVE AND THE ANT.

THE same instruction we may get
From another couple, smaller yet.

A dove came to a brook to drink,
When, leaning o'er its crumbling brink,
An ant fell in, and vainly tried,
In this to her an ocean tide,
To reach the land ; whereat the dove,
With every living thing in love,
Was prompt a spire of grass to throw her,
By which the ant regain'd the shore.

A barefoot scamp, both mean and sly,
Soon after chanced this dove to spy ;
And, being arm'd with bow and arrow,
  The hungry codger doubted not
  The bird of Venus, in his pot, ·
Would make a soup before the morrow.
  Just as his deadly bow he drew,
  Our pismire stung his heel.
Roused by the villain's squeal,
The dove took timely hint, and flew
  Far from the rascal's coop ;—
  And with her flew his soup.

XIII.—THE ASTROLOGER WHO STUMBLED INTO A WELL.

To an astrologer who fell
Plump to the bottom of a well,
Poor blockhead ! cried a passer-by,
Not see your feet, and read the sky ?

This upshot of a story will suffice
  To give a useful hint to most ;
For few there are in this our world so wise
As not to trust in star or ghost,
  Or cherish secretly the creed
That men the book of destiny may read.
This book, by Homer and his pupils sung,
What is it, in plain common sense,
But what was chance those ancient folks among,
  And with ourselves, God's providence ?
  Now chance doth bid defiance
  To every thing like science ;
  'Twere wrong, if not,
To call it hazard, fortune, lot—
  Things palpably uncertain.
  But from the purposes divine,
  The deep of infinite design,
Who boasts to lift the curtain ?
Whom but himself doth God allow
To read his bosom thoughts, and how ?
Would he imprint upon the stars sublime
The shrouded secrets of the night of time ?
And all for what ? To exercise the wit
Of those who on astrology have writ ?
To help us shun inevitable ills ?
To poison for us even pleasure's rills ?
  The choicest blessings to destroy,
  Exhausting, ere they come, their joy ? '
Such faith is worse than error—'tis a crime.
The sky-host moves and marks the course of time ;
The sun sheds on our nicely-measured days
The glory of his night-dispelling rays ;

And all from this we can divine
Is, that they need to rise and shine,—
To roll the seasons, ripen fruits,
· And cheer the hearts of men and brutes.
How tallies this revolving universe
With human things, eternally diverse ?
Ye horoscopers, waning quacks,
Please turn on Europe's courts your backs,
  And, taking on your travelling lists
  The bellows-blowing alchemists,
  Budge off together to the land of mists.
But I've digress'd.   Return we now, bethinking
Of our poor star-man, whom we left a drinking.
Besides the folly of his lying trade,
  This man the type may well be made
  Of those who at chimeras stare
  When they should mind the things that are.

XIV.—THE HARE AND THE FROGS.

ONCE in his bed deep mused the hare,
(What else but muse could he do there ?)
And soon by gloom was much afflicted ;—
To gloom the creature's much addicted.
  Alas ! these constitutions nervous,
  He cried, how wretchedly they serve us !
  We timid people, by their action,
  Can't eat nor sleep with satisfaction ;
  We can't enjoy a pleasure single,
  But with some misery it must mingle.
  Myself, for one, am forced by cursed fear
  To sleep with open eye as well as ear.
  Correct yourself, says some adviser.
  Grows fear, by such advice, the wiser ?
  Indeed, I well enough descry
  That men have fear, as well as I.
With such revolving thoughts our hare
Kept watch in soul-consuming care.
A passing shade, or leaflet's quiver
Would give his blood a boiling fever.
  Full soon, his melancholy soul
  Aroused from dreaming doze
  By noise too slight for foes,
  He scuds in haste to reach his hole.
He pass'd a pond ; and from its border bogs,
Plunge after plunge, in leap'd the timid frogs,
  Aha ! I do to them, I see,
  He cried, what others do to me.
  The sight of even me, a hare,
  Sufficeth some, I find, to scare.
  And here, the terror of my tramp
  Hath put to rout, it seems, a camp.
The trembling fools ! they take me for
The very thunderbolt of war !
I see, the coward never skulk'd a foe
That might not scare a coward still below.

XV.—THE COCK AND THE FOX.

UPON a tree there mounted guard
  A veteran cock, adroit and cunning,
  When to the roots a fox up running,
Spoke thus, in tones of kind regard :—
  Our quarrel, brother, 's at an end ;
  Henceforth I hope to live your friend ;
    For peace now reigns
    Throughout the animal domains.

I bear the news :—come down, I pray,
  And give me the embrace fraternal ;
And please, my brother, don't delay.
  So much the tidings do concern all,
That I must spread them far to-day.
Now you and yours can take your walks
Without a fear or thought of hawks.
And should you clash with them or others,
In us you'll find the best of brothers ;—
For which you may, this joyful night,
  Your merry bonfires light.
    But, first, let's seal the bliss
    With one fraternal kiss.
Good friend, the cock replied, upon my word,
A better thing I never heard ;
    And doubly I rejoice
    To hear it from your voice ;
And, really there must be something in it,
For yonder come two greyhounds, which I flatter
Myself are couriers on this very matter.
  They come so fast, they'll be here in a minute.
I'll down, and all of us will seal the blessing
  With general kissing and caressing.
Adieu, said fox ; my errand 's pressing ;
    I'll hurry on my way,
    And we'll rejoice some other day.
So off the fellow scamper'd, quick and light,
To gain the fox-holes of a neighbouring height,
Less happy in his stratagem than flight.
  The cock laugh'd sweetly in his sleeve ;—
  'Tis doubly sweet deceiver to deceive.

——◆——

XVI.—THE RAVEN WISHING TO IMITATE
        THE EAGLE.
——

THE bird of Jove bore off a mutton,
  A raven being witness.
That weaker bird, but equal glutton,
  Not doubting of his fitness
  To do the same with ease,
  And bent his taste to please,
  Took round the flock his sweep,
And mark'd among the sheep,
The one of fairest flesh and size,
A real sheep of sacrifice—
A dainty titbit bestial,
Reserved for mouth celestial.
Our gormand, gloating round,
  Cried, Sheep, I wonder much
  Who could have made you such.
You're far the fattest I have found ;
I'll take you for my eating.
And on the creature bleating
He settled down. Now, sooth to say,
This sheep would weigh
    More than a cheese ;
    And had a fleece
    Much like that matting famous
Which graced the chin of Polyphemus ;
  So fast it clung to every claw,
  It was not easy to withdraw.
The shepherd came, caught, caged, and, to their joy,
Gave croaker to his children for a toy.

Ill plays the pilferer, the bigger thief ;
One's self one ought to know ;—in brief,
Example is a dangerous lure ;
Death strikes the gnat, where flies the wasp secure.

XVII.—THE PEACOCK COMPLAINING TO JUNO.
——

THE peacock to the queen of heaven
  Complain'd in some such words :—
Great goddess, you have given
  To me, the laughing-stock of birds,
A voice which fills, by taste quite just,
    All nature with disgust ;
Whereas that little paltry thing,
  The nightingale, pours from her throat
So sweet and ravishing a note,
She bears alone the honours of the spring.

      In anger Juno heard,
And cried, Shame on you, jealous bird !
Grudge you the nightingale her voice,
Who in the rainbow neck rejoice,
Than costliest silks more richly tinted,
In charms of grace and form unstinted,—
    Who strut in kingly pride,
    Your glorious tail spread wide
With brilliants which in sheen do
Outshine the jeweller's bow window ?
  Is there a bird beneath the blue
    That has more charms than you ?
  No animal in everything can shine.
  By just partition of our gifts divine,
  Each has its full and proper share ;
  Among the birds that cleave the air,
The hawk's a swift, the eagle is a brave one,
For omens serves the hoarse old raven,
The rook 's of coming ills the prophet ;
    And if there 's any discontent,
    I've heard not of it.

  Cease, then, your envious complaint ;
  Or I, instead of making up your lack,
Will take your boasted plumage from your back.

——◆——

XVIII.—THE CAT METAMORPHOSED INTO A
        WOMAN.
——

A BACHELOR caress'd his cat,
A darling, fair, and delicate ;
So deep in love, he thought her mew
The sweetest voice he ever knew.
By prayers, and tears, and magic art,
The man got Fate to take his part ;
And, lo ! one morning at his side
His cat, transform'd, became his bride.
In wedded state our man was seen
The fool in courtship he had been.
No lover e'er was so bewitch'd
    By any maiden's charms
As was this husband, so enrich'd
    By hers within his arms.
He praised her beauties, this and that,
And saw there nothing of the cat.
In short, by passion's aid, he
Thought her a perfect lady.

'Twas night : some carpet-gnawing mice
    Disturb'd the nuptial joys.
      Excited by the noise,
The bride sprang at them in a trice
    The mice were scared and fled.
    The bride, scarce in her bed,

The gnawing heard, and sprang again,—
  And this time not in vain,
For, in this novel form array'd,
Of her the mice were less afraid.
Through life she loved this mousing course,
So great is stubborn nature's force.

In mockery of change, the old
  Will keep their youthful bent.
When once the cloth has got its fold,
  The smelling-pot its scent,
In vain your efforts and your care
To make them other than they are.
To work reform, do what you will,
  Old habit will be habit still.
Nor fork* nor strap can mend its manners,
Nor cudgel-blows beat down its banners.
Secure the doors against the renter,
And through the windows it will enter.

———◆———

XIX.—THE LION AND THE ASS HUNTING.

THE king of animals, with royal grace,
Would celebrate his birthday in the chase.
  'Twas not with bow and arrows
  To slay some wretched sparrows ;
The lion hunts the wild boar of the wood,
The antlered deer and stags, the fat and good.
  This time, the king, t' insure success,
  Took for his aide-de-camp an ass,
  A creature of stentorian voice,
  That felt much honour'd by the choice.
The lion hid him in a proper station,
And order'd him to bray, for his vocation,
  Assured that his tempestuous cry
  The boldest beasts would terrify,
  And cause them from their lairs to fly.
And, sooth, the horrid noise the creature made
Did strike the tenants of the wood with dread ;
  And, as they headlong fled,
All fell within the lion's ambuscade.
  Has not my service glorious
  Made both of us victorious ?
  Cried out the much-elated ass.
Yes, said the lion ; bravely bray'd !
  Had I not known yourself and race,
I should have been myself afraid !
  If he had dared, the donkey
  Had shown himself right spunky
At this retort, though justly made ;
.For who could suffer boasts to pass
So ill-befitting to an ass ?

———◆———

XX.—THE WILL EXPLAINED BY ÆSOP.

IF what old story says of Æsop 's true,
  The oracle of Greece he was,
And more than Areopagus he knew,
  With all its wisdom in the laws.
The following tale gives but a sample
Of what has made his fame so ample.
Three daughters shared a father's purse,
  Of habits totally diverse.
The first, bewitch'd with drinks delicious ;
The next, coquettish and capricious ;
The third, supremely avaricious.

* Naturam expellas furca, tamen usque recurret.—Hor.

The sire, expectant of his fate,
  Bequeathed his whole estate,
  In equal shares, to them,
  And to their mother just the same,—
To her then payable, and not before,
Each daughter should possess her part no more.
The father died. The females three
Were much in haste the will to see.
  They read and read, but still
  Saw not the willer's will.
For could it well be understood
That each of this sweet sisterhood,
When she possess'd her part no more,
Should to her mother pay it o'er ?
'Twas surely not so easy saying
How lack of means would help the paying.
What meant their honour'd father, then ?
Th' affair was brought to legal men,
Who, after turning o'er the case
Some hundred thousand different ways,
  Threw down the learned bonnet,
  Unable to decide upon it ;
  And then advised the heirs,
Without more thought, t' adjust affairs.
As to the widow's share, the counsel say,
We hold it just the daughters each should pay
  One third to her upon demand,
  Should she not choose to have it stand
  Commuted as a life annuity,
Paid from her husband's death, with due congruity.
  The thing thus order'd, the estate
  Is duly cut in portions three.
  And in the first they all agree
  To put the feasting-lodges, plate,
    Luxurious cooling mugs,
    Enormous liquor jugs,
Rich cupboards,—built beneath the trellised vine,—
The stores of ancient, sweet Malvoisian wine,
  The slaves to serve it at a sign ;
In short, whatever, in a great house,
There is of feasting apparatus.
  The second part is made
Of what might help the jilting trade—
  The city house and furniture,
  Exquisite and genteel, be sure,
The eunuchs, milliners, and laces,
The jewels, shawls, and costly dresses.
The third is made of household stuff,
More vulgar, rude, and rough—
Farms, fences, flocks, and fodder—
And men and beasts to turn the sod o'er.
  This done, since it was thought
  To give the parts by lot
  Might suit, or it might not,
Each paid her share of fees dear
And took the part that pleased her.
  'Twas in great Athens town,
  Such judgment gave the gown.
  And there the public voice
Applauded both the judgment and the choice.
  But Æsop well was satisfied
  The learned men had set aside,
  In judging thus the testament,
  The very gist of its intent.
The dead, quoth he, could he but know of it,
Would heap reproaches on such Attic wit.
What ! men who proudly take their place
As sages of the human race,
  Lack they the simple skill
  To settle such a will ?

This said, he undertook himself
  The task of portioning the pelf;
And straightway gave each maid the part
  The least according to her heart—
The prim coquette, the drinking stuff,
  The drinker, then, the farms and cattle;
And on the miser, rude and rough,
  The robes and lace did Æsop settle;
  For thus, he said, an early date
  Would see the sisters alienate
  Their several shares of the estate.
No motive now in maidenhood to tarry,
They all would seek, post haste, to marry;
  And, having each a splendid bait,
  Each soon would find a well-bred mate;
And, leaving thus their father's goods intact,
Would to their mother pay them all, in fact,—
    Which of the testament
    Was plainly the intent.
The people, who had thought a slave an ass,
Much wonder'd how it came to pass
  That one alone should have more sense
  Than all their men of most pretence.

BOOK III.

I.—THE MILLER, HIS SON, AND THE ASS.

TO M. DE MAUCROIX.

BECAUSE the arts are plainly birthright matters,
For fables we to ancient Greece are debtors;
But still this field could not be reap'd so clean
As not to let us, later comers, glean.
The fiction-world hath deserts yet to dare,
And, daily, authors make discoveries there.
I'd fain repeat one which our man of song,
Old Malherbe, told one day to young Racan.
Of Horace they the rivals and the heirs,
Apollo's pets,—my masters, I should say,—
Sole by themselves were met, I'm told, one day,
Confiding each to each their thoughts and cares.
Racan begins :—Pray end my inward strife,
For well you know, my friend, what's what in life,
Who through its varied course, from stage to stage,
Have stored the full experience of age;
What shall I do? 'Tis time I chose profession.
You know my fortune, birth, and disposition.
Ought I to make the country my resort,
Or seek the army, or to rise at court?
There's nought but mixeth bitterness with charms;
War hath its pleasures; hymen, its alarms.
'Twere nothing hard to take my natural bent,—
But I've a world of people to content.
Content a world! old Malherbe cries; who can, sir?
Why, let me tell a story are I answer.

A miller and his son, I've somewhere read,
The first in years, the other but a lad,—
A fine, smart boy, however, I should say,—
To sell their ass went to a fair one day.
In order there to get the highest price,
They needs must keep their donkey fresh and nice;
So, tying fast his feet, they swung him clear,
And bore him hanging like a chandelier.
Alas! poor, simple-minded country fellows!
The first that sees their load, loud laughing, bellows,

What farce is this to split good people's sides!
The most an ass is not the one that rides!
The miller, much enlighten'd by this talk,
Untied his precious beast, and made him walk.
The ass, who liked the other mode of travel,
Bray'd some complaint at trudging on the gravel;
Whereat, not understanding well the beast,
The miller caused his hopeful son to ride,
And walk'd behind, without a spark of pride.
Three merchants pass'd, and, mightily displeased,
The eldest of these gentlemen cried out,
Ho there! dismount, for shame, you lubber lout,
Nor make a foot-boy of your grey-beard sire;
Change places, as the rights of age require.
To please you, sirs, the miller said, I ought.
So down the young and up the old man got.
Three girls next passing, What a shame, says one,
That boy should be obliged on foot to run,
While that old chap, upon his ass astride,
Should play the calf, and like a bishop ride!
Please save your wit, the miller made reply,
Tough veal, my girls, the calf as old as I.
But joke on joke repeated changed his mind;
So up he took, at last, his son behind.
Not thirty yards ahead, another set
Found fault. The biggest fools I ever met,
Says one of them, such burdens to impose.
The ass is faint, and dying with their blows.
Is this, indeed, the mercy which these rustics
Show to their honest, faithful, old domestics!
If to the fair these lazy fellows ride,
'Twill be to sell thereat the donkey's hide!
Zounds! cried the miller, precious little brains
Hath he who takes, to please the world, such pains;
But since we're in, we'll try what can be done.
So off the ass they jump'd, himself and son,
And, like a prelate, donkey march'd alone.
Another man they met. These folks, said he,
Enslave themselves to let their ass go free—
The darling brute! If I might be so bold,
I'd counsel them to have him set in gold.
Not so went Nicholas his Jane to woo,
Who rode, we sing, his ass to save his shoe.
Ass! ass! our man replied; we're asses three!
I do avow myself an ass to be;
But since my sage advisers can't agree,
  Their words henceforth shall not be heeded;
  I'll suit myself. And he succeeded.

For you, choose army, love, or court;
  In town, or country, make resort;
Take wife, or cowl; ride you, or walk;
Doubt not but tongues will have their talk.

II.—THE MEMBERS AND THE BELLY

PERHAPS, had I but shown due loyalty,
This book would have begun with royalty,
  Of which, in certain points of view,
  Boss* Belly is the image true,
In whose bereavements all the members share;
  Of whom the latter once so weary were,

---

* A word probably more familiar to hod-carriers than to
lexicographers; qu. derived from the French *bosseman*,
or the English *boatswain*, pronounced *bos'n*? It denotes a
"master" of some practical "art." Master Belly, says
Rabelais, was the first Master of Arts in the world.—TRANS.

As all due service to forbear,
On what they called his idle plan
Resolved to play the gentleman,
And let his lordship live on air.
    Like burden-beasts, said they,
    We sweat from day to day;
    And all for whom, and what!
    Ourselves we profit not.
Our labour has no object but one,
That is, to feed this lazy glutton.
We'll learn the resting trade
    By his example's aid.
So said, so done; all labour ceased;
The hands refused to grasp, the arms to strike;
    All other members did the like.
Their boss might labour if he pleased!
It was an error which they soon repented,
With pain of languid poverty acquainted.
The heart no more the blood renew'd,
And hence repair no more accrued
    To ever-wasting strength;
    Whereby the mutineers, at length,
Saw that the idle belly, in its way,
Did more for common benefit than they.

For royalty our fable makes,
A thing that gives as well as takes.
    Its power all labour to sustain,
Nor for themselves turns out their labour vain.
It gives the artist bread, the merchant riches;
Maintains the diggers in their ditches;
    Pays man of war and magistrate;
    Supports the swarms in place,
    That live on sovereign grace;
In short, is caterer for the state.

    Menenius told the story well,
When Rome, of old, in pieces fell,
The commons parting from the senate.
The ills, said they, that we complain at
Are, that the honours, treasures, power, and dignity,
Belong to them alone; while we
    Get nought our labour for
But tributes, taxes, and fatigues of war.
Without the walls the people had their stand
Prepared to march in search of other land,
    When by this noted fable
    Menenius was able
    To draw them, hungry, home
    To duty and to Rome*.

III.—THE WOLF TURNED SHEPHERD.

A WOLF, whose gettings from the flocks
    Began to be but few,
Bethought himself to play the fox
    In character quite new.
A shepherd's hat and coat he took,
    A cudgel for a crook,
    Nor e'en the pipe forgot;
And more to seem what he was not,
Himself upon his hat he wrote,
I'm Willie, shepherd of these sheep.
    His person thus complete,

* According to our republican notions of government,
these people were somewhat imposed upon. Perhaps the
fable finds a more appropriate application in the relation
of employer to employed. I leave the fabulists and the
political economists to settle the question between them.
—TRANSLATOR.

His crook in upraised feet,
The impostor Willie stole upon the keep.
The real Willie, on the grass asleep,
    Slept there, indeed, profoundly,
His dog and pipe slept, also soundly;
    His drowsy sheep around lay.
    As for the greatest number,
Much bless'd the hypocrite their slumber,
And hoped to drive away the flock,
Could he the shepherd's voice but mock.
He thought undoubtedly he could.
He tried: the tone in which he spoke,
    Loud echoing from the wood,
    The plot and slumber broke;
    Sheep, dog, and man awoke.
    The wolf, in sorry plight,
    In hampering coat bedight,
    Could neither run nor fight.

There's always leakage of deceit
Which makes it never safe to cheat.
    Whoever is a wolf had better
    Keep clear of hypocritic fetter.

IV.—THE FROGS ASKING A KING.

A CERTAIN commonwealth aquatic,
    Grown tired of order democratic,
By clamouring in the ears of Jove, effected
    Its being to a monarch's power subjected.
Jove flung it down, at first, a king pacific.
Who nathless fell with such a splash terrific,
    The marshy folks, a foolish race and timid,
    Made breathless haste to get from him hid.
They dived into the mud beneath the water,
Or found among the reeds and rushes quarter.
    And long it was they dared not see
    The dreadful face of majesty,
    Supposing that some monstrous frog
    Had been sent down to rule the bog.
    The king was really a log,
    Whose gravity inspired with awe
        The first that, from his hiding-place
    Forth venturing, astonish'd, saw
        The royal blockhead's face.
    With trembling and with fear,
    At last he drew quite near.
Another follow'd, and another yet,
Till quite a crowd at last were met;
Who, growing fast and strangely bolder,
Perch'd soon upon the royal shoulder.
His gracious majesty kept still,
And let his people work their will.
Clack, clack! what din beset the ears of Jove?
We want a king, the people said, to move!
    The god straight sent them down a crane,
Who caught and slew them without measure,
And gulp'd their carcasses at pleasure;
    Whereat the frogs more wofully complain.
What! what! great Jupiter replied;
By your desires must I be tied?
Think you such government is bad?
You should have kept what first you had;
Which having blindly fail'd to do,
It had been prudent still for you
To let that former king suffice,
More meek and mild, if not so wise.
With this now make yourselves content,
Lest for your sins a worse be sent.

V.—THE FOX AND THE GOAT.

A FOX once journey'd, and for company
A certain bearded, horned goat had he ;
Which goat no further than his nose could see.
The fox was deeply versed in trickery.
   These travellers did thirst compel
   To seek the bottom of a well.
   There, having drunk enough for two,
   Says fox, My friend, what shall we do ?
   'Tis time that we were thinking
   Of something else than drinking.
   Raise you your feet upon the wall,
   And stick your horns up straight and tall ;
   Then up your back I'll climb with ease,
   And draw you after, if you please.
   Yes, by my beard, the other said,
   'Tis just the thing. I like a head
   Well stock'd with sense, like thine.
     Had it been left to mine,
      I do confess,
   I never should have thought of this.
     So Renard clamber'd out,
     And, leaving there the goat,
     Discharged his obligations
     By preaching thus on patience :—
Had Heaven put sense thy head within,
To match the beard upon thy chin,
Thou wouldst have thought a bit,
Before descending such a pit.
     I'm out of it ; good bye :
     With prudent effort try
     Yourself to extricate.
     For me, affairs of state
     Permit me not to wait.

     Whatever way you wend,
     Consider well the end.

VI.—THE EAGLE, THE WILD SOW, AND THE CAT.

   A CERTAIN hollow tree
   Was tenanted by three.
   An eagle held a lofty bough,
   The hollow root a wild wood sow,
   A female cat between the two.
All busy with maternal labours,
They lived awhile obliging neighbours.
   At last the cat's deceitful tongue
   Broke up the peace of old and young.
   Up climbing to the eagle's nest,
   She said, with whisker'd lips compress'd,
Our death, or, what as much we mothers fear,
   That of our helpless offspring dear,
     Is surely drawing near.
   Beneath our feet, see you not how
   Destruction's plotted by the sow ?
   Her constant digging, soon or late,
   Our proud old castle will uproot.
And then—O, sad and shocking fate !—
She'll eat our young ones as the fruit !
Were there but hope of saving one,
'Twould soothe somewhat my bitter moan.
Thus leaving apprehensions hideous,
Down went the puss perfidious
To where the sow, no longer digging,
Was in the very act of pigging.
   Good friend and neighbour, whisper'd she
I warn you on your guard to be.

Your pigs should you but leave a minute,
This eagle here will seize them in it.
   Speak not of this, I beg, at all,
   Lest on my head her wrath should fall.
   Another breast with fear inspired,
   With fiendish joy the cat retired.
   The eagle ventured no egress
   To feed her young, the sow still less.
   Fools they, to think that any curse
   Than ghastly famine could be worse !
Both staid at home, resolved and obstinate,
To save their young ones from impending fate,—
   The royal bird for fear of mine,
   For fear of royal claws the swine.
   All died, at length, with hunger,
   The older and the younger ;
   There staid, of eagle race or boar,
Not one this side of death's dread door ;—
     A sad misfortune, which
     The wicked cats made rich.
   O, what is there of hellish plot
   The treacherous tongue dares not !
Of all the ills Pandora's box outpour'd,
Deceit, I think, is most to be abhorr'd.

VII.—THE DRUNKARD AND HIS WIFE.

   EACH has his fault, to which he clings
   In spite of shame or fear.
   This apophthegm a story brings,
   To make its truth more clear.
   A sot had lost health, mind, and purse ;
     And, truly, for that matter,
     Sots mostly lose the latter
   Ere running half their course.
When wine, one day, of wit had fill'd the room,
His wife inclosed him in a spacious tomb.
   There did the fumes evaporate
   At leisure from his drowsy pate.
   When he awoke, he found
   His body wrapp'd around
   With grave-clothes, chill and damp,
   Beneath a dim sepulchral lamp.
How 's this ? My wife a widow sad ?
He cried, and I a ghost ? Dead ! dead ?
   Thereat his spouse, with snaky hair,
   And robes like those the Furies wear,
   With voice to fit the realms below,
     Brought boiling caudle to his bier—
     For Lucifer the proper cheer ;
   By which her husband came to know—
   For he had heard of those three ladies—
   Himself a citizen of Hades.
     What may your office be ?
     The phantom question'd he.
   I'm server up of Pluto's meat,
   And bring his guests the same to eat.
Well, says the sot, not taking time to think,
And don't you bring us anything to drink ?

VIII.—THE GOUT AND THE SPIDER.

   WHEN Nature angrily turn'd out
   Those plagues, the spider and the gout,—
See you, said she, those huts so meanly built,
These palaces so grand and richly gilt ?

By mutual agreement fix
Your choice of dwellings ; or if not,
To end th' affair by lot,
Draw out these little sticks.
The huts are not for me, the spider cried ;
And not for me the palace, cried the gout ;
For there a sort of men she spied
Call'd doctors, going in and out,
From whom she could not hope for ease.
So hied her to the huts the fell disease,
And, fastening on a poor man's toe,
Hoped there to fatten on his woe,
And torture him, fit after fit,
Without a summons e'er to quit,
From old Hippocrates.
The spider, on the lofty ceiling,
As if she had a life-lease feeling,
Wove wide her cunning toils,
Soon rich with insect spoils.
A maid destroy'd them as she swept the
room :
Repair'd, again they felt the fatal broom.
The wretched creature, every day,
From house and home must pack away.
At last, her courage giving out,
She went to seek her sister gout,
And in the field descried her,
Quite starved : more evils did betide her
Than e'er befel the poorest spider—
Her toiling host enslaved her so,
And made her chop, and dig, and hoe !
(Says one, Kept brisk and busy,
The gout is made half easy.)
O, when, exclaim'd the sad disease,
Will this my misery stop !
O, sister spider, if you please,
Our places let us swop.
The spider gladly heard,
And took her at her word,—
And flourish'd in the cabin-lodge,
Not forced the tidy broom to dodge.
The gout, selecting her abode
With an ecclesiastic judge,
Turn'd judge herself, and, by her code,
He from his couch no more could budge.
The salves and cataplasms Heaven knows,
That mock'd the misery of his toes ;
While aye, without a blush, the curse,
Kept driving onward worse and worse.
Needless to say, the sisterhood
Thought their exchange both wise and good.

IX.—THE WOLF AND THE STORK.

THE wolves are prone to play the glutton.
One, at a certain feast, 'tis said,
So stuff'd himself with lamb and mutton,
He seem'd but little short of dead.
Deep in his throat a bone stuck fast.
Well for this wolf, who could not speak,
That soon a stork quite near him pass'd.
By signs invited, with her beak
The bone she drew
With slight ado,
And for this skilful surgery
Demanded, modestly, her fee.

Your fee ! replied the wolf,
In accents rather gruff ;
And is it not enough
Your neck is safe from such a gulf ?
Go, for a wretch ingrate,
Nor tempt again your fate !

X.—THE LION BEATEN BY THE MAN.

A PICTURE once was shown,
In which one man, alone,
Upon the ground had thrown
A lion fully grown.
Much gloried at the sight the rabble.
A lion thus rebuked their babble :—
That you have got the victory there,
There is no contradiction.
But, gentles, possibly you are
The dupes of easy fiction :
Had we the art of making pictures,
Perhaps our champion had beat yours !

XI.—THE FOX AND THE GRAPES.

A FOX, almost with hunger dying,
Some grapes upon a trellis spying,
To all appearance ripe, clad in
Their tempting russet skin,
Most gladly would have eat them ;
But since he could not get them,
So far above his reach the vine,—
They 're sour, he said ; such grapes as these,
The dogs may eat them if they please !

Did he not better than to whine !

XII.—THE SWAN AND THE COOK.

THE pleasures of a poultry yard
Were by a swan and gosling shared.
The swan was kept there for his looks,
The thrifty gosling for the cooks ;
The first the garden's pride, the latter
A greater favourite on the platter.
They swam the ditches, side by side,
And oft in sports aquatic vied,
Plunging, splashing far and wide,
With rivalry ne'er satisfied.
One day the cook, named Thirsty John,
Sent for the gosling, took the swan,
In haste his throat to cut,
And put him in the pot.
The bird's complaint resounded
In glorious melody ;
Whereat the cook, astounded
His sad mistake to see,
Cried, What ! make soup of a musician !
Please God, I'll never set such dish on.
No, no ; I'll never cut a throat
That sings so sweet a note.

'Tis thus, whatever peril may alarm us,
Sweet words will never harm us.

XIII.—THE WOLVES AND THE SHEEP.

BY-GONE a thousand years of war,
　The wearers of the fleece
　And wolves at last made peace ;
Which both appear'd the better for ;
For if the wolves had now and then
　Eat up a straggling ewe or wether,
As often had the shepherd men
　Turn'd wolf-skins into leather.
Fear always spoil'd the verdant herbage,
And so it did the bloody carnage.
Hence peace was sweet; and, lest it should be riven,
　On both sides hostages were given.
The sheep, as by the terms arranged,
For pups of wolves their dogs exchanged ;
　Which being done above suspicion,
　Confirm'd and seal'd by high commission,
What time the pups were fully grown,
And felt an appetite for prey,
And saw the sheepfold left alone,
　The shepherds all away,
They seized the fattest lambs they could,
And, choking, dragg'd them to the wood ;
Of which, by secret means apprised,
　Their sires, as is surmised,
Fell on the hostage guardians of the sheep,
　And slew them all asleep.
So quick the deed of perfidy was done,
There fled to tell the tale not one !

From which we may conclude
That peace with villains will be rued.
　Peace in itself, 'tis true,
　May be a good for you ;
　But 'tis an evil, nathless,
　When enemies are faithless.

XIV.—THE LION GROWN OLD.

A LION, mourning, in his age, the wane
Of might once dreaded through his wild domain,
　Was mock'd, at last, upon his throne,
　By subjects of his own,
　Strong through his weakness grown.
The horse his head saluted with a kick ;
　The wolf snapp'd at his royal hide ;
　The ox, too, gored him in the side ;
The unhappy lion, sad and sick,
　Could hardly growl, he was so weak.
　In uncomplaining, stoic pride,
He waited for the hour of fate,
Until the ass approach'd his gate ;
Whereat, This is too much, he saith ;
I willingly would yield my breath ;
But, ah ! thy kick is double death !

XV.—PHILOMEL AND PROGNE.

FROM home and city spires, one day,
The swallow Progne flew away,
　And sought the bosky dell
　Where sang poor Philomel.

My sister, Progne said, how do you do ?
'Tis now a thousand years since you
Have been conceal'd from human view ;
I'm sure I have not seen your face
　Once since the times of Thrace.
Pray, will you never quit this dull retreat ?
Where could I find, said Philomel, so sweet ?
　What ! sweet ? cried Progne—sweet to waste
　Such tones on beasts devoid of taste,
　Or on some rustic, at the most !
　Should you by deserts be engross'd ?
Come, be the city's pride and boast.
Besides, the woods remind of harms
　That Tereus in them did your charms.
Alas ! replied the bird of song,
The thought of that so cruel wrong
　Makes me, from age to age,
　Prefer this hermitage ;
For nothing like the sight of men
Can call up what I suffer'd then.

XVI.—THE WOMAN DROWNED.

I HATE that saying, old and savage,
" 'Tis nothing but a woman drowning."
That's much, I say.　What grief more keen
　should have edge
Than loss of her, of all our joys the crowning ?
Thus much suggests the fable I am borrowing.
A woman perish'd in the water,
　Where, anxiously, and sorrowing,
　Her husband sought her,
To ease the grief he could not cure,
By honour'd rites of sepulture.
It chanced that near the fatal spot,
　Along the stream which had
　Produced a death so sad,
There walk'd some men that knew it not.
The husband ask'd if they had seen
His wife, or aught that hers had been.
One promptly answer'd, No !
But search the stream below :
It must have borne her in its flow.
No, said another ; search above.
　In that direction
She would have floated, by the love
　Of contradiction.
This joke was truly out of season ;—
I don't propose to weigh its reason.
But whether such propensity
　The sex's fault may be,
Or not, one thing is very sure,
　Its own propensities endure.
Up to the end they'll have their will,
　And, if it could be, further still.

XVII.—THE WEASEL IN THE GRANARY.

A WEASEL through a hole contrived to squeeze,
　(She was recovering from disease,)
　Which led her to a farmer's hoard.
There lodged, her wasted form she cherish'd ;
　Heaven knows the lard and victuals stored
　That by her gnawing perish'd !
　Of which the consequence
　Was sudden corpulence.

A week or so was past,
When having fully broken fast,
A noise she heard, and hurried
To find the hole by which she came,
And seem'd to find it not the same ;
So round she ran, most sadly flurried ;
And, coming back, thrust out her head,
Which, sticking there, she said,
This is the hole, there can't be blunder :
What makes it now so small, I wonder,
Where, but the other day, I pass'd with ease?
    A rat her trouble sees,
And cries, But with an emptier belly ;
You enter'd lean, and lean must sally.
    What I have said to you
Has eke been said to not a few,
Who, in a vast variety of cases,
Have ventured into such-like places.

XVIII.—THE CAT AND THE OLD RAT.

A STORY-WRITER of our sort
Historifies, in short,
Of one that may be reckon'd
A Rodilard the Second,—
The Alexander of the cats,
The Attila, the scourge of rats,
Whose fierce and whisker'd head
Among the latter spread,
A league around, its dread ;
Who seem'd, indeed, determined
The world should be unvermined.
The planks with props more false than slim,
The tempting heaps of poison'd meal,
The traps of wire and traps of steel,
Were only play compared with him.
At length, so sadly were they scared,
The rats and mice no longer dared
    To show their thievish faces
    Outside their hiding-places,
Thus shunning all pursuit ; whereat
Our crafty General Cat
Contrived to hang himself, as dead,
Beside the wall with downward head,
Resisting gravitation's laws
.By clinging with his hinder claws
    To some small bit of string.
    The rats esteem'd the thing
A judgment for some naughty deed,
    Some thievish snatch,
    Or ugly scratch ;
And thought their foe had got his meed
    By being hung indeed.
    With hope elated all
    Of laughing at his funeral,
They thrust their noses out in air ;
And now to show their heads they dare ;
Now dodging back, now venturing more ;
    At last upon the larder's store
    They fall to filching, as of yore.
A scanty feast enjoy'd these shallows ;
Down dropp'd the hung one from his gallows,
    And of the hindmost caught.
Some other tricks to me are known,
Said he, while tearing bone from bone,
    By long experience taught ;
The point is settled, free from doubt,
That from your holes you shall come out.

His threat as good as prophecy
Was proved by Mr. Mildandsly ;
For, putting on a mealy robe,
He squatted in an open tub,
And held his purring and his breath ;—
Out came the vermin to their death.
On this occasion, one old stager,
A rat as grey as any badger,
Who had in battle lost his tail,
Abstained from smelling at the meal ;
And cried, far off, Ah ! General Cat,
I much suspect a heap like that ;
Your meal is not the thing, perhaps,
For one who knows somewhat of traps ;
Should you a sack of meal become,
I'd let you be, and stay at home.

    Well said, I think, and prudently,
    By one who knew distrust to be
    The parent of security.

BOOK IV.

I.—THE LION IN LOVE.
TO MADEMOISELLE DE SÉVIGNÉ.

SÉVIGNÉ, type of every grace
In female form and face,
In your regardlessness of men,
Can you show favour when
The sportive fable craves your ear,
And see, unmoved by fear,
    A lion's haughty heart
Thrust through by Love's audacious dart ?
Strange conqueror, Love ! And happy he,
And strangely privileged and free,
    Who only knows by story
    Him and his feats of glory !
If on this subject you are wont
To think the simple truth too blunt,
The fabulous may less affront ;
Which now, inspired with gratitude,
Yea, kindled into zeal most fervent,
    Doth venture to intrude
    Within your maiden solitude,
And kneel, your humble servant.—
In times when animals were speakers,
Among the quadrupedal seekers
    Of our alliance
    There came the lions.
And wherefore not ? for then
They yielded not to men
In point of courage or of sense,
Nor were in looks without pretence.
A high-born lion, on his way
Across a meadow, met one day
A shepherdess, who charm'd him so,
That, as such matters ought to go,
He sought the maiden for his bride.
Her sire, it cannot be denied,
Had much preferr'd a son-in-law
Of less terrific mouth and paw.
It was not easy to decide—
The lion might the gift abuse—
'Twas not quite prudent to refuse.

And if refusal there should be,
Perhaps a marriage one would see,
Some morning, made clandestinely.
  For, over and above
The fact that she could bear
With none but males of martial air,
  The lady was in love
With him of shaggy hair.
Her sire, much wanting cover
To send away the lover,
Thus spoke :—My daughter, sir,
Is delicate.   I fear to her
    Your fond caressings
    Will prove rough blessings
    To banish all alarm
    About such sort of harm,
Permit us to remove the cause,
By filing off your teeth and claws.
In such a case, your royal kiss
Will be to her a safer bliss,
    And to yourself a sweeter ;
Since she will more respond
To those endearments fond
    With which you greet her.
The lion gave consent at once,
By love so great a dunce !
Without a tooth or claw now view him—
A fort with cannon spiked.
The dogs, let loose upon him, slew him,
All biting safely where they liked.

O, tyrant Love ! when held by you,
We may to prudence bid adieu.

———◆———

II.—THE SHEPHERD AND THE SEA.

A SHEPHERD, neighbour to the sea,
Lived with his flock contentedly.
    His fortune, though but small,
    Was safe within his call.
At last some stranded kegs of gold
Him tempted, and his flock he sold,
Turn'd merchant, and the ocean's waves
Bore all his treasure—to its caves.
Brought back to keeping sheep once more,
But not chief shepherd, as before,
When sheep were his that grazed the shore,
He who, as Corydon or Thyrsis,
Might once have shone in pastoral verses, ·
Bedeck'd with rhyme and metre,
Was nothing now but Peter.
But time and toil redeem'd in full
Those harmless creatures rich in wool ;
And as the lulling winds, one day,
The vessels wafted with a gentle motion,
Want you, he cried, more money, Madam Ocean ?
Address yourself to some one else, I pray ;
    You shall not get it out of me !
    I know too well your treachery.

    This tale 's no fiction, but a fact,
    Which, by experience back'd,
    Proves that a single penny,
      At present held, and certain,
    Is worth five times as many
      Of Hope's beyond the curtain ;

That one should be content with his condition,
And shut his ears to counsels of ambition,
More faithless than the wreck-strown sea, and
    which
Doth thousands beggar where it makes one
    rich,—
Inspires the hope of wealth, in glorious forms,
And blasts the same with piracy and storms.

———◆———

III.—THE FLY AND THE ANT.

A FLY and ant, upon a sunny bank,
Discuss'd the question of their rank.
O Jupiter ! the former said,
Can love of self so turn the head,
    That one so mean and crawling,
    And of so low a calling,
To boast equality shall dare
With me, the daughter of the air ?
In palaces I am a guest,
And even at thy glorious feast.
Whene'er the people that adore thee
    May immolate for thee a bullock,
I'm sure to taste the meat before them.
    Meanwhile this starveling, in her hillock,
Is living on some bit of straw
Which she has labour'd home to draw.
But tell me now, my little thing,
Do you camp ever on a king,
An emperor, or lady ?
I do, and have full many a play-day
On fairest bosom of the fair,
And sport myself upon her hair.
Come now, my hearty, rack your brain
To make a case about your grain.
Well, have you done ? replied the ant.
You enter palaces, I grant,
And for it get right soundly cursed.
    Of sacrifices, rich and fat,
Your taste, quite likely, is the first ;—
    Are they the better off for that ?
You enter with the holy train ;
So enters many a wretch profane.
On heads of kings and asses you may squat ;
Deny your vaunting—I will not ;
But well such impudence, I know,
Provokes a sometimes fatal blow.
The name in which your vanity delights
Is own'd as well by parasites,
And spies that die by ropes—as you soon will
By famine or by ague-chill, .
    When Phœbus goes to cheer
    The other hemisphere,—
The very time to me most dear.
    Not forced abroad to go
    Through wind, and rain, and snow,
My summer's work I then enjoy,
And happily my mind employ,
From care by care exempted.
By which this truth I leave to you,
That by two sorts of glory we are tempted,
    The false one and the true.
Work waits, time flies ; adieu :—
    This gabble does not fill
    My granary or till.

IV.—THE GARDENER AND HIS LORD.

A LOVER of gardens, half cit and half clown,
Possess'd a nice garden beside a small town ;
And with it a field by a live hedge inclosed,
Where sorrel and lettuce, at random disposed,
A little of jasmine, and much of wild thyme,
   Grew gaily, and all in their prime
   To make up Miss Peggy's bouquet,
   The grace of her bright wedding day.
For poaching in such a nice field—'twas a shame ;
A foraging, cud-chewing hare was to blame.
   Whereof the good owner bore down
   This tale to the lord of the town :—
Some mischievous animal, morning and night,
In spite of my caution, comes in for his bite.
He laughs at my cunning-set dead-falls and
        snares ;
For clubbing and stoning as little he cares.
I think him a wizard. A wizard ! the coot !
I'd catch him if he were a devil to boot !
The lord said, in haste to have sport for his hounds,
I'll clear him, I warrant you, out of your grounds ;
To-morrow I'll do it without any fail.

The thing thus agreed on, all hearty and hale,
The lord and his party, at crack of the dawn,
With hounds at their heels canter'd over the lawn.
Arrived, said the lord in his jovial mood,
We'll breakfast with you, if your chickens are good.
That lass, my good man, I suppose is your daughter :
No news of a son-in-law ? Any one sought her ?
No doubt, by the score. Keep an eye on the docket,
Eh ? Dost understand me ? I speak of the pocket.
So saying, the daughter he graciously greeted,
And close by his lordship he bade her be seated ;
Avow'd himself pleased with so handsome a maid,
And then with her kerchief familiarly play'd,—
Impertinent freedoms the virtuous fair
Repell'd with a modest and lady-like air,—
So much that her father a little suspected
The girl had already a lover elected.
Meanwhile in the kitchen what bustling and cooking !
For what are your hams ? They are very good looking.
They're kept for your lordship. I take them, said he ;
Such elegant flitches are welcome to me.
He breakfasted finely ;—his troop, with delight,—
Dogs, horses, and grooms of the best appetite.
Thus he govern'd his host in the shape of a guest,
Unbottled his wine, and his daughter caress'd.
To breakfast, the huddle of hunters succeeds,
The yelping of dogs and the neighing of steeds,
All cheering and fixing for wonderful deeds ;
The horns and the bugles make thundering din ;
Much wonders our gardener what it can mean.
The worst is, his garden most wofully fares ;
Adieu to its arbours, and borders, and squares ;
Adieu to its succory, onions, and leeks ;
Adieu to whatever good cookery seeks.

Beneath a great cabbage the hare was in bed,
Was started, and shot at, and hastily fled.
Off went the wild chase, with a terrible screech,
And not through a hole, but a horrible breach,
Which some one had made, at the beck of the lord,
Wide through the poor hedge ! 'Twould have been
      quite absurd
Should lordship not freely from garden go out,
On horseback, attended by rabble and rout.

Scarce suffer'd the gard'ner his patience to wince,
Consoling himself—'Twas the sport of a prince ;
While bipeds and quadrupeds served to devour,
And trample, and waste, in the space of an hour,
Far more than a nation of foraging hares
Could possibly do in a hundred of years.

   Small princes, this story is true.
   When told in relation to you.
In settling your quarrels with kings for your tools,
You prove yourselves losers and eminent fools.

V.—THE ASS AND THE LITTLE DOG.

ONE's native talent from its course
Cannot be turned aside by force ;
But poorly apes the country clown
The polish'd manners of the town.
Their Maker chooses but a few
With power of pleasing to imbue ;
Where wisely leave it we, the mass,
Unlike a certain fabled ass,
That thought to gain his master's blessing
By jumping on him and caressing.
   What ! said the donkey in his heart ;
   Ought it to be that puppy's part
     To lead his useless life
      In full companionship
     With master and his wife,
     While I must bear the whip ?
What doth the cur a kiss to draw ?
Forsooth, he only gives his paw !
If that is all there needs to please,
I'll do the thing myself, with ease.
   Possess'd with this bright notion,—
His master sitting on his chair,
At leisure in the open air,—
   He ambled up, with awkward motion,
And put his talents to the proof ;
Upraised his bruised and batter'd hoof,
And, with an amiable mien,
His master patted on the chin,
The action gracing with a word—
The fondest bray that e'er was heard !
O, such caressing was there ever ?
Or melody with such a quaver ?
Ho ! Martin ! here ! a club, a club bring !
Out cried the master, sore offended.
So Martin gave the ass a drubbing,—
And so the comedy was ended.

VI.—THE BATTLE OF THE RATS AND THE WEASELS.

THE weasels live, no more than cats,
On terms of friendship with the rats ;
   And, were it not that these
   Through doors contrive to squeeze
     Too narrow for their foes,
     The animals long-snouted
     Would long ago have routed,
     And from the planet scouted
     Their race, as I suppose.

   One year it did betide,
   When they were multiplied,
   An army took the field
   Of rats, with spear and shield,

Whose crowded ranks led on
A king named Ratapon.
  The weasels, too, their banner
  Unfurl'd in warlike manner.
  As Fame her trumpet sounds,
    The victory balanced well ;
Enrich'd were fallow grounds
  Where slaughter'd legions fell ;
But by said trollop's tattle,
The loss of life in battle
Thinn'd most the rattish race
In almost every place ;
And finally their rout
Was total, spite of stout
Artarpax and Psicarpax,
And valiant Meridarpax*,
Who, cover'd o'er with dust,
Long time sustain'd their host
Down sinking on the plain.
Their efforts were in vain ;
Fate ruled that final hour,
(Inexorable power !)
And so the captains fled
As well as those they led ;
The princes perish'd all.
The undistinguish'd small
In certain holes found shelter,
In crowding, helter-skelter ;
But the nobility
Could not go in so free,
Who proudly had assumed
Each one a helmet plumed ;
We know not, truly, whether
For honour's sake the feather,
Or foes to strike with terror ;
But, truly, 'twas their error.
Nor hole, nor crack, nor crevice
  Will let their head-gear in ;
While meaner rats in bevies
  An easy passage win ;—
So that the shafts of fate
Do chiefly hit the great.

A feather in the cap
Is oft a great mishap.
An equipage too grand
Comes often to a stand
Within a narrow place.
The small, whate'er the case,
With ease slip through a strait,
Where larger folks must wait.

VII.—THE MONKEY AND THE DOLPHIN.

It was a custom of the Greeks
For passengers o'er sea to carry
  Both monkeys full of tricks
And funny dogs to make them merry.
A ship, that had such things on deck,
Not far from Athens, went to wreck.
But for the dolphins, all had drown'd.
  They are a philanthropic fish,
Which fact in Pliny may be found ;—
  A better voucher who could wish !
They did their best on this occasion.
A monkey even, on their plan

Well nigh attain'd his own salvation ;
  A dolphin took him for a man,
And on his dorsal gave him place.
So grave the silly creature's face,
That one might well have set him down
That old musician of renown*.
The fish had almost reach'd the land,
  When, as it happen'd,—what a pity !—
He ask'd, Are you from Athens grand ?
  Yes ; well they know me in that city.
If ever you have business there,
  I'll help you do it, for my kin
  The highest offices are in.
My cousin, sir, is now lord mayor.
The dolphin thank'd him, with good grace,
Both for himself and all his race,
And ask'd, You doubtless know Piræus,
Where, should we come to town, you'll see us
Piræus ! yes, indeed I know ;
He was my crony long ago.
The dunce knew not the harbour's name,
And for a man's mistook the same.
  The people are by no means few,
Who never went ten miles from home,
Nor know their market-town from Rome,
  Yet cackle just as if they knew.
The dolphin laugh'd, and then began
His rider's form and face to scan,
And found himself about to save
From fishy feasts, beneath the wave,
A mere resemblance of a man.
So, plunging down, he turn'd to find
Some drowning wight of human kind.

VIII.—THE MAN AND THE WOODEN GOD.

A pagan kept a god of wood,—
  A sort that never hears,
  Though furnish'd well with ears,—
From which he hoped for wondrous good.
The idol cost the board of three ;
  So much enrich'd was he
  With vows and offerings vain,
With bullocks garlanded and slain :
  No idol ever had, as that,
  A kitchen quite so full and fat.
But all this worship at his shrine
Brought not from this same block divine
Inheritance, or hidden mine,
  Or luck at play, or any favour.
  Nay, more, if any storm whatever
Brew'd trouble here or there,
The man was sure to have his share,
  And suffer in his purse,
Although the god fared none the worse.
At last, by sheer impatience bold,
  The man a crowbar seizes,
  His idol breaks in pieces,
And finds it richly stuff'd with gold.
How 's this ! Have I devoutly treated,
Says he, your godship, to be cheated !
Now leave my house, and go your way,
And search for altars where you may.
You're like those natures, dull and gross,
From which comes nothing but by blows.
The more I gave, the less I got ;
I'll now be rich, and you may rot.

----

* Names of rats, invented by Homer.

* Arion.

IX.—THE JAY IN THE FEATHERS OF THE PEACOCK.

A PEACOCK moulted : soon a jay was seen
Bedeck'd with Argus tail of gold and green,
High strutting, with elated crest,
As much a peacock as the rest.
　His trick was recognised and bruited,
　His person jeer'd at, hiss'd, and hooted.
　The peacock gentry flock'd together,
　And pluck'd the fool of every feather.
Nay more, when back he sneak'd to join his race,
They shut their portals in his face.

　　There is another sort of jay,
　　The number of its legs the same,
　Which makes of borrow'd plumes display,
　　And plagiary is its name.
　　But hush ! the tribe I'll not offend ;
　　'Tis not my work their ways to mend.

X.—THE CAMEL AND THE FLOATING STICKS.

THE first who saw the humpback'd camel
Fled off for life ; the next approach'd with care ;
The third with tyrant rope did boldly dare
The desert wanderer to trammel.
　Such is the power of use to change
　The face of objects new and strange ;
　Which grow, by looking at, so tame,
　They do not even seem the same.
And since this theme is up for our attention,
A certain watchman I will mention,
　Who, seeing something far
　　Away upon the ocean,
　　Could not but speak his notion
　That 'twas a ship of war.
Some minutes more had past,—
　A bomb-ketch 'twas without a sail,
　And then a boat, and then a bale,
And floating sticks of wood at last !

　　Full many things on earth, I wot,
　Will claim this tale,—and well they may ;
　They're something dreadful far away,
　　But near at hand—they're not.

XI.—THE FROG AND THE RAT.

THEY to bamboozle are inclined,
　Saith Merlin, who bamboozled are.
The word, though rather unrefined,
Has yet an energy we ill can spare ;
So by its aid I introduce my tale.
　A well-fed rat, rotund and hale,
　Not knowing either Fast or Lent,
　Disporting round a frog-pond went.
A frog approach'd, and, with a friendly greeting,
　Invited him to see her at her home,
And pledged a dinner worth his eating,—
To which the rat was nothing loath to come.
Of words persuasive there was little need :
　She spoke, however, of a grateful bath ;
Of sports and curious wonders on their path ;
Of rarities of flower, and rush, and reed :

One day he would recount with glee
To his assembled progeny
The various beauties of these places,
The customs of the various races,
And laws that sway the realms aquatic,
(She did not mean the hydrostatic !)
One thing alone the rat perplex'd,—
He was but moderate as a swimmer.
The frog this matter nicely fix'd
　By kindly lending him her
Long paw, which with a rush she tied
To his ; and off they started, side by side.
Arrived upon the lakelet's brink,
There was but little time to think.
The frog leap'd in, and almost brought her
Bound guest to land beneath the water.
Perfidious breach of law and right !
　She meant to have a supper warm
　Out of his sleek and dainty form.
Already did her appetite
Dwell on the morsel with delight.
The gods, in anguish, he invokes ;
His faithless hostess rudely mocks ;
He struggles up, she struggles down.
　A kite, that hovers in the air,
　Inspecting everything with care,
Now spies the rat bolike to drown,
　And, with a rapid wing,
　　Upbears the wretched thing,
The frog, too, dangling by the string !
The joy of such a double haul
Was to the hungry kite not small.
It gave him all that he could wish—
A double meal of flesh and fish.

　　The best contrived deceit
　　　Can hurt its own contriver,
　And perfidy doth often cheat
　　　Its author's purse of every stiver.

XII.—THE ANIMALS SENDING TRIBUTE TO ALEXANDER.

A FABLE flourish'd with antiquity
Whose meaning I could never clearly see.
Kind reader, draw the moral if you're able :
　I give you here the naked fable.
Fame having bruited that a great commander,
A son of Jove, a certain Alexander,
Resolved to leave nought free on this our ball,
Had to his footstool gravely summon'd all
Men, quadrupeds, and nullipeds, together
With all the bird-republics, every feather,—
The goddess of the hundred mouths, I say,
　Thus having spread dismay,
　By widely publishing abroad
This mandate of the demigod,
The animals, and all that do obey
Their appetite alone, mistrusted now
That to another sceptre they must bow.
　Far in the desert met their various races,
　All gathering from their hiding-places.
　Discuss'd was many a notion.
　At last, it was resolved, on motion,
To pacify the conquering banner,
By sending homage in, and tribute.
With both the homage and its manner
They charged the monkey, as a glib brute ;

And, lest the chap should too much chatter,
In black on white they wrote the matter.
Nought but the tribute served to fash,
As that must needs be paid in cash.
A prince, who chanced a mine to own,
At last, obliged them with a loan.
The mule and ass, to bear the treasure,
Their service tender'd, full of pleasure ;
And then the caravan was none the worse,
Assisted by the camel and the horse.
Forthwith proceeded all the four
Behind the new ambassador,
And saw, erelong, within a narrow place,
Monseigneur Lion's quite unwelcome face.
Well met, and all in time, said he ;
Myself your fellow traveller will be.
I went my tribute by itself to bear ;
And though 'tis light, I well might spare
The unaccustom'd load.
Take each a quarter, if you please,
And I will guard you on the road ;
More free and at my ease—
In better plight, you understand,
To fight with any robber band.
A lion to refuse, the fact is,
Is not a very usual practice :
So in he comes, for better and for worse ;
Whatever he demands is done,
And, spite of Jove's heroic son,
He fattens freely from the public purse.
While wending on their way,
They found a spot one day,
With waters hemm'd, of crystal sheen ;
Its carpet, flower-besprinkled green ;
Where pastured at their ease
Both flocks of sheep and dainty heifers,
And play'd the cooling breeze—
The native land of all the zephyrs.
No sooner is the lion there
Than of some sickness he complains.
Says he, You on your mission fare.
A fever, with its thirst and pains,
Dries up my blood, and bakes my brains ;
And I must search some herb,
Its fatal power to curb.
For you, there is no time to waste ;
Pay me my money, and make haste.
The treasures were unbound,
And placed upon the ground.
Then, with a look which testified
His royal joy, the lion cried,
My coins, good heavens, have multiplied !
And see the young ones of the gold
As big already as the old !
The increase belongs to me, no doubt ;
And eagerly he took it out !
'Twas little staid beneath the lid ;
The wonder was that any did.
Confounded were the monkey and his suite.
And, dumb with fear, betook them to their way,
And bore complaint to Jove's great son, they say—
Complaint without a reason meet ;
For what could he ! Though a celestial scion,
He could but fight, as lion versus lion.

When corsairs battle, Turk with Turk,
They're not about their proper work.

XIII.—THE HORSE WISHING TO BE REVENGED UPON THE STAG.

The horses have not always been
The humble slaves of men.
When, in the far-off past,
The fare of gentlemen was mast,
And even hats were never felt,
Horse, ass, and mule in forests dwelt.
Nor saw one then, as in these ages,
So many saddles, housings, pillions ;
Such splendid equipages,
With golden-lace postilions ;
Such harnesses for cattle,
To be consumed in battle ;
As one saw not so many feasts,
And people married by the priests.
The horse fell out, within that space,
With the antler'd stag, so fleetly made :
He could not catch him in a race,
And so he came to man for aid.
Man first his suppliant bitted ;
Then, on his back well seated,
Gave chase with spear, and rested not
Till to the ground the foe he brought.
This done, the honest horse, quite blindly,
Thus thank'd his benefactor kindly :—
Dear sir, I'm much obliged to you ;
I'll back to savage life. Adieu !
O, no, the man replied ;
You'd better here abide ;
I know too well your use.
Here, free from all abuse,
Remain a liege to me,
And large your provender shall be.
Alas ! good housing or good cheer,
That costs one's liberty, is dear.
The horse his folly now perceived,
But quite too late he grieved.
No grief his fate could alter ;
His stall was built, and there he lived,
And died there in his halter.
Ah ! wise had he one small offence forgot !
Revenge, however sweet, is dearly bought
By that one good, which gone, all else is nought.

XIV.—THE FOX AND THE BUST.

The great are like the maskers of the stage ;
Their show deceives the simple of the age.
For all that they appear to be they pass,
With only those whose type 's the ass.
The fox, more wary, looks beneath the skin,
And looks on every side, and, when he sees
That all their glory is a semblance thin,
He turns, and saves the hinges of his knees,
With such a speech as once, 'tis said,
He utter'd to a hero's head.
A bust, somewhat colossal in its size,
Attracted crowds of wondering eyes.
The fox admired the sculptor's pains :
Fine head, said he, but void of brains !
The same remark to many a lord applies.

XV.—THE WOLF, THE GOAT, AND THE KID.

As went the goat her pendent dugs to fill,
And browse the herbage of a distant hill,
    She latch'd her door, and bid,
    With matron care, her kid ;—
      My daughter, as you live,
      This portal don't undo
      To any creature who
      This watchword does not give :
    " Deuce take the wolf and all his race !"
The wolf was passing near the place
By chance, and heard the words with pleasure,
    And laid them up as useful treasure ;
And hardly need we mention,
Escaped the goat's attention.
    No sooner did he see
    The matron off, than he,
With hypocritic tone and face,
Cried out before the place,
" Deuce take the wolf and all his race !"
    Not doubting thus to gain admission,
The kid, not void of all suspicion,
Peer'd through a crack, and cried,
    Show me white paw before
    You ask me to undo the door.
The wolf could not, if he had died,
    For wolves have no connexion
    With paws of that complexion.
So, much surprised, our gormandiser
Retired to fast till he was wiser.
How would the kid have been undone.
    Had she but trusted to the word
    The wolf by chance had overheard !
Two sureties better are than one ;
    And caution 's worth its cost,
    Though sometimes seeming lost.

XVI.—THE WOLF, THE MOTHER, AND HER CHILD.

This wolf another brings to mind,
Who found dame Fortune more unkind,
  . In that the greedy, pirate sinner,
    Was balk'd of life as well as dinner.
As saith our tale, a villager
    Dwelt in a by, unguarded place ;
There, hungry, watch'd our pillager
For luck and chance to mend his case.
For there his thievish eyes had seen
All sorts of game go out and in—
Nice sucking calves, and lambs and sheep ;
    And turkeys by the regiment,
    With steps so proud, and necks so bent,
They'd make a daintier glutton weep.
The thief at length began to tire
Of being gnaw'd by vain desire.
Just then a child set up a cry :
Be still, the mother said, or I
Will throw you to the wolf, you brat !
Ha, ha ! thought he, what talk is that !
The gods be thank'd for luck so good !
And ready at the door he stood,
When soothingly the mother said,
    Now cry no more, my little dear ;
    That naughty wolf, if he comes here,
Your dear papa shall kill him dead.

Humph ! cried the veteran mutton-eater.
    Now this, now that ! Now hot, now cool !
Is this the way they change their metre !
    And do they take me for a fool !
Some day, a nutting in the wood,
That young one yet shall be my food.
But little time has he to dote
    On such a feast ; the dogs rush out
And seize the caitiff by the throat ;
    And country ditchers, thick and stout,
With rustic spears and forks of iron,
The hapless animal environ.
What brought you here, old head ! cried one.
    He told it all, as I have done,
Why, bless my soul ! the frantic mother said,—
    You, villain, eat my little son !
    And did I nurse the darling boy,
    Your fiendish appetite to cloy !
With that they knock'd him on the head.
His feet and scalp they bore to town,
    To grace the seigneur's hall,
    Where, pinn'd against the wall,
This verse completed his renown :—
    " Ye honest wolves, believe not all
That mothers say, when children squall !"

XVII.—THE WORDS OF SOCRATES.

A house was built by Socrates
That failed the public taste to please.
Some blamed the inside ; some, the out ; and all
    Agreed that the apartments were too small.
Such rooms for him, the greatest sage of Greece !
    I ask, said he, no greater bliss
    Than real friends to fill e'en this.
    And reason had good Socrates
To think his house too large for these.
A crowd to be your friends will claim,
    Till some unhandsome test you bring.
There's nothing plentier than the name ;
    There's nothing rarer than the thing.

XVIII.—THE OLD MAN AND HIS SONS.

All power is feeble with dissension :
    For this I quote the Phrygian slave.
If aught I add to his invention,
    It is our manners to engrave,
    And not from any envious wishes ;—
    I'm not so foolishly ambitious.
Phædrus enriches oft his story,
    In quest—I doubt it not—of glory !
    Such thoughts were idle in my breast.
An aged man, near going to his rest,
His gather'd sons thus solemnly address'd :—
To break this bunch of arrows you may try ;
And, first, the string that binds them I untie.
The elders, having tried with might and main,
    Exclaim'd, This bundle I resign
    To muscles sturdier than mine.
The second tried, and bow'd himself in vain.
The youngest took them with the like success.
All were obliged their weakness to confess.
Unharm'd the arrows pass'd from son to son ;
Of all they did not break a single one.
Weak fellows ! said their sire, I now must show
What in the case my feeble strength can do.

They laugh'd, and thought their father but in joke,
Till, one by one, they saw the arrows broke.
See concord's power ! replied the sire ; as long
As you in love agree, you will be strong.
I go, my sons, to join our fathers good ;
Now promise me to live as brothers should,
And soothe by this your dying father's fears.
Each strictly promised with a flood of tears.
Their father took them by the hand, and died ;
And soon the virtue of their vows was tried.
 Their sire had left a large estate
 Involved in lawsuits intricate ;
 Here seized a creditor, and there
 A neighbour levied for a share.
 At first the trio nobly bore
 The brunt of all this legal war.
 But short their friendship as 'twas rare.
Whom blood had join'd—and small the wonder !—
 The force of interest drove asunder ;
 And, as is wont in such affairs,
 Ambition, envy, were coheirs.
 In parcelling their sire's estate,
 They quarrel, quibble, litigate,
 Each aiming to supplant the other.
 The judge, by turns, condemns each brother.
 Their creditors make new assault,
 Some pleading error, some default.
 The sunder'd brothers disagree ;
 For counsel one, have counsels three.
All lose their wealth ; and now their sorrows
Bring fresh to mind those broken arrows.

XIX.—THE ORACLE AND THE ATHEIST.

THAT man his Maker can deceive,
Is monstrous folly to believe.
The labyrinthine mazes of the heart
Are open to His eyes in every part.
Whatever one may do, or think, or feel,
From Him no darkness can the thing conceal.
A pagan once, of graceless heart and hollow,
 Whose faith in gods, I'm apprehensive,
 Was quite as real as expensive,
Consulted, at his shrine, the god Apollo.
 Is what I hold alive, or not ?
Said he,—a sparrow having brought,
Prepared to wring its neck, or let it fly,
As need might be, to give the god the lie.
 Apollo saw the trick,
 And answer'd quick,
Dead or alive, show me your sparrow,
 And cease to set for me a trap
 Which can but cause yourself mishap.
I see afar, and far I shoot my arrow.

XX.—THE MISER WHO HAD LOST HIS TREASURE.

'TIS use that constitutes possession.
I ask that sort of men, whose passion
 It is to get and never spend,
 Of all their toil what is the end ;
What they enjoy of all their labours
Which do not equally their neighbours ?
Throughout this upper mortal strife,
The miser leads a beggar's life.

Old Æsop's man of hidden treasure
May serve the case to demonstrate.
He had a great estate,
But chose a second life to wait
Ere he began to taste his pleasure.
This man, whom gold so little bless'd,
Was not possessor, but possess'd.
His cash he buried under ground,
Where only might his heart be found ;
It being, then, his sole delight
To ponder of it day and night,
And consecrate his rusty pelf,
A sacred offering, to himself.
In all his eating, drinking, travel,
Most wondrous short of funds he seem'd ;
One would have thought he little dream'd
Where lay such sums beneath the gravel.
A ditcher mark'd his coming to the spot,
 So frequent was it,
And thus at last some little inkling got
 Of the deposit.
He took it all, and babbled not.
 One morning, ere the dawn,
 Forth had our miser gone
To worship what he loved the best,
When, lo ! he found an empty nest !
Alas ! what groaning, wailing, crying !
What deep and bitter sighing !
 His torment makes him tear
 Out by the roots his hair.
A passenger demandeth why
 Such marvellous outcry.
They've got my gold ! it's gone—it's gone !
Your gold ! pray where ?—Beneath this stone.
Why, man, is this a time of war,
That you should bring your gold so far ?
You'd better kept it in your drawer ;
And I'll be bound, if once but in it,
You could have got it any minute.
At any minute ! Ah, Heaven knows
That cash comes harder than it goes !
I touch'd it not.—Then have the grace
To explain to me that rueful face,
 Replied the man ; for, if 'tis true
You touch'd it not, how plain the case,
That, put the stone back in its place,
 And all will be as well for you !

XXI.—THE EYE OF THE MASTER.

A STAG took refuge from the chase
 Among the oxen of a stable,
 Who counsel'd him, as saith the fable,
To seek at once some safer place.
My brothers, said the fugitive,
Betray me not, and, as I live,
The richest pasture I will show,
That e'er was grazed on, high or low ;
Your kindness you will not regret,
For well some day I'll pay the debt.
 The oxen promised secrecy.
Down crouch'd the stag, and breathed more free.
 At eventide they brought fresh hay,
 As was their custom day by day ;
 And often came the servants near,
 As did indeed the overseer,

But with so little thought or care,
That neither horns, nor hide, nor hair
Reveal'd to them the stag was there.
Already thank'd the wild-wood stranger
The oxen for their treatment kind,
And there to wait made up his mind,
Till he might issue free from danger.
Replied an ox that chew'd the cud,
Your case looks fairly in the bud ;
But then I fear the reason why
Is, that the man of sharpest eye
Hath not yet come his look to take.
I dread his coming, for your sake ;
Your boasting may be premature ;
Till then, poor stag, you're not secure.
'Twas but a little while before
The careful master oped the door.
    How's this, my boys ? said he ;
These empty racks will never do.
Go, change this dirty litter too.
    More care than this I want to see
    Of oxen that belong to me.
Well, Jim, my boy, you're young and stout ;
What would it cost to clear these cobwebs out ?
And put these yokes, and hames, and traces,
All as they should be, in their places ?
    Thus looking round, he came to see
    One head he did not usually.
        The stag is found ; his foes
        Deal heavily their blows.
        Down sinks he in the strife ;
        No tears can save his life.
They slay, and dress, and salt the beast,
And cook his flesh in many a feast,
And many a neighbour gets a taste.
    As Phædrus says it, pithily,
    The master's is the eye to see :—
    I add the lover's, as for me.

XXII.—THE LARK AND HER YOUNG ONES WITH
        THE OWNER OF A FIELD.

" DEPEND upon yourself alone,"
Has to a common proverb grown.
'Tis thus confirm'd in Æsop's way :—
The larks to build their nests are seen
Among the wheat-crops young and green ;
        That is to say,
What time all things, dame Nature heeding,
Betake themselves to love and breeding—
        The monstrous whales and sharks
            Beneath the briny flood,
            The tigers in the wood,
        And in the fields, the larks.
One she, however, of these last,
Found more than half the spring-time past
Without the taste of spring-time pleasures ;
    When firmly she set up her will
    That she would be a mother still,
    And resolutely took her measures ;—
First, got herself by Hymen match'd ;
Then built her nest, laid, sat, and hatch'd.
    All went as well as such things could.
    The wheat-crop ripening ere the brood
Were strong enough to take their flight,
Aware how perilous their plight,
    The lark went out to search for food,

And told her young to listen well,
And keep a constant sentinel.
The owner of this field, said she,
Will come, I know, his grain to see.
Hear all he says ; we little birds
Must shape our conduct by his words.
    No sooner was the lark away,
Than came the owner with his son.
This wheat is ripe, said he : now run
        And give our friends a call
        To bring their sickles all,
        And help us, great and small,
    To-morrow, at the break of day.
The lark, returning, found no harm,
Except her nest in wild alarm.
Says one, We heard the owner say,
Go, give our friends a call
To help, to-morrow, break of day.
    Replied the lark, If that is all,
    We need not be in any fear,
But only keep an open ear.
As gay as larks, now eat your victuals.—
They ate and slept—the great and littles.
The dawn arrives, but not the friends ;
The lark soars up, the owner wends
His usual round to view his land.
This grain, says he, ought not to stand.
Our friends do wrong ; and so does he
Who trusts that friends will friendly be.
My son, go call our kith and kin
To help us get our harvest in.
    This second order made
The little larks still more afraid.
He sent for kindred, mother, by his son ;
The work will now, indeed, be done.
    No, darlings ; go to sleep ;
    Our lowly nest we'll keep.
With reason said, for kindred there came none.
Thus, tired of expectation vain,
Once more the owner view'd his grain.
My son, said he, we're surely fools
To wait for other people's tools ;
As if one might, for love or pelf,
Have friends more faithful than himself !
Engrave this lesson deep, my son.
And know you now what must be done ?
We must ourselves our sickles bring,
And, while the larks their matins sing,
Begin the work ; and, on this plan,
Get in our harvest as we can.
This plan the lark no sooner knew,
Than, Now's the time, she said, my chicks ;
And, taking little time to fix,
        Away they flew ;
All fluttering, soaring, often grounding,
Decamp'd without a trumpet sounding.

~~~~~~~~~~~~~~~

BOOK V.

I.—THE WOODMAN AND MERCURY.
TO M. THE CHEVALIER DE BOUILLON.

YOUR taste has served my work to guide ;
To gain its suffrage I have tried.
You'd have me shun a care too nice,
Or beauty at too dear a price,
Or too much effort, as a vice.

My taste with yours agrees :
Such effort cannot please ;
And too much pains about the polish
Is apt the substance to abolish ;
Not that it would be right or wise
The graces all to ostracize.
You love them much when delicate ;
Nor is it left for me to hate.
As to the scope of Æsop's plan,
I fail as little as I can.
If this my rhymed and measured speech
Availeth not to please or teach,
I own it not a fault of mine ;
Some unknown reason I assign.
   With little strength endued
   For battles rough and rude,
Or with Herculean arm to smite,
I show to vice its foolish plight.
In this my talent wholly lies ;
Not that it does at all suffice.
My fable sometimes brings to view
The face of vanity purblind
With that of restless envy join'd ;
And life now turns upon these pivots two.
Such is the silly little frog
That aped the ox upon her bog.
A double image sometimes shows
How vice and folly do oppose
The ways of virtue and good sense ;
As lambs with wolves so grim and gaunt,
The silly fly and frugal ant.
Thus swells my work—a comedy immense—
Its acts unnumber'd and diverse,
Its scene the boundless universe.
Gods, men, and brutes, all play their part
In fields of nature or of art,
And Jupiter among the rest.
Here comes the god who's wont to bear
Jove's frequent errands to the fair,
With wingéd heels and haste ;
But other work 's in hand to-day.

A man that labour'd in the wood
Had lost his honest livelihood ;
    That is to say,
   His axe was gone astray.
   He had no tools to spare ;
   This wholly earn'd his fare.
   Without a hope beside,
   He sat him down and cried,
Alas, my axe ! where can it be ?
O Jove ! but send it back to me,
And it shall strike good blows for thee.
His prayer in high Olympus heard,
Swift Mercury started at the word.
Your axe must not be lost, said he :
Now will you know it when you see ?
An axe I found upon the road.
With that an axe of gold he show'd.
Is't this ? The woodman answer'd, Nay.
An axe of silver, bright and gay,
Refused the honest woodman too.
At last the finder brought to view
An axe of iron, steel, and wood.
That's mine, he said, in joyful mood ;
With that I'll quite contented be.
The god replied, I give the three,
As due reward of honesty.
This luck when neighbouring choppers knew,
They lost their axes, not a few,

And sent their prayers to Jupiter
So fast, he knew not which to hear.
His wingéd son, however, sent
With gold and silver axes, went.
Each would have thought himself a fool
Not to have own'd the richest tool.
But Mercury promptly gave, instead
Of it, a blow upon the head.
With simple truth to be contented,
Is surest not to be repented ;
   But still there are who would
   With evil trap the good,—
   Whose cunning is but stupid,
   For Jove is never dupéd.

II.—THE EARTHEN POT AND THE IRON POT.

An iron pot proposed
   To an earthen pot a journey.
The latter was opposed,
   Expressing the concern he
Had felt about the danger
Of going out a ranger.
He thought the kitchen hearth
The safest place on earth
For one so very brittle.
For thee, who art a kettle,
And hast a tougher skin,
There's nought to keep thee in.
I'll be thy body-guard,
   Replied the iron pot,
If anything that's hard
   Should threaten thee a jot,
Between you I will go,
And save thee from the blow.
This offer him persuaded.
The iron pot paraded
Himself as guard and guide
Close at his cousin's side.
Now, in their tripod way,
They hobble as they may;
And eke together bolt
At every little jolt,—
   Which gives the crockery pain ;
   But presently his comrade hits
   So hard, he dashes him to bits,
Before he can complain.

Take care that you associate
With equals only, lest your fate
Between these pots should find its mate.

III.—THE LITTLE FISH AND THE FISHER.

A little fish will grow,
   If life be spared, a great;
But yet to let him go,
   And for his growing wait,
May not be very wise,
   As 'tis not sure your bait
Will catch him when of size.
Upon a river bank, a fisher took
A tiny troutling from his hook.
Said he, 'Twill serve to count, at least,
As the beginning of my feast ;
And so I'll put it with the rest.
   This little fish, thus caught,
   His clemency besought.

What will your honour do with me !
I'm not a mouthful, as you see.
Pray let me grow to be a trout,
And then come here and fish me out.
Some alderman, who likes things nice,
Will buy me then at any price.
But now, a hundred such you'll have to fish,
To make a single good-for-nothing dish.
    Well, well, be it so, replied the fisher,
My little fish, who play the preacher,
The frying-pan must be your lot,
Although, no doubt, you like it not :
I fry the fry that can be got.

    In some things, men of sense
Prefer the present to the future tense.

IV.—THE EARS OF THE HARE.

Some beast with horns did gore
    The lion; and that sovereign dread,
Resolved to suffer so no more,
    Straight banish'd from his realm, 'tis said,
All sorts of beasts with horns—
Rams, bulls, goats, stags, and unicorns.
    Such brutes all promptly fled.
A hare, the shadow of his ears perceiving,
    Could hardly help believing
That some vile spy for horns would take them,
And food for accusation make them.
Adieu, said he, my neighbour cricket ;
I take my foreign ticket.
    My ears, should I stay here,
    Will turn to horns, I fear ;
And were they shorter than a bird's,
I fear the effect of words.
These horns ! the cricket answer'd ; why,
God made them ears who can deny ?
Yes, said the coward, still they'll make them horns,
And horns, perhaps of unicorns !
    In vain shall I protest,
With all the learning of the schools :
    My reasons they will send to rest
    In th' Hospital of Fools.

V.—THE FOX WITH HIS TAIL CUT OFF.

A cunning old fox, of plundering habits,
Great crauncher of fowls, great catcher of rabbits,
Whom none of his sort had caught in a nap,
Was finally caught in somebody's trap.
By luck he escaped, not wholly and hale,
For the price of his luck was the loss of his tail.
Escaped in this way, to save his disgrace,
He thought to get others in similar case.
One day that the foxes in council were met,
Why wear we, said he, this cumbering weight,
Which sweeps in the dirt wherever it goes ?
Pray tell me its use if any one knows.
    If the council will take my advice,
    We shall dock off our tails in a trice.
Your advice may be good, said one on the ground;
But, ere I reply, pray turn yourself round ;
Whereat such a shout from the council was heard,
Poor bob-tail, confounded, could say not a word.
To urge the reform would have wasted his breath:
Long tails were the mode till the day of his death.

VI.—THE OLD WOMAN AND HER TWO SERVANTS.

A beldam kept two spinning maids,
Who plied so handily their trades,
Those spinning sisters down below
Were bunglers when compared with these.
No care did this old woman know
But giving tasks as she might please.
No sooner did the god of day
    His glorious locks enkindle,
Than both the wheels began to play,
    And from each whirling spindle
Forth danced the thread right merrily,
And back was coil'd unceasingly.
Soon as the dawn, I say, its tresses show'd,
A graceless cock most punctual crow'd.
The beldam roused, more graceless yet,
    In greasy petticoat bedight,
    Struck up her farthing light,
And then forthwith the bed beset,
Where deeply, blessedly did snore
Those two maid-servants tired and poor.
One oped an eye, an arm one stretch'd,
And both their breath most sadly fetch'd,
This threat concealing in the sigh—
That cursed cock shall surely die !
And so he did :—they cut his throat,
And put to sleep his rousing note.
And yet this murder mended not
The cruel hardship of their lot ;
For now the twain were scarce in bed
Before they heard the summons dread.
The beldam, full of apprehension
Lest oversleep should cause detention,
Ran like a goblin through her mansion.
    Thus often, when one thinks
    To clear himself from ill,
    His effort only sinks
    Him in the deeper still.
    The beldam acting for the cock,
    Was Scylla for Charybdis' rock.

VII.—THE SATYR AND THE TRAVELLER.

Within a savage forest grot
    A satyr and his chips
Were taking down their porridge hot;
    Their cups were at their lips.

You might have seen in mossy den,
    Himself, his wife, and brood ;
They had not tailor-clothes, like men,
    But appetites as good.

In came a traveller, benighted,
    All hungry, cold, and wet,
Who heard himself to eat invited
    With nothing like regret.

He did not give his host the pain
    His asking to repeat;
But first he blew with might and main
    To give his fingers heat.

Then in his steaming porridge dish
  He delicately blew.
The wondering satyr said, I wish
  The use of both I knew.

Why, first, my blowing warms my hand,
  And then it cools my porridge.
Ah! said his host, then understand
  I cannot give you storage.

To sleep beneath one roof with you,
  I may not be so bold.
Far be from me that mouth untrue
  Which blows both hot and cold.

VIII.—THE HORSE AND THE WOLF.

A WOLF, what time the thawing breeze
Renews the life of plants and trees,
And beasts go forth from winter lair
To seek abroad their various fare,—
A wolf, I say, about those days,
In sharp look-out for means and ways,
Espied a horse turn'd out to graze.
His joy the reader may opine.
Once got, said he, this game were fine;
But if a sheep, 'twere sooner mine.
I can't proceed my usual way;
Some trick must now be put in play.
          This said,
He came with measured tread,
As if a healer of disease,—
Some pupil of Hippocrates,—
And told the horse, with learned verbs,
He knew the power of roots and herbs,— .
Whatever grew about those borders,—
  And not at all to flatter
  Himself in such a matter,
  Could cure of all disorders.
If he, Sir Horse, would not conceal
  The symptoms of his case,
He, Doctor Wolf, would gratis heal;
For that to feed in such a place,
  And run about untied,
Was proof itself of some disease,
  As all the books decide.
I have, good doctor, if you please,
Replied the horse, as I presume,
Beneath my foot, an aposthume.
My son, replied the learned leech,
That part, as all our authors teach,
Is strikingly susceptible
Of ills which make acceptable
What you may also have from me—
The aid of skilful surgery;
Which noble art, the fact is,
For horses of the blood I practise.
The fellow, with this talk sublime,
Watch'd for a snap the fitting time.
Meanwhile, suspicious of some trick,
  The wary patient nearer draws,
And gives his doctor such a kick,
  As makes a chowder of his jaws.
Exclaim'd the wolf, in sorry plight,
I own those heels have served me right.
  I err'd to quit my trade,
    As I will not in future;
  Me nature surely made
    For nothing but a butcher.

IX.—THE PLOUGHMAN AND HIS SONS.

  THE farmer's patient care and toil
  Are oftener wanting than the soil.

A wealthy ploughman drawing near his end,
Call'd in his sons apart from every friend,
  And said, When of your sire bereft,
  The heritage our fathers left
  Guard well, nor sell a single field.
  A treasure in it is conceal'd:
  The place, precisely, I don't know,
  But industry will serve to show.
  The harvest past, Time's forelock take,
  And search with plough, and spade, and rake;
  Turn over every inch of sod,
  Nor leave unsearch'd a single clod.
The father died. The sons—and not in vain—
  Turn'd o'er the soil, and o'er again;
  That year their acres bore
  More grain than e'er before.
  Though hidden money found they none,
  Yet had their father wisely done,
    To show by such a measure,
    That toil itself is treasure.

X.—THE MOUNTAIN IN LABOUR.

  A MOUNTAIN was in travail pang;
  The country with her clamour rang.
    Out ran the people all, to see,
    Supposing that the birth would be
    A city, or at least a house.
      It was a mouse!

  In thinking of this fable,
    Of story feign'd and false,
  But meaning veritable,
    My mind the image calls
  Of one who writes, "The war I sing
Which Titans waged against the Thunder-king."
  As on the sounding verses ring,
    What will be brought to birth?
      Why, dearth.

XI.—FORTUNE AND THE BOY

  BESIDE a well, uncurb'd and deep,
  A schoolboy laid him down to sleep:
  (Such rogues can do so anywhere.)
  If some kind man had seen him there,
  He would have leap'd as if distracted;
  But Fortune much more wisely acted;
For, passing by, she softly waked the child,
Thus whispering in accents mild:
    I save your life, my little dear,
    And beg you not to venture here
    Again, for had you fallen in,
  I should have had to bear the sin;
  But I demand, in reason's name,
  If for your rashness I'm to blame.
With this the goddess went her way.
I like her logic, I must say.

There takes place nothing on this planet,
But Fortune ends, whoe'er began it.
In all adventures good or ill,
We look to her to foot the bill.
Has one a stupid, empty pate,
That serves him never till too late?
He clears himself by blaming Fate.

XII.—THE DOCTORS.

THE selfsame patient put to test
Two doctors, Fear-the-worst and Hope-the-best.
The latter hoped; the former did maintain
The man would take all medicine in vain.
By different cures the patient was beset,
But erelong cancell'd nature's debt,
      While nursed
As was prescribed by Fear-the-worst.
But over the disease both triumph'd still.
Said one, I well foresaw his death.
Yes, said the other, but my pill
Would certainly have saved his breath.

XIII.—THE HEN WITH THE GOLDEN EGGS.

How avarice loseth all,
   By striving all to gain,
I need no witness call
   But him whose thrifty hen,
As by the fable we are told,
Laid every day an egg of gold.
She hath a treasure in her body,
Bethinks the avaricious noddy.
He kills and opens—vexed to find
All things like hens of common kind.
Thus spoil'd the source of all his riches,
To misers he a lesson teaches.
   In these last changes of the moon,
   How often doth one see
   Men made as poor as he
By force of getting rich too soon!

XIV.—THE ASS CARRYING RELICS.

AN ass, with relics for his load,
Supposed the worship on the road
   Meant for himself alone,
   And took on lofty airs,
   Receiving as his own
   The incense and the prayers.
Some one, who saw his great mistake,
Cried, Master Donkey, do not make
   Yourself so big a fool.
Not you they worship, but your pack;
They praise the idols on your back,
   And count yourself a paltry tool.

'Tis thus a brainless magistrate
Is honour'd for his robe of state.

XV.—THE STAG AND THE VINE.

A STAG, by favour of a vine,
Which grew where suns most genial shine,
And form'd a thick and matted bower
Which might have turn'd a summer shower,
Was saved from ruinous assault.
The hunters thought their dogs at fault,
And call'd them off. In danger now no more,
The stag, a thankless wretch and vile,
Began to browse his benefactress o'er.
The hunters, listening the while,
   The rustling heard, came back
   With all their yelping pack,
And seized him in that very place.
This is, said he, but justice, in my case.
   Let every black ingrate
   Henceforward profit by my fate.
The dogs fell to—'twere wasting breath
To pray those hunters at the death.
They left, and we will not revile 'em,
A warning for profaners of asylum.

XVI.—THE SERPENT AND THE FILE.

A SERPENT, neighbour to a smith,
(A neighbour bad to meddle with,)
Went through his shop, in search of food,
But nothing found, 'tis understood,
To eat, except a file of steel,
Of which he tried to make a meal.
The file, without a spark of passion,
Address'd him in the following fashion :—
Poor simpleton! you surely bite
With less of sense than appetite ;
   For ere from me you gain
   One quarter of a grain,
You'll break your teeth from ear to ear.
Time's are the only teeth I fear.

This tale concerns those men of letters,
Who, good for nothing, bite their betters.
Their biting so is quite unwise.
   Think you, ye literary sharks,
   Your teeth will leave their marks
Upon the deathless works you criticise?
   Fie! fie! fie! men!
To you they're brass—they're steel—they're diamond.

XVII.—THE HARE AND THE PARTRIDGE.

BEWARE how you deride
The exiles from life's sunny side :
   To you is little known
   How soon their case may be your own.
On this, sage Æsop gives a tale or two,
As in my verses I propose to do.
   A field in common share
   A partridge and a hare,
   And live in peaceful state,
   Till, woeful to relate !
   The hunters' mingled cry
   Compels the hare to fly.

He hurries to his fort,
And spoils almost the sport
By faulting every hound
That yelps upon the ground.
At last his reeking heat
Betrays his snug retreat.
Old Tray, with philosophic nose,
Snuffs carefully, and grows
So certain, that he cries,
    The hare is here ; bow wow !
    And veteran Ranger now,—
The dog that never lies,—
The hare is gone, replies.
Alas ! poor, wretched hare,
Back comes he to his lair,
To meet destruction there !
The partridge, void of fear,
Begins her friend to jeer :—
You bragg'd of being fleet ;
How serve you, now, your feet ?
Scarce has she ceased to speak,—
The laugh yet in her beak,—
When comes her turn to die,
From which she could not fly.
She thought her wings, indeed,
Enough for every need ;
But in her laugh and talk,
Forgot the cruel hawk !

XVIII.—THE EAGLE AND THE OWL.

THE eagle and the owl, resolved to cease
Their war, embraced in pledge of peace.
On faith of king, on faith of owl, they swore
That they would eat each other's chicks no more.
    But know you mine ? said Wisdom's bird.
    Not I, indeed, the eagle cried.
    The worse for that, the owl replied :
I fear your oath 's a useless word ;
    I fear that you, as king, will not
    Consider duly who or what :
You kings and gods, of what 's before ye,
Are apt to make one category.
Adieu, my young, if you should meet them !
Describe them, then, or let me greet them,
And, on my life, I will not eat them,
The eagle said.   The owl replied :
My little ones, I say with pride,
For grace of form cannot be match'd,—
The prettiest birds that e'er were hatch'd ;
By this you cannot fail to know them ;
'Tis needless, therefore, that I show them.
Pray don't forget, but keep this mark in view,
Lest fate should curse my happy nest by you.
At length God gives the owl a set of heirs,
And while at early eve abroad he fares,
    In quest of birds and mice for food,
    Our eagle haply spies the brood,
    As on some craggy rock they sprawl,
    Or nestle in some ruined wall,
    (But which it matters not at all,)
    And thinks them ugly little frights,
    Grim, sad, with voice like shrieking sprites.
These chicks, says he, with looks almost infernal,
Can't be the darlings of our friend nocturnal.
I'll sup of them.   And so he did, not slightly :—
He never sups, if he can help it, lightly.

The owl return'd ; and, sad, he found
    Nought left but claws upon the ground.
He pray'd the gods above and gods below
To smite the brigand who had caused his woe.
Quoth one, On you alone the blame must fall ;
    Or rather on the law of nature,
    Which wills that every earthly creature
Shall think its like the loveliest of all.
You told the eagle of your young ones' graces ;
    You gave the picture of their faces :—
    Had it of likeness any traces ?

XIX.—THE LION GOING TO WAR.

THE lion had an enterprise in hand ;
    Held a war-council, sent his provost-marshal,
    And gave the animals a call impartial—
Each, in his way, to serve his high command.
    The elephant should carry on his back
    The tools of war, the mighty public pack,
    And fight in elephantine way and form ;
    The bear should hold himself prepared to storm ;
    The fox all secret stratagems should fix ;
    The monkey should amuse the foe by tricks.
Dismiss, said one, the blockhead asses,
    And hares, too cowardly and fleet.
No, said the king ; I use all classes ;
    Without their aid my force were incomplete.
The ass shall be our trumpeter, to scare
Our enemy.   And then the nimble hare
Our royal bulletins shall homeward bear.

    A monarch provident and wise
Will hold his subjects all of consequence,
    And know in each what talent lies.
There's nothing useless to a man of sense.

XX.—THE BEAR AND THE TWO COMPANIONS.

    Two fellows, needing funds, and bold,
    A bearskin to a furrier sold,
    Of which the bear was living still,
    But which they presently would kill—
        At least they said they would.
    And, if their word was good,
    It was a king of bears—an Ursa Major—
        The biggest bear beneath the sun.
    Its skin, the chaps would wager,
        Was cheap at double cost ;
        'Twould make one laugh at frost—
        And make two robes as well as one.
    Old Dindenaut*, in sheep who dealt,
    Less prized his sheep, than they their pelt—
        (In their account 'twas theirs,
        But in his own, the bear's.)
    By bargain struck upon the skin,
    Two days at most must bring it in.
Forth went the two.   More easy found than got,
The bear came growling at them on the trot.
Behold our dealers both confounded,
As if by thunderbolt astounded !
Their bargain vanish'd suddenly in air ;
For who could plead his interest with a bear ?
    One of the friends sprung up a tree ;
    The other, cold as ice could be,

---

* Vide Rabelais, *Pantagruel*, Book IV. Chap. viii.

Fell on his face, feign'd death,
And closely held his breath,—
He having somewhere heard it said
The bear ne'er preys upon the dead.
Sir Bear, sad blockhead, was deceived—
The prostrate man a corpse believed ;
But, half suspecting some deceit,
He feels and snuffs from head to feet,
And in the nostrils blows.
The body's surely dead, he thinks.
I'll leave it, says he, for it stinks ;
    And off into the woods he goes.
The other dealer, from his tree
Descending cautiously, to see
His comrade lying in the dirt,
    Consoling, says, It is a wonder
    That, by the monster forced asunder,
We're, after all, more scared than hurt.
But, addeth he, what of the creature's skin ?
He held his muzzle very near ;
What did he whisper in your ear ?
He gave this caution,—" Never dare
Again to sell the skin of bear
Its owner has not ceased to wear."

———

XXI.—THE ASS DRESSED IN THE LION'S SKIN.

CLAD in a lion's shaggy hide,
An ass spread terror far and wide,
And, though himself a coward brute,
Put all the world to scampering rout :
    But, by a piece of evil luck,
    A portion of an ear outstuck,
    Which soon reveal'd the error
    Of all the panic-terror.
Old Martin did his office quick.
Surprised were all who did not know the trick,
    To see that Martin, at his will,
    Was driving lions to the mill !

    In France, the men are not a few
    Of whom this fable proves too true ;
    Whose valour chiefly doth reside
    In coat they wear and horse they ride.

———

BOOK VI.

—

I.—THE SHEPHERD AND THE LION.

OF fables judge not by their face ;
They give the simplest brute a teacher's place.
Bare precepts were inert and tedious things ;
The story gives them life and wings.
    But story for the story's sake
    Were sorry business for the wise ;
As if, for pill that one should take,
    You gave the sugary disguise.
    For reasons such as these,
Full many writers great and good
Have written in this frolic mood,
    And made their wisdom please.
But tinsel'd style they all have shunn'd with care ;
With them one never sees a word to spare.
Of Phædrus some have blamed the brevity,
While Æsop uses fewer words than he.

A certain Greek, however, beats
Them both in his laconic feats.
Each tale he locks in verses four ;
The well or ill I leave to critic lore.
At Æsop's side to see him let us aim,
Upon a theme substantially the same.
The one selects a lover of the chase ;
A shepherd comes, the other's tale to grace.
Their tracks I keep, though either tale may grow
A little in its features as I go.

The one which Æsop tells is nearly this :—
A shepherd from his flock began to miss,
And long'd to catch the stealer of his sheep.
    Before a cavern, dark and deep,
    Where wolves retired by day to sleep,
    Which he suspected as the thieves,
    He set his trap among the leaves ;
    And, ere he left the place,
    He thus invoked celestial grace :—
    O king of all the powers divine,
Against the rogue but grant me this delight,
That this my trap may catch him in my sight,
    And I, from twenty calves of mine,
    Will make the fattest thine.
But while the words were on his tongue,
Forth came a lion great and strong.
Down crouch'd the man of sheep, and said,
    With shivering fright half dead,
Alas ! that man should never be aware
Of what may be the meaning of his prayer !
    To catch the robber of my flocks,
    O king of gods, I pledged a calf to thee :
    If from his clutches thou wilt rescue me,
    I'll raise my offering to an ox.

'Tis thus the master-author tells the stor
    Now hear the rival of his glory.

———

II.—THE LION AND THE HUNTER.

A BRAGGART, lover of the chase,
Had lost a dog of valued race,
And thought him in a lion's maw.
He ask'd a shepherd whom he saw,
Pray show me, man, the robber's place,
And I'll have justice in the case.
    'Tis on this mountain side,
    The shepherd man replied.
The tribute of a sheep I pay,
Each month, and where I please I stray.
Out leap'd the lion as he spake,
    And came that way, with agile feet.
The braggart, prompt his flight to take,
    Cried, Jove, O grant a safe retreat !

    A danger close at hand
    Of courage is the test.
    It shows us who will stand—
    Whose legs will run their best.

———

III.—PHŒBUS AND BOREAS.

OLD Boreas and the sun, one day
Espied a traveller on his way,
Whose dress did happily provide
Against whatever might betide.

The time was autumn, when, indeed,
All prudent travellers take heed.
The rains that then the sunshine dash,
And Iris with her splendid sash,
Warn one who does not like to soak
To wear abroad a good thick cloak.
Our man was therefore well bedight
With double mantle, strong and tight.
This fellow, said the wind, has meant
To guard from every ill event ;
But little does he wot that I
Can blow him such a blast
That, not a button fast,
His cloak shall cleave the sky.
Come, here's a pleasant game, Sir Sun !
Wilt play ? Said Phœbus, Done !
We'll bet between us here
Which first will take the gear
From off this cavalier.
Begin, and shut away
The brightness of my ray.
Enough. Our blower, on the bet,
Swell'd out his pursy form
With all the stuff for storm—
The thunder, hail, and drenching wet,
And all the fury he could muster ;
Then, with a very demon's bluster,
He whistled, whirl'd, and splash'd,
And down the torrents dash'd,
Full many a roof uptearing
He never did before,
Full many a vessel bearing
To wreck upon the shore,—
And all to doff a single cloak.
But vain the furious stroke ;
The traveller was stout,
And kept the tempest out,
Defied the hurricane,
Defied the pelting rain ;
And as the fiercer roar'd the blast,
His cloak the tighter held he fast.
The sun broke out, to win the bet ;
He caused the clouds to disappear,
Refresh'd and warm'd the cavalier,
And through his mantle made him sweat,
Till off it came, of course,
In less than half an hour ;
And yet the sun saved half his power.—
So much doth mildness more than force.

———◆———

IV.—JUPITER AND THE FARMER.

Of yore, a farm had Jupiter to rent ;
To advertise it, Mercury was sent.
The farmers, far and near,
Flock'd round, the terms to hear ;
And, calling to their aid
The various tricks of trade,
One said 'twas rash a farm to hire
Which would so much expense require ;
Another, that, do what you would,
The farm would still be far from good.
While thus, in market style, its faults were told,
One of the crowd, less wise than bold,
Would give so much, on this condition,
That Jove would yield him altogether
The choice and making of his weather,—
That, instantly on his decision,

His various crops should feel the power
Of heat or cold, of sun or shower.

Jove yields. The bargain closed, our man
Rains, blows, and takes the care
Of all the changes of the air,
On his peculiar, private plan.
His nearest neighbours felt it not,
And all the better was their lot.
Their year was good, by grace divine ;
The grain was rich, and full the vine.
The renter, failing altogether,
The next year made quite different weather ;
And yet the fruit of all his labours
Was far inferior to his neighbours'.
What better could he do ? To Heaven
He owns at last his want of sense,
And so is graciously forgiven.
Hence we conclude that Providence
Knows better what we need
Than we ourselves, indeed.

———◆———

V.—THE COCKEREL, THE CAT, AND THE YOUNG MOUSE.

A youthful mouse, not up to trap,
Had almost met a sad mishap.
The story hear him thus relate,
With great importance, to his mother :—
I pass'd the mountain bounds of this estate,
And off was trotting on another,
Like some young rat with nought to do
But see things wonderful and new,
When two strange creatures came in view.
The one was mild, benign, and gracious ;
The other, turbulent, rapacious,
With voice terrific, shrill, and rough,
And on his head a bit of stuff
That look'd like raw and bloody meat,
Raised up a sort of arms, and beat
The air, as if he meant to fly,
And bore his plumy tail on high.

A cock, that just began to crow,
As if some nondescript,
From far New Holland shipp'd,
Was what our mousling pictured so.
He beat his arms, said he, and raised his voice,
And made so terrible a noise,
That I, who, thanks to Heaven, may justly boast
Myself as bold as any mouse,
Scud off, (his voice would even scare a ghost !)
And cursed himself and all his house ;
For, but for him, I should have staid,
And doubtless an acquaintance made
With her who seem'd so mild and good.
Like us, in velvet cloak and hood,
She wears a tail that's full of grace,
A very sweet and humble face,—
No mouse more kindness could desire,—
And yet her eye is full of fire.
I do believe the lovely creature
A friend of rats and mice by nature.
Her ears, though, like herself, they're bigger,
Are just like ours in form and figure.
To her I was approaching, when,
Aloft on what appear'd his den,
The other scream'd,—and off I fled.
My son, his cautious mother said,

That sweet one was the cat,
The mortal foe of mouse and rat,
Who seeks by smooth deceit,
Her appetite to treat.
So far the other is from that,
     We yet may eat
     His dainty meat ;
Whereas the cruel cat,
Whene'er she can, devours
No other meat than ours.

Remember while you live,
It is by looks that men deceive.

VI.—THE FOX, THE MONKEY, AND THE ANIMALS.

LEFT kingless by the lion's death,
The beasts once met, our story saith,
Some fit successor to install.
Forth from a dragon-guarded, moated place,
The crown was brought, and, taken from its case,
  And being tried by turns on all,
The heads of most were found too small ;
Some hornèd were, and some too big ;
  Not one would fit the regal gear.
For ever ripe for such a rig,
  The monkey, looking very queer,
Approach'd with antics and grimaces,
  And, after scores of monkey faces,
With what would seem a gracious stoop,
Pass'd through the crown as through a hoop.
  The beasts, diverted with the thing,
  Did homage to him as their king.
The fox alone the vote regretted,
But yet in public never fretted.
When he his compliments had paid
To royalty, thus newly made,
Great sire, I know a place, said he,
  Where lies conceal'd a treasure,
Which, by the right of royalty,
  Should bide your royal pleasure.
The king lack'd not an appetite
  For such financial pelf,
And, not to lose his royal right,
  Ran straight to see it for himself.
It was a trap, and he was caught.
Said Renard, Would you have it thought,
You ape, that you can fill a throne,
And guard the rights of all, alone,
Not knowing how to guard your own ?

The beasts all gather'd from the farce,
That stuff for kings is very scarce.

VII.—THE MULE BOASTING OF HIS GENEALOGY.

A PRELATE's mule of noble birth was proud,
  And talk'd, incessantly and loud,
  Of nothing but his dam, the mare,
Whose mighty deeds by him recounted were,—
This had she done, and had been present there,—
  By which her son made out his claim
  To notice on the scroll of Fame.
Too proud, when young, to bear a doctor's pill ;
  When old, he had to turn a mill.
  As there they used his limbs to bind,
  His sire, the ass, was brought to mind.

Misfortune, were its only use
  The claims of folly to reduce,
And bring men down to sober reason,
Would be a blessing in its season.

VIII.—THE OLD MAN AND THE ASS.

AN old man, riding on his ass,
Had found a spot of thrifty grass,
And there turn'd loose his weary beast.
Old Grizzle, pleased with such a feast,
Flung up his heels, and caper'd round,
Then roll'd and rubb'd upon the ground,
And frisk'd and browsed and bray'd,
And many a clean spot made.
Arm'd men came on them as he fed :
Let's fly, in haste the old man said.
And wherefore so ? the ass replied.
With heavier burdens will they ride ?
  No, said the man, already started.
  Then, cried the ass, as he departed,
I'll stay, and be—no matter whose ;
Save you yourself, and leave me loose.
But let me tell you, ere you go,
(I speak plain French, you know,)
My master is my only foe.

IX.—THE STAG SEEING HIMSELF IN THE WATER.

BESIDE a placid, crystal flood,
A stag admired the branching wood
That high upon his forehead stood,
But gave his Maker little thanks
For what he call'd his spindle shanks.
What limbs are these for such a head !—
So mean and slim ! with grief he said.
  My glorious head o'ertops
  The branches of the copse ;
  My legs are my disgrace.
As thus he talk'd, a bloodhound gave him chase.
  To save his life he flew
  Where forests thickest grew.
His horns,—pernicious ornament !—
Arresting him where'er he went,
  Did unavailing render
    What else, in such a strife,
    Had saved his precious life—
His legs, as fleet as slender.
Obliged to yield, he cursed the gear
Which nature gave him every year.

  Too much the beautiful we prize ;
  The useful, often, we despise :
  Yet oft, as happen'd to the stag,
  The former doth to ruin drag.

X.—THE HARE AND THE TORTOISE.

To win a race, the swiftness of a dart
Availeth not without a timely start.
The hare and tortoise are my witnesses.
Said tortoise to the swiftest thing that is,
I'll bet that you'll not reach so soon as I
  The tree on yonder hill we spy.
So soon ! Why, madam, are you frantic ?
Replied the creature, with an antic ;

Pray take, your senses to restore,
A grain or two of hellebore.
Say, said the tortoise, what you will ;
I dare you to the wager still.
'Twas done ; the stakes were paid,
And near the goal tree laid—
Of what, is not a question for this place,
Nor who it was that judged the race.
Our hare had scarce five jumps to make,
Of such as he is wont to take,
When, starting just before their beaks
He leaves the hounds at leisure,
Thence till the kalends of the Greeks,
The sterile heath to measure.
Thus having time to browse and doze,
And list which way the zephyr blows,
He makes himself content to wait,
And let the tortoise go her gait
In solemn, senatorial state.
She starts ; she moils on, modestly and lowly,
And with a prudent wisdom hastens slowly ;
But he, meanwhile, the victory despises,
Thinks lightly of such prizes,
Believes it for his honour
To take late start and gain upon her.
So, feeding, sitting at his ease,
He meditates of what you please,
Till his antagonist he sees
Approach the goal ; then starts,
Away like lightning darts :
But vainly does he run ;
The race is by the tortoise won.
Cries she, My senses do I lack !
What boots your boasted swiftness now ?
You're beat ! and yet, you must allow,
I bore my house upon my back.

— • —

XI.—THE ASS AND HIS MASTERS.

A GARDENER's ass complain'd to Destiny
Of being made to rise before the dawn.
The cocks their matins have not sung, said he,
Ere I am up and gone.
And all for what ? To market herbs, it seems.
Fine cause, indeed, to interrupt my dreams !
Fate, moved by such a prayer,
Sent him a currier's load to bear,
Whose hides so heavy and ill-scented were,
They almost choked the foolish beast.
I wish me with my former lord, he said ;
For then, whene'er he turn'd his head,
If on the watch, I caught
A cabbage-leaf, which cost me nought.
But, in this horrid place, I find
No chance or windfall of the kind ;—
Or if, indeed, I do,
The cruel blows I rue.
Anon it came to pass
He was a collier's ass.
Still more complaint.   What now ? said Fate,
Quite out of patience.
If on this jackass I must wait,
What will become of kings and nations ?
Has none but he aught here to tease him ?
Have I no business but to please him ?
And Fate had cause ;—for all are so.
Unsatisfied while here below

Our present lot is aye the worst.
Our foolish prayers the skies infest.
Were Jove to grant all we request,
The din renew'd, his head would burst.

— • —

XII.—THE SUN AND THE FROGS.

REJOICING on their tyrant's wedding-day,
The people drown'd their care in drink ;
While from the general joy did Æsop shrink,
And show'd its folly in this way.
The sun, said he, once took it in his head
To have a partner for his bed.
From swamps, and ponds, and marshy bogs,
Up rose the wailings of the frogs.
What shall we do, should he have progeny ?
Said they to Destiny ;
One sun we scarcely can endure,
And half-a-dozen, we are sure,
Will dry the very sea.
Adieu to marsh and fen !
Our race will perish then,
Or be obliged to fix
Their dwelling in the Styx !
For such an humble animal,
The frog, I take it, reason'd well.

—•—

XIII.—THE COUNTRYMAN AND THE SERPENT.

A COUNTRYMAN, as Æsop certifies,
A charitable man, but not so wise,
One day in winter found,
Stretch'd on the snowy ground,
A chill'd or frozen snake,
As torpid as a stake,
And, if alive, devoid of sense.
He took him up, and bore him home,
And, thinking not what recompense
For such a charity would come,
Before the fire he stretch'd him,
And back to being fetch'd him.
The snake scarce felt the genial heat
Before his heart with native malice beat.
He raised his head, thrust out his forkèd tongue,
Coil'd up, and at his benefactor sprung.
Ungrateful wretch ! said he, is this the way
My care and kindness you repay ?
Now you shall die.   With that his axe he takes,
And with two blows three serpents makes.
Trunk, head, and tail were separate snakes ;
And, leaping up with all their might,
They vainly sought to reunite.

'Tis good and lovely to be kind ;
But charity should not be blind ;
For as to wretchedness ingrate,
You cannot raise it from its wretched state.

— • —

XIV.—THE SICK LION AND THE FOX.

SICK in his den, we understand,
The king of beasts sent out command
That of his vassals every sort
Should send some deputies to court—
With promise well to treat
Each deputy and suite ;

On faith of lion, duly written,
None should be scratch'd, much less be bitten.
The royal will was executed,
And some from every tribe deputed;
The foxes, only, would not come.
One thus explain'd their choice of home :—
Of those who seek the court, we learn,
　The tracks upon the sand
　Have one direction, and
Not one betokens a return.
This fact begetting some distrust,
His majesty at present must
Excuse us from his great levee.
His plighted word is good, no doubt ;
But while how beasts get in we see,
　We do not see how they get out.

XV.—THE FOWLER, THE HAWK, AND THE LARK.

FROM wrongs of wicked men we draw
　Excuses for our own :—
Such is the universal law.
　Would you have mercy shown,
　Let yours be clearly known.

A fowler's mirror served to snare
The little tenants of the air.
A lark there saw her pretty face,
And was approaching to the place.
　A hawk, that sailed on high
　Like vapour in the sky,
Came down, as still as infant's breath,
On her who sang so near her death.
She thus escaped the fowler's steel,
The hawk's malignant claws to feel.
　While in his cruel way,
　The pirate pluck'd his prey,
Upon himself the net was sprung.
O fowler, pray'd he in the hawkish tongue,
　Release me in thy clemency !
　I never did a wrong to thee.
　The man replied, 'Tis true ;
　And did the lark to you ?

XVI.—THE HORSE AND THE ASS.

IN such a world, all men, of every grade,
Should each the other kindly aid ;
For, if beneath misfortune's goad
A neighbour falls, on you will fall his load.

There jogg'd in company an ass and horse ;
Nought but his harness did the last endorse ;
The other bore a load that crush'd him down,
　And begg'd the horse a little help to give,
Or otherwise he could not reach the town.
This prayer, said he, is civil, I believe ;
One half this burden you would scarcely feel.
The horse refused, flung up a scornful heel,
And saw his comrade die beneath the weight :—
　And saw his wrong too late ;
　For on his own proud back
　They put the ass's pack,
　And over that, beside,
　They put the ass's hide.

XVII.—THE DOG THAT DROPPED THE SUBSTANCE FOR THE SHADOW.

THIS world is full of shadow-chasers,
　Most easily deceived.
Should I enumerate these racers,
　I should not be believed.
I send them all to Æsop's dog,
Which, crossing water on a log,
Espied the meat he bore, below ;
　To seize its image, let it go ;
Plunged in ; to reach the shore was glad,
With neither what he hoped, nor what he'd had.

XVIII.—THE CARTER IN THE MIRE.

THE Phaëton who drove a load of hay
　Once found his cart bemired.
Poor man ! the spot was far away
　From human help—retired,
In some rude country place,
In Brittany, as near as I can trace,
　Near Quimper Corentan,—
　A town that poet never sang,—
Which Fate, they say, puts in the traveller's path,
When she would rouse the man to special wrath.
　May Heaven preserve us from that route !
But to our carter, hale and stout :—
Fast stuck his cart ; he swore his worst,
　And, fill'd with rage extreme,
The mud-holes now he cursed,
　And now he cursed his team,
And now his cart and load,—
Anon, the like upon himself bestow'd.
Upon the god he call'd at length,
Most famous through the world for strength.
　O, help me, Hercules ! cried he ;
　For if thy back of yore
　This burly planet bore,
　Thy arm can set me free.
This prayer gone up, from out a cloud there broke
A voice which thus in godlike accents spoke :—
　The suppliant must himself bestir,
　Ere Hercules will aid confer.
Look wisely in the proper quarter,
　To see what hindrance can be found ;
Remove the execrable mud and mortar,
Which, axle-deep, besets thy wheels around.
　Thy sledge and crowbar take,
　And pry me up that stone, or break ;
　Now fill that rut upon the other side.
Hast done it ! Yes, the man replied.
Well, said the voice, I'll aid thee now ;
Take up thy whip. I have.....but, how !
　My cart glides on with ease !
　I thank thee, Hercules.
Thy team, rejoin'd the voice, has light ado ;
So help thyself, and Heaven will help thee too.

XIX.—THE CHARLATAN.

THE world has never lack'd its charlatans;
More than themselves have lack'd their plans.
　One sees them on the stage at tricks
　Which mock the claims of sullen Styx.

What talents in the streets they post !
One of them used to boast
Such mastership of eloquence
That he could make the greatest dunce
Another Tully Cicero
In all the arts that lawyers know.
Ay, sirs, a dunce, a country clown,
The greatest blockhead of your town,—
Nay more, an animal, an ass,—
The stupidest that nibbles grass,—
Needs only through my course to pass,
And he shall wear the gown
With credit, honour, and renown.
The prince heard of it, call'd the man, thus spake :
    My stable holds a steed
    Of the Arcadian breed,
Of which an orator I wish to make.
    Well, sire, you can,
    Replied our man.
    At once his majesty
    Paid the tuition fee.
Ten years must roll, and then the learned ass
Should his examination pass,
    According to the rules
    Adopted in the schools ;
If not, his teacher was to tread the air,
With halter'd neck, above the public square,—
    His rhetoric bound on his back,
    And on his head the ears of jack.
A courtier told the rhetorician,
    With bows and terms polite,
    He would not miss the sight
Of that last pendent exhibition ;
For that his grace and dignity
Would well become such high degree ;
And, on the point of being hung,
He would bethink him of his tongue,
And show the glory of his art,—
The power to melt the hardest heart,—
    And wage a war with time
    By periods sublime—
A pattern speech for orators thus leaving,
Whose work is vulgarly call'd thieving.
    Ah ! was the charlatan's reply,
    Ere that, the king, the ass, or I,
Shall, one or other of us, die.
And reason good had he ;
We count on life most foolishly,
    Though hale and hearty we may be.
In each ten years, death cuts down one in three.

XX.—DISCORD.

The goddess Discord, having made, on high,
    Among the gods a general grapple,
    And thence a lawsuit, for an apple,
Was turn'd out, bag and baggage, from the sky.
The animal call'd man, with open arms,
Received the goddess of such naughty charms,—
Herself and Whether-or-no, her brother,
With Thine-and-mine, her stingy mother.
In this, the lower universe,
Our hemisphere she chose to curse :
For reasons good she did not please
To visit our antipodes—
Folks rude and savage like the beasts,
Who, wedding free from forms and priests,

In simple tent or leafy bower,
    Make little work for such a power.
That she might know exactly where
    Her direful aid was in demand,
    Renown flew courier through the land,
Reporting each dispute with care ;
Then she, outrunning Peace, was quickly there ;
And if she found a spark of ire,
Was sure to blow it to a fire.
At length, Renown got out of patience
At random hurrying o'er the nations,
And, not without good reason, thought
A goddess, like her mistress, ought
To have some fix'd and certain home,
To which her customers might come ;
For now they often search'd in vain.
With due location, it was plain
She might accomplish vastly more,
And more in season than before.
To find, howe'er, the right facilities,
Was harder, then, than now it is ;
For then there were no nunneries.

So, Hymen's inn at last assign'd,
Thence lodged the goddess to her mind.

XXI.—THE YOUNG WIDOW.

A husband's death brings always sighs ;
The widow sobs, sheds tears—then dries.
Of Time the sadness borrows wings ;
And Time returning pleasure brings.
Between the widow of a year
And of a day, the difference
    Is so immense,
That very few who see her
Would think the laughing dame
And weeping one the same.
The one puts on repulsive action,
The other shows a strong attraction.
The one gives up to sighs, or true or false ;
The same sad note is heard, whoever calls.
    Her grief is inconsolable,
    They say ; not so our fable,
    Or, rather, not so says the truth.

    To other worlds a husband went
And left his wife in prime of youth.
Above his dying couch she bent,
And cried, My love, O wait for me !
My soul would gladly go with thee !
    (But yet it did not go.)
The fair one's sire, a prudent man,
Check'd not the current of her woe.
At last he kindly thus began :—
My child, your grief should have its bound.
What boots it him beneath the ground
That you should drown your charms ?
    Live for the living, not the dead.
    I don't propose that you be led
At once to Hymen's arms ;
But give me leave, in proper time,
To rearrange the broken chime
With one who is as good, at least,
In all respects, as the deceased.
Alas ! she sigh'd, the cloister vows
Befit me better than a spouse.
The father left the matter there.
About one month thus mourn'd the fair ;

Another month, her weeds arranged ;
Each day some robe or lace she changed.
Till mourning dresses served to grace,
And took of ornament the place.
   The frolic band of loves
   Came flocking back like doves.
   Jokes, laughter, and the dance,
   The native growth of France,
   Had finally their turn ;
   And thus, by night and morn,
   She plunged, to tell the truth,
   Deep in the fount of youth.
   Her sire no longer fear'd
   The dead so much endear'd ;
    But, as he never spoke,
    Herself the silence broke :—
Where is that youthful spouse, said she,
Whom, sir, you lately promised me ?

EPILOGUE.

HERE check we our career :
Long books I greatly fear.
I would not quite exhaust my stuff ;
The flower of subjects is enough.
To me, the time is come, it seems,
To draw my breath for other themes.
Love, tyrant of my life, commands
That other work be on my hands.
   I dare not disobey.
Once more shall Psyche be my lay.
I'm call'd by Damon to portray
   Her sorrows and her joys.
I yield : perhaps, while she employs,
My muse will catch a richer glow ;
   And well if this my labour'd strain
   Shall be the last and only pain
Her spouse shall cause me here below.

BOOK VII.

TO MADAME DE MONTESPAN. O

THE apologue is from the immortal gods ;
Or, if the gift of man it is,
   Its author merits apotheosis.
Whoever magic genius lauds
   Will do what in him lies
To raise this art's inventor to the skies.
It hath the potence of a charm,
On dulness lays a conquering arm,
Subjects the mind to its control,
And works its will upon the soul.
O lady, arm'd with equal power,
If e'er within celestial bower,
With messmate gods reclined,
My muse ambrosially hath dined,
Lend me the favour of a smile
On this her playful toil.
If you support, the tooth of time will shun,
And let my work the envious years outrun.
If authors would themselves survive,
To gain your suffrage they should strive.
On you my verses wait to get their worth ;—
To you my beauties all will owe their birth,—
   For beauties you will recognise
   Invisible to other eyes.

Ah ! who can boast a taste so true,
   Of beauty or of grace,
   In either thought or face ?
For words and looks are equal charms in you.
Upon a theme so sweet, the truth to tell,
   My muse would gladly dwell :
But this employ to others I must yield ;—
A greater master claims the field.
For me, fair lady, 'twere enough
Your name should be my wall and roof.
Protect henceforth the favour'd book
Through which for second life I look.
   In your auspicious light,
   These lines, in envy's spite,
   Will gain the glorious meed,
   That all the world shall read.
'Tis not that I deserve such fame ;—
I only ask in Fable's name,
(You know what credit that should claim ;)
And, if successfully I sue,
A fane will be to Fable due,—
A thing I would not build—except for you.

✓ I.—THE ANIMALS SICK OF THE PLAGUE. O

THE sorest ill that Heaven hath
Sent on this lower world in wrath,—
The plague (to call it by its name,)
   One single day of which
   Would Pluto's ferryman enrich,—
Waged war on beasts, both wild and tame.
They died not all, but all were sick :
No hunting now, by force or trick,
To save what might so soon expire.
No food excited their desire ;
Nor wolf nor fox now watch'd to slay
The innocent and tender prey.
   The turtles fled ;
So love and therefore joy were dead.
The lion council held, and said :
My friends, I do believe
This awful scourge, for which we grieve,
Is for our sins a punishment
Most righteously by Heaven sent.
Let us our guiltiest beast resign,
A sacrifice to wrath divine.
Perhaps this offering, truly small,
May gain the life and health of all.
By history we find it noted
That lives have been just so devoted.
Then let us all turn eyes within,
And ferret out the hidden sin.
Himself let no one spare nor flatter,
But make clean conscience in the matter.
For me, my appetite has play'd the glutton
Too much and often upon mutton.
What harm had e'er my victims done ?
   I answer, truly, None.
Perhaps, sometimes, by hunger press'd,
I've eat the shepherd with the rest.
I yield myself, if need there be ;
   And yet I think, in equity,
Each should confess his sins with me ;
   For laws of right and justice cry,
   The guiltiest alone should die.
Sire, said the fox, your majesty
Is humbler than a king should be,
And over-squeamish in the case.

What ! eating stupid sheep a crime ?
No, never, sire, at any time.
It rather was an act of grace,
A mark of honour to their race.
And as to shepherds, one may swear,
The fate your majesty describes,
Is recompense less full than fair
For such usurpers o'er our tribes.

Thus Renard glibly spoke,
And loud applause from flatterers broke.
Of neither tiger, boar, nor bear,
Did any keen inquirer dare
To ask for crimes of high degree;
The fighters, biters, scratchers, all
From every mortal sin were free ;
The very dogs, both great and small,
Were saints, as far as dogs could be.

The ass, confessing in his turn,
Thus spoke in tones of deep concern :—
I happen'd through a mead to pass ;
The monks, its owners, were at mass ;
Keen hunger, leisure, tender grass,
And add to these the devil too,
All tempted me the deed to do.
I browsed the bigness of my tongue ;
Since truth must out, I own it wrong.

On this, a hue and cry arose,
As if the beasts were all his foes :'
A wolf, haranguing lawyer-wise,
Denounced the ass for sacrifice—
The bald-pate, scabby, ragged lout,
By whom the plague had come, no doubt.
His fault was judged a hanging crime.
What ! eat another's grass ? O shame !
The noose of rope and death sublime,
For that offence, were all too tame !
And soon poor Grizzle felt the same.

Thus human courts acquit the strong,
And doom the weak, as therefore wrong

II.—THE ILL-MARRIED.

IF worth and beauty always wedded were,
To-morrow I would seek a wife ;
But since divorce has come between the pair,
Fair forms not being homes of souls as fair,
Excuse my choice of single life.

Of married folks a multitude
I've seen, but still have never rued
Or long'd to quit my solitude.
Yet of our race almost four quarters
Brave Hymen's torch—intrepid martyrs.
Four quarters, also, soon repent—
Too late, however, to recant.
My tale makes one of these poor fellows,
Who sought relief from marriage vows,
Send back again his tedious spouse,
Contentious, covetous, and jealous.
With nothing pleased or satisfied,
This restless, comfort-killing bride
Some fault in every one descried.
Her good man went to bed too soon,
Or lay in bed till almost noon.

Too cold, too hot,—too black, too white,—
Were on her tongue from morn till night.
The servants mad and madder grew ;
The husband knew not what to do.
'Twas, Dear, you never think or care ;
And, Dear, that price we cannot bear ;
And, Dear, you never stay at home ;
And, Dear, I wish you would just come ;—
Till, finally, such ceaseless dearing
Upon her husband's patience wearing,
Back to her sire's he sent his wife,
To taste the sweets of country life,
To dance at will the country jigs,
And feed the turkeys, geese, and pigs.
In course of time, he hoped his bride
Might have her temper mollified ;
Which hope he duly put to test.
His wife recall'd, said he,
How went with you your rural rest,
From vexing cares and fashions free ?
Its peace and quiet did you gain,—
Its innocence without a stain ?
Enough of all, said she ; but then
To see those idle, worthless men
Neglect the flocks, it gave me pain.
I told them, plainly, what I thought,
And thus their hatred quickly bought ;
For which I do not care—not I.
Ah, madam, did her spouse reply,
If still your temper's so morose,
And tongue so virulent, that those
Who only see you morn and night
Are quite grown weary of the sight,
What, then, must be your servants' case,
Who needs must see you face to face,
Throughout the day ?
And what must be the harder lot
Of him, I pray,
Whose days and nights
With you must be by marriage rights ?
Return you to your father's cot.
If I recall you in my life,
Or even wish for such a wife,
Let Heaven, in my hereafter, send
Two such, to tease me without end !

III.—THE RAT RETIRED FROM THE WORLD.

THE sage Levantines have a tale
About a rat that weary grew
Of all the cares which life assail,
And to a Holland cheese withdrew.
His solitude was there profound,
Extending through his world so round.
Our hermit lived on that within ;
And soon his industry had been
With claws and teeth so good,
That in his novel hermitage,
He had in store, for wants of age,
Both house and livelihood.
What more could any rat desire ?
He grew fair, fat, and round.
God's blessings thus redound
To those who in His vows retire.
One day this personage devout,
Whose kindness none might doubt,
Was ask'd, by certain delegates
That came from Rat-United-States,

For some small aid, for they
To foreign parts were on their way,
For succour in the great cat-war.
Ratopolis beleaguer'd sore,
  Their whole republic drain'd and poor,
No morsel in their scrips they bore.
  Slight boon they craved, of succour sure
In days at utmost three or·four.
My friends, the hermit said,
To worldly things I'm dead.
How can a poor recluse
To such a mission be of use !
What can he do but pray
That God will aid it on its way !
And so, my friends, it is my prayer
That God will have you in his care.
His well-fed saintship said no more,
But in their faces shut the door.
What think you, reader, is the service
For which I use this niggard rat !
To paint a monk ! No, but a dervise.
  A monk, I think, however fat,
  Must be more bountiful than that.

---•---

IV.—THE HERON.

ONE day,—no matter when or where,—
A long-legg'd heron chanced to fare
  By a certain river's brink,
  With his long, sharp beak
  Helved on his slender neck ;—
  'Twas a fish-spear, you might think.
The water was clear and still,
The carp and the pike there at will
  Pursued their silent fun,
  Turning up, ever and anon,
  A golden side to the sun.
With ease might the heron have made
Great profits in his fishing trade.
So near came the scaly fry,
They might be caught by the passer-by.
But he thought he better might
Wait for a better appetite—
For he lived by rule, and could not eat,
Except at his hours, the best of meat.
Anon his appetite return'd once more ;
So, approaching again the shore,
He saw some tench taking their leaps,
Now and then, from their lowest deeps.
With as dainty a taste as Horace's rat,
He turn'd away from such food as that.
What, tench for a heron ! poh !
I scorn the thought, and let them go.
The tench refused, there came a gudgeon ;
For all that, said the bird, I budge on.
I'll ne'er open my beak, if the gods please,
For such mean little fishes as these.
      He did it for less ;
      For it came to pass,
That not another fish could he see ;
And, at last, so hungry was he,
That he thought it of some avail
To find on the bank a single snail.
    Such is the sure result
    Of being too difficult.
    Would you be strong and great,
    Learn to accommodate.

Get what you can, and trust for the rest ;
The whole is oft lost by seeking the best.
Above all things beware of disdain :
Where, at most, you have little to gain.
The people are many that make
Every day this sad mistake.
'Tis not for the herons I put this case,
Ye featherless people, of the human race.
  —List to another tale as true,
And you'll hear the lesson brought home to you.

---•---

V.—THE MAID.

A CERTAIN maid, as proud as fair,
  A husband thought to find
  Exactly to her mind—
Well-form'd and young, genteel in air,
Not cold nor jealous ;—mark this well.
Whoe'er would wed this dainty belle
Must have, besides, rank, wealth, and wit,
And all good qualities to fit—
A man 'twere difficult to get.
Kind Fate, however, took great care
To grant, if possible, her prayer.
There came a-wooing men of note ;
  The maiden thought them all,
  By half, too mean and small.
They marry me ! the creatures dote :—
  Alas ! poor souls ! their case I pity.
(Here mark the bearing of the beauty.)
Some were less delicate than witty ;
Some had the nose too short or long ;
In others something else was wrong ;
Which made each in the maiden's eyes
An altogether worthless prize.
Profound contempt is aye the vice
Which springs from being over-nice.
Thus were the great dismiss'd ; and then
Came offers from inferior men.
The maid, more scornful than before,
  Took credit to her tender heart
For giving them an open door.
  They think me much in haste to part
With independence ! God be thank'd
My lonely nights bring no regret ;
  Nor shall I pine, or greatly fret,
Should I with ancient maids be rank'd.
Such were the thoughts that pleased the fair :
Age made them only thoughts that were.
Adieu to lovers :—passing years
Awaken doubts and chilling fears.
Regret, at last, brings up the train.
Day after day she sees, with pain,
Some smile or charm take final flight,
And leave the features of a " fright."
Then came a hundred sorts of paint ;
But still no trick, nor ruse, nor feint,
Avail'd to hide the cause of grief,
Or bar out Time, that graceless thief.
A house, when gone to wreck and ruin,
May be repair'd and made a new one.
Alas ! for ruins of the face
No such rebuilding e'er takes place.
Her daintiness now changed its tune ;
Her mirror told her, Marry soon !
So did a certain wish within,
With more of secrecy than sin,—

A wish that dwells with even prudes,
Annihilating solitudes.
This maiden's choice was past belief,
She soothing down her restless grief,
And smoothing it of every ripple,
    By marrying a cripple.

———•———

VI.—THE WISHES.

WITHIN the Great Mogul's domains there are
Familiar sprites of much domestic use :
They sweep the house, and take a tidy care
Of equipage, nor garden work refuse ;
But, if you meddle with their toil,
The whole, at once, you're sure to spoil.
One, near the mighty Ganges flood,
The garden of a burgher good
    Work'd noiselessly and well ;
To master, mistress, garden, bore
A love that time and toil outwore,
    And bound him like a spell.
    Did friendly zephyrs blow,
    The demon's pains to aid?
    (For so they do, 'tis said.)
    I own I do not know.
But for himself he rested not,
And richly bless'd his master's lot.
What mark'd his strength of love,
He lived a fixture on the place,
In spite of tendency to rove
    So natural to his race.
But brother sprites conspiring
With importunity untiring,
So teased their goblin chief, that he,
Of his caprice or policy,
Our sprite commanded to attend
A house in Norway's farther end,
Whose roof was snow-clad through the year,
And shelter'd human kind with deer.
Before departing to his hosts
Thus spake this best of busy ghosts :—
To foreign parts I'm forced to go !
For what sad fault I do not know ;—
But go I must ; a month's delay,
Or week's perhaps, and I'm away.
Seize time ; three wishes make at will ;
For three I'm able to fulfil—
No more.   Quick at their easy task,
Abundance first these wishers ask—
Abundance, with her stores unlock'd—
Barns, coffers, cellars, larder, stock'd—
    Corn, cattle, wine, and money,—
    The overflow of milk and honey.
But what to do with all this wealth !
    What inventories, cares, and worry !
What wear of temper and of health !
    Both lived in constant, slavish hurry.
Thieves took by plot, and lords by loan ;
The king by tax, the poor by tone.
    Thus felt the curses which
    Arise from being rich,—
Remove this affluence, they pray ;
The poor are happier than they
Whose riches make them slaves.
Go, treasures, to the winds and waves ;
Come, goddess of the quiet breast,
Who sweet'nest toil with rest,

    Dear Mediocrity, return !
The prayer was granted as we learn.
    Two wishes thus expended,
        Had simply ended
    In bringing them exactly where,
    When they set out they were.
        So, usually, it fares
With those who waste in such vain prayers
The time required by their affairs.
The goblin laugh'd, and so did they
However, ere he went away,
To profit by his offer kind,
They ask'd for wisdom, wealth of mind,—
A treasure void of care and sorrow—
A treasure fearless of the morrow,
Let who will steal, or beg, or borrow.

———•———

VII.—THE LION'S COURT.

HIS lion majesty would know, one day,
What bestial tribes were subject to his sway.
He therefore gave his vassals, all,
    By deputies a call,
    Despatching everywhere
    A written circular,
Which bore his seal, and did import
His majesty would hold his court
A month most splendidly ;—
A feast would open his levee,
Which done, Sir Jocko's sleight
Would give the court delight.
By such sublime magnificence
The king would show his power immense.

    Now were they gather'd all
    Within the royal hall—
And such a hall ! The charnel scent
Would make the strongest nerves relent.
The bear put up his paw to close
The double access of his nose.
The act had better been omitted ;
His throne at once the monarch quitted,
And sent to Pluto's court the bear,
To show his delicacy there.
The ape approved the cruel deed,
A thorough flatterer by breed.
He praised the prince's wrath and claws ;
He praised the odour and its cause.
Judged by the fragrance of that cave,
The amber of the Baltic wave,
The rose, the pink, the hawthorn bank,
Might with the vulgar garlic rank.
The mark his flattery overshot,
And made him share poor Bruin's lot,
This lion playing in his way,
The part of Don Caligula.
The fox approach'd. Now, said the king,
Apply your nostrils to this thing,
And let me hear, without disguise,
The judgment of a beast so wise.
The fox replied, Your Majesty will please
Excuse—and here he took good care to sneeze;—
Afflicted with a dreadful cold,
Your majesty need not be told
My sense of smell is mostly gone.

From danger thus withdrawn,
    He teaches us the while,
    That one, to gain the smile

Of kings, must hold the middle place
'Twixt blunt rebuke and fulsome praise ;
And sometimes use with easy grace,
The language of the Norman race*.

VIII.—THE VULTURES AND THE PIGEONS.

MARS once made havoc in the air .
Some cause aroused a quarrel there
Among the birds ;—not those that sing,
The courtiers of the merry Spring,
And by their talk, in leafy bowers,
Of loves they feel, enkindle ours ;
Nor those which Cupid's mother yokes
To whirl on high her golden spokes ;
But naughty hawk and vulture folks,
Of hooked beak and talons keen.
　　The carcass of a dog, 'tis said,
　　Had to this civil carnage led.
Blood rain'd upon the swarded green,
And valiant deeds were done, 1 ween.
But time and breath would surely fail
To give the fight in full detail ;
Suffice to say, that chiefs were slain,
And heroes strow'd the sanguine plain,
Till old Prometheus, in his chains,
Began to hope an end of pains.
'Twas sport to see the battle rage,
And valiant hawk with hawk engage ;
'Twas pitiful to see them fall,—
Torn, bleeding, weltering, gasping, all.
Force, courage, cunning, all were plied ;
Intrepid troops on either side
No effort spared to populate
The dusky realms of hungry Fate.
This woful strife awoke compassion
Within another feather'd nation,
　　Of iris neck and tender heart.
They tried their hand at mediation—
　　To reconcile the foes, or part.
The pigeon people duly chose
　　Ambassadors, who work'd so well
As soon the murderous rage to quell,
And stanch the source of countless woes.
A truce took place, and peace ensued.
　　Alas ! the people dearly paid
　　Who such pacification made !
Those cursed hawks at once pursued
The harmless pigeons, slew and ate,
Till towns and fields were desolate.
Small prudence had the friends of peace
To pacify such foes as these !

The safety of the rest requires
The bad should flesh each other's spears :
　　Whoever peace with them desires
　　Had better set them by the ears.

IX.—THE COACH AND THE FLY.

UPON a sandy, uphill road,
Which naked in the sunshine glow'd,
　　Six lusty horses drew a coach.
Dames, monks, and invalids, its load,

---

* The Normans are proverbial among the French for
the oracular non-committal of their responses. — Un
Normand, says the proverb, a son dit et son dédit.

On foot, outside, at leisure trode.
The team, all weary, stopp'd and blow'd :
　　Whereon there did a fly approach,
And, with a vastly business air.
　　Cheer'd up the horses with his buzz,—
Now prick'd them here, now prick'd them there,
　　As neatly as a jockey does,—
And thought the while—he knew 'twas so—
He made the team and carriage go,—
On carriage-pole sometimes alighting—
Or driver's nose—and biting.
And when the whole did get in motion,
Confirm'd and settled in the notion,
He took, himself, the total glory,—
Flew back and forth in wondrous hurry,
And, as he buzz'd about the cattle,
Seem'd like a sergeant in a battle,
The files and squadrons leading on
To where the victory is won.
Thus charged with all the commonweal,
This single fly began to feel
Responsibility too great,
And cares, a grievous, crushing weight ;
And made complaint that none would aid
　　The horses up the tedious hill—
The monk his prayers at leisure said—
　　Fine time to pray!—the dames, at will,
Were singing songs— not greatly needed !
　　Thus in their ears he sharply sang,
　　And notes of indignation ran,—
Notes, after all, not greatly heeded.
Erelong the coach was on the top :
Now, said the fly, my hearties, stop
And breathe ;—I've got you up the hill ;
　　And, Messrs. Horses, let me say,
1 need not ask you if you will
　　A proper compensation pay.

Thus certain ever-bustling noddies
　　Are seen in every great affair ;
Important, swelling, busy-bodies,
　　And bores 'tis easier to bear
Than chase them from their needless care.

X.—THE DAIRYWOMAN AND THE POT OF MILK.

A POT of milk upon her cushion'd crown,
Good Peggy hasten'd to the market town ;
Short clad and light, with speed she went,
Not fearing any accident ;
　　Indeed, to be the nimbler tripper,
　　　　Her dress that day,
　　　　The truth to say,
　　Was simple petticoat and slipper.
　　　　And, thus bedight,
　　　　Good Peggy, light,—
Her gains already counted,—
　　　　Laid out the cash
　　　　At single dash,
Which to a hundred eggs amounted.
　　　　Three nests she made,
　　　　Which, by the aid
Of diligence and care were hatch'd.
　　　　To raise the chicks,
　　　　I'll easy fix,
Said she, beside our cottage thatch'd.
　　　　The fox must get
　　　　More cunning yet,

Or leave enough to buy a pig.
    With little care
    And any fare,
He'll grow quite fat and big ;
    And then the price
    Will be so nice,
For which the pork will sell !
    'Twill go quite hard
    But in our yard
I'll bring a cow and calf to dwell—
    A calf to frisk among the flock !
The thought made Peggy do the same ;
And down at once the milk-pot came,
    And perish'd with the shock.
Calf, cow, and pig, and chicks, adieu !
Your mistress' face is sad to view ;—
She gives a tear to fortune spilt ;
Then with the downcast look of guilt,
Home to her husband empty goes,
Somewhat in danger of his blows.

Who buildeth not, sometimes, in air
His cots, or seats, or castles fair ?
From kings to dairywomen,—all,—
The wise, the foolish, great and small,—
Each thinks his waking dream the best.
Some flattering error fills the breast :
The world with all its wealth is ours,
Its honours, dames, and loveliest bowers.
Instinct with valour, when alone,
I hurl the monarch from his throne ;
The people, glad to see him dead,
Elect me monarch in his stead,
And diadems rain on my head.
Some accident then calls me back,
And I'm no more than simple Jack.

XI.—THE CURATE AND THE CORPSE.

A DEAD man going slowly, sadly,
    To occupy his last abode,
A curate by him, rather gladly,
    Did holy service on the road.
Within a coach the dead was borne,
A robe around him, duly worn,
Of which I wot he was not proud—
That ghostly garment call'd a shroud.
In summer's blaze and winter's blast,
That robe is changeless—'tis the last.
The curate, with his priestly dress on,
    Recited all the church's prayers,
The psalm, the verse, response, and lesson,
    In fullest style of such affairs.
Sir Corpse, we beg you, do not fear
A lack of such things on your bier ;
They'll give abundance every way,
Provided only that you pay.
The Reverend John Cabbagepate
Watch'd o'er the corpse, as if it were
A treasure, needing guardian care ;
And all the while his looks elate,
This language seem'd to hold :
The dead will pay so much in gold,
So much in lights of molten wax,
So much in other sorts of tax :
With all he hoped to buy a cask of wine,
The best which thereabouts produced the vine.
A pretty niece, on whom he doted,
And eke his chambermaid, should be promoted,
    By being newly petticoated.

The coach upset, and dash'd to pieces,
Cut short these thoughts of wine and nieces !
There lay poor John with broken head,
Beneath the coffin of the dead !
His rich parishioner in lead
    Drew on the priest the doom
Of riding with him to the tomb !

    The Pot of Milk, and fate
    Of Curate Cabbagepate,
    As emblems, do but give
The history of most that live.

XII.—THE MAN WHO RAN AFTER FORTUNE, AND THE MAN WHO WAITED FOR HER IN HIS BED.

WHO joins not with his restless race
To give Dame Fortune eager chase !
O, had I but some lofty perch,
    From which to view the panting crowd
    Of care-worn dreamers, poor and proud,
As on they hurry in the search,
From realm to realm, o'er land and water,
Of Fate's fantastic, fickle daughter !
Ah ! slaves sincere of flying phantom !
    Just as their goddess they would clasp,
    The jilt divine eludes their grasp,
And flits away to Bantam !
Poor fellows ! I bewail their lot.
    And here's the comfort of my ditty ;
For fools the mark of wrath are not
    So much, I'm sure, as pity.
That man, say they, and feed their hope,
Raised cabbages—and now he's pope !
Don't we deserve as rich a prize !
Ay, richer ! But hath Fortune eyes !
And then the popedom, is it worth
    The price that must be given ?—
Repose ?—the sweetest bliss of earth,
    And, ages since, of gods in heaven ?
'Tis rarely Fortune's favourites
Enjoy this cream of all delights.
Seek not the dame, and she will you—
A truth which of her sex is true.

Snug in a country town
A pair of friends were settled down.
One sigh'd unceasingly to find
A fortune better to his mind,
And, as he chanced his friend to meet,
Proposed to quit their dull retreat.
No prophet can to honour come,
Said he, unless he quits his home ;
Let's seek our fortune far and wide.
Seek, if you please, his friend replied ;
For one, I do not wish to see
A better clime or destiny.
I leave the search and prize to you ;
Your restless humour please pursue !
You'll soon come back again.
I vow to nap it here till then.
The enterprising, or ambitious,
Or, if you please, the avaricious,
    Betook him to the road.
The morrow brought him to a place
The flaunting goddess ought to grace
    As her particular abode—

I mean the court whereat he staid,
And plans for seizing Fortune laid.
He rose, and dress'd, and dined, and went to
          bed,
    Exactly as the fashion led :
In short, he did whate'er he could,
But never found the promised good.
Said he, Now somewhere else I'll try—
And yet I fail'd I know not why ;
For Fortune here is much at home ;
To this and that I see her come,
Astonishingly kind to some.
And, truly, it is hard to see
The reason why she slips from me.
'Tis true, perhaps, as I've been told,
That spirits here may be too bold.
To courts and courtiers all I bid adieu ;
Deceitful shadows they pursue.
The dame has temples in Surat ;
I'll go and see them—that is flat.
To say so was t' embark at once.
O, human hearts are made of bronze !
His must have been of adamant,
Beyond the power of Death to daunt,
Who ventured first this route to try,
And all its frightful risks defy.
'Twas more than once our venturous wight
Did homeward turn his aching sight,
When pirates, rocks, and calms and storms,
Presented death in frightful forms—
Death sought with pains on distant shores,
Which soon as wish'd for would have come,
Had he not left the peaceful doors
Of his despised but blessed home.
    Arrived, at length, in Hindostan,
The people told our wayward man
That Fortune, ever void of plan,
Dispensed her favours in Japan.
And on he went, the weary sea
His vessel bearing lazily.
    This lesson, taught by savage men,
Was after all his only gain :—
Contented in thy country stay,
And seek thy wealth in nature's way.
Japan refused to him, no less
Than Hindostan, success ;
And hence his judgment came to make
His quitting home a great mistake.
    Renouncing his ungrateful course,
He hasten'd back with all his force ;
And when his village came in sight,
His tears were proof of his delight.
Ah, happy he, exclaim'd the wight,
Who, dwelling there with mind sedate,
Employs himself to regulate
His ever-hatching, wild desires ;
Who checks his heart when it aspires
To know of courts, and seas, and glory,
More than he can by simple story ;
Who seeks not o'er the treacherous wave—
More treacherous Fortune's willing slave—
The bait of wealth and honours fleeting,
Held by that goddess, aye retreating.
Henceforth from home I budge no more !
    Pop on his sleeping friends he came,
    Thus purposing against the dame,
And found her sitting at his door.

XIII.—THE TWO COCKS.

Two cocks in peace were living, when
A war was kindled by a hen.
O love, thou bane of Troy ! 'twas thine
The blood of men and gods to shed
Enough to turn the Xanthus red
          As old Port wine !
And long the battle doubtful stood :
    (I mean the battle of the cocks ;)
    They gave each other fearful shocks:
The fame spread o'er the neighbourhood,
And gather'd all the crested brood.
And Helens more than one, of plumage bright,
Led off the victor of that bloody fight.
    The vanquish'd, drooping, fled,
    Conceal'd his batter'd head,
    And in a dark retreat
    Bewail'd his sad defeat.
    His loss of glory and the prize
His rival now enjoy'd before his eyes.
While this he every day beheld,
His hatred kindled, courage swell'd :
He whet his beak, and flapp'd his wings,
And meditated dreadful things.
Waste rage ! His rival flew upon a roof
And crow'd to give his victory proof.—
    A hawk this boasting heard.
      Now perish'd all his pride,
      As suddenly he died
    Beneath that savage bird.
    In consequence of this reverse,
The vanquish'd sallied from his hole,
And took the harem, master sole,
    For moderate penance not the worse.
      Imagine the congratulation,
      The proud and stately leading,
      Gallanting, coaxing, feeding,
      Of wives almost a nation.
'Tis thus that Fortune loves to flee
The insolent by victory.
We should mistrust her when we beat,
Lest triumph lead us to defeat.

XIV.—THE INGRATITUDE AND INJUSTICE OF MEN TOWARDS FORTUNE.

A TRADER on the sea to riches grew ;
Freight after freight the winds in favour blew ;
    Fate steer'd him clear ; gulf, rock, nor shoal
    Of all his bales exacted toll.
Of other men the powers of chance and storm
Their dues collected in substantial form ;
While smiling Fortune, in her kindest sport,
Took care to waft his vessels to their port.
His partners, factors, agents, faithful proved ;
    His goods—tobacco, sugar, spice—
    Were sure to fetch the highest price.
      By fashion and by folly loved,
      His rich brocades and laces,
      And splendid porcelain vases,
      Enkindling strong desires,
      Most readily found buyers.
In short, gold rain'd where'er he went—
Abundance, more than could be spent—
Dogs, horses, coaches, downy bedding—
His very fasts were like a wedding.

A bosom friend, a look his table giving,
Inquired whence came such sumptuous living.
Whence should it come, said he, superb of brow,
But from the fountain of my knowing how?
I owe it simply to my skill and care
In risking only where the marts will bear.
And now, so sweet his swelling profits were,
He risk'd anew his former gains:
Success rewarded not his pains—
His own imprudence was the cause.
One ship, ill-freighted, went awreck;
Another felt of arms the lack,
When pirates, trampling on the laws,
O'ercame, and bore it off a prize!
A third, arriving at its port,
Had fail'd to sell its merchandise,—
The style and folly of the court
Not now requiring such a sort.
His agents, factors, fail'd;—in short,
The man himself, from pomp and princely cheer,
And palaces, and parks, and dogs, and deer,
Fell down to poverty most sad and drear.
His friend, now meeting him in shabby plight,
Exclaim'd, And whence comes this to pass?
From Fortune, said the man, alas!
Console yourself, replied the friendly wight:
For, if to make you rich the dame denies,
She can't forbid you to be wise.

What faith he gain'd, I do not wis;
I know, in every case like this,
Each claims the credit of his bliss,
And with a heart ingrate
Imputes his misery to Fate.

———•———

XV.—THE FORTUNE-TELLERS.

'Tis oft from chance opinion takes its rise,
And into reputation multiplies.
This prologue finds pat applications
In men of all this world's vocations;
For fashion, prejudice, and party strife,
Conspire to crowd poor justice out of life.
What can you do to counteract
This reckless, rushing cataract?
'Twill have its course for good or bad,
As it, indeed, has always had.

A dame in Paris play'd the Pythoness
With much of custom, and, of course, success.
Was any trifle lost, or did
Some maid a husband wish,
Or wife of husband to be rid,
Or either sex for fortune fish,
Resort was had to her with gold,
To get the hidden future told.
Her art was made of various tricks,
Wherein the dame contrived to mix,
With much assurance, learned terms.
Now, chance, of course, sometimes confirms;
And just as often as it did,
The news was anything but hid.
In short, though, as to ninety-nine per cent.,
The lady knew not what her answers meant,
Borne up by ever-babbling Fame,
An oracle she soon became.
A garret was this woman's home,
Till she had gain'd of gold a sum

That raised the station of her spouse—
Bought him an office and a house.
As she could then no longer bear it,
Another tenanted the garret.
To her came up the city crowd,—
Wives, maidens, servants, gentry proud,—
To ask their fortunes, as before;
A Sibyl's cave was on her garret floor:
Such custom had its former mistress drawn,
It lasted even when herself was gone.
It sorely tax'd the present mistress' wits
To satisfy the throngs of teasing cits.
I tell your fortunes! joke, indeed!
Why, gentlemen, I cannot read!
What can you, ladies, learn from me,
Who never learn'd my A, B, C?
Avaunt with reasons! tell she must,—
Predict as if she understood,
And lay aside more precious dust
Than two the ablest lawyers could.
The stuff that garnish'd out her room—
Four crippled chairs, a broken broom—
Help'd mightily to raise her merits,—
Full proof of intercourse with spirits!
Had she predicted e'er so truly,
On floor with carpet cover'd duly,
Her word had been a mockery made.
The fashion set upon the garret.
Doubt that! none bold enough to dare it!
The other woman lost her trade.

All shopmen know the force of signs,
And so, indeed, do some divines.
In palaces, a robe awry
Has sometimes set the wearer high;
And crowds his teaching will pursue
Who draws the greatest listening crew.
Ask, if you please, the reason why.

———•———

XVI.—THE CAT, THE WEASEL, AND THE YOUNG RABBIT.

John Rabbit's palace under ground
Was once by Goody Weasel found.
She, sly of heart, resolved to seize
The place, and did so at her ease.
She took possession while its lord
Was absent on the dewy sward,
Intent upon his usual sport,
A courtier at Aurora's court.
When he had browsed his fill of clover,
And cut his pranks all nicely over,
Home Johnny came to take his drowse,
All snug within his cellar-house.
The weasel's nose he came to see,
Outsticking through the open door.
Ye gods of hospitality!
Exclaim'd the creature, vexèd sore,
Must I give up my father's lodge?
Ho! Madam Weasel, please to budge,
Or, quicker than a weasel's dodge,
I'll call the rats to pay their grudge!
The sharp-nosed lady made reply,
That she was first to occupy.
The cause of war was surely small—
A house where one could only crawl!
And though it were a vast domain,
Said she, I'd like to know what will
Could grant to John perpetual reign,—
The son of Peter or of Bill,—

More than to Paul, or even me.
John Rabbit spoke—great lawyer he—
Of custom, usage, as the law,
   Whereby the house, from sire to son,
As well as all its store of straw,
   From Peter came at length to John.
Who could present a claim so good
As he, the first possessor, could ?
Now, said the dame, let 's drop dispute,
   And go before Raminagrobis,
Who'll judge, not only in this suit,
   But tell us truly whose the globe is.
This person was a hermit cat,
   A cat that play'd the hypocrite,
A saintly mouser, sleek and fat,
   An arbiter of keenest wit.
John Rabbit in the judge concurr'd,
   And off went both their case to broach
Before his majesty, the furr'd.
   Said Clapperclaw, My kits, approach,
And put your noses to my ears :
I'm deaf, almost, by weight of years.
And so they did, not fearing aught.
   The good apostle, Clapperclaw,
Then laid on each a well-arm'd paw,
And both to an agreement brought,
   By virtue of his tuskèd jaw.
This brings to mind the fate
Of little kings before the great.

XVII.—THE HEAD AND THE TAIL OF THE SERPENT.

    Two parts the serpent has—
    Of men the enemies—
    The head and tail : the same
    Have won a mighty fame,
       Next to the cruel Fates ;—
    So that, indeed, hence
       They once had great debates
    About precedence.
The first had always gone ahead ;
The tail had been for ever led ;
And now to Heaven it pray'd,
    And said,
O, many and many a league,
    Dragg'd on in sore fatigue,
    Behind his back I go.
Shall he for ever use me so ?
Am I his humble servant ;
No.   Thanks to God most fervent !
    His brother I was born,
    And not his slave forlorn.
The self-same blood in both,
I'm just as good as he :
A poison dwells in me
As virulent as doth *
In him. In mercy, heed
And grant me this decree,
That I in turn may lead—
My brother, follow me.
My course shall be so wise.
That no complaint shall rise.

With cruel kindness Heaven granted
   The very thing he blindly wanted :
To such desires of beasts and men,
   Though often deaf, it was not then.

   * An ancient mistake in natural history.

At once this novel guide,
   That saw no more in broad daylight
Than in the murk of darkest night,
   His powers of leading tried,
Struck trees, and men, and stones, and bricks,
   And led his brother straight to Styx..
   And to the same unlovely home,
   Some states by such an error come.

XVIII.—AN ANIMAL IN THE MOON.*

WHILE one philosopher affirms
   That by our senses we're deceived,
Another swears, in plainest terms,
   The senses are to be believed.
The twain are right. Philosophy
Correctly calls us dupes whene'er
Upon mere senses we rely ;
But when we wisely rectify
   The raw report of eye or ear,
By distance, medium, circumstance,
In real knowledge we advance.
These things hath nature wisely plann'd—
Whereof the proof shall be at hand.
I see the sun : its dazzling glow
Seems but a hand-breadth here below ;
But should I see it in its home,
That azure, star-besprinkled dome,
Of all the universe the eye,
Its blaze would fill one half the sky.
The powers of trigonometry
Have set my mind from blunder free.
The ignorant believe it flat ;
I make it round, instead of that.
I fasten, fix, on nothing ground it,
And send the earth to travel round it.
In short, I contradict my eyes,
And sift the truth from constant lies.
The mind, not hasty at conclusion,
Resists the onset of illusion,
Forbids the sense to get the better,
And ne'er believes it to the letter.
Between my eyes, perhaps too ready,
   And ears as much or more too slow,
A judge with balance true and steady,
   I come, at last, some things to know.
Thus when the water crooks a stick,
My reason straightens it as quick—
Kind Mistress Reason—foe of error,
And best of shields from needless terror.
The creed is common with our race,
The moon contains a woman's face.
True ! No. Whence, then, the notion,
From mountain top to ocean ?
The roughness of that satellite,
   Its hills and dales, of every grade,
   Effect a change of light and shade
Deceptive to our feeble sight ;
So that, besides the human face,
All sorts of creatures one might trace.
Indeed, a living beast, I ween,
Has lately been by England seen.
All duly placed the telescope,
And keen observers full of hope,
An animal entirely new,

   * This fable is founded on a fact which occurred in the experience of the astronomer Sir Paul Neal, a member of the Royal Society of London.

In that fair planet, came to view.
Abroad and fast the wonder flew ;—
Some change had taken place on high,
Presaging earthly changes nigh ;
Perhaps, indeed, it might betoken
The wars that had already broken
Out wildly o'er the Continent.
The king to see the wonder went :
(As patron of the sciences,
No right to go more plain than his.)
To him, in turn, distinct and clear,
This lunar monster did appear.—
A mouse, between the lenses caged,
Had caused these wars, so fiercely waged !
No doubt the happy English folks
Laugh'd at it as the best of jokes.
How soon will Mars afford the chance
For like amusements here in France !
He makes us reap broad fields of glory.
   Our foes may fear the battle-ground ;
   For us, it is no sooner found,
   Than Louis, with fresh laurels crown'd,
Bears higher up our country's story.
   The daughters, too, of Memory,—
   The Pleasures and the Graces,—
   Still show their cheering faces :
We wish for peace, but do not sigh.
The English Charles the secret knows
To make the most of his repose.
And more than this, he'll know the way,
   By valour working sword in hand,
   To bring his sea-encircled land
To share the fight it only sees to-day.
Yet, could he but this quarrel quell,
What incense-clouds would grateful swell !
What deed more worthy of his fame ! *
Augustus, Julius—pray, which Cæsar's name
Shines now on story's page with purest flame ?
O people happy in your sturdy hearts !
Say, when shall Peace pack up these bloody darts,
And send us all, like you, to softer arts ?

BOOK VIII.

I.—DEATH AND THE DYING.

DEATH never taketh by surprise
The well-prepared, to wit, the wise—
   They knowing of themselves the time
   To meditate the final change of clime.
That time, alas ! embraces all
Which into hours and minutes we divide ;
   There is no part, however small,
   That from this tribute one can hide.

---

* This fable appears to have been composed about the beginning of the year 1677. The European powers then found themselves exhausted by war and desirous of peace. England, the only neutral, became. of course, the arbiter of the negotiations which ensued at Nimeguen. All the belligerent parties invoked her mediation. Charles II., however, felt himself exceedingly embarrassed by his secret connections with Louis XIV., which made him desire to prescribe conditions favourable to that monarch ; while, on the other hand, he feared the people of England, if, treacherous to her interests, he should fail to favour the nations allied and combined against France.

The very moment, oft, which bids
   The heirs of empire see the light
Is that which shuts their fringèd lids
   In everlasting night.
Defend yourself by rank and wealth,
Plead beauty, virtue, youth, and health,—
   Unblushing Death will ravish all ;
The world itself shall pass beneath his pall.
No truth is better known ; but, truth to say,
   No truth is oftener thrown away.

A man, well in his second century,
Complain'd that Death had call'd him suddenly ;
   Had left no time his plans to fill,
   To balance books, or make his will.
O Death, said he, d'ye call it fair,
   Without a warning to prepare,
   To take a man on lifted leg ?
   O, wait a little while, I beg.
My wife cannot be left alone ;
I must set out my nephew's son ;
And let me build my house a wing,
Before you strike, O cruel king !
Old man, said Death, one thing is sure,—
   My visit here's not premature.
Hast thou not lived a century !
Darest thou engage to find for me,
In Paris' walls two older men ?
Has France, among her millions ten ?
Thou say'st I should have sent thee word
Thy lamp to trim, thy loins to gird ;
And then my coming had been meet—
      Thy will engross'd,
      Thy house complete !
Did not thy feelings notify ?
Did not they tell thee thou must die ?
Thy taste and hearing are no more ;
Thy sight itself is gone before ;
For thee the sun superfluous shines,
And all the wealth of Indian mines.
Thy mates I've shown thee dead or dying.
What's this, indeed, but notifying !
Come on, old man, without reply ;
   For to the great and common weal
It doth but little signify
   Whether thy will shall ever feel
   The impress of thy hand and seal.

And Death had reason,—ghastly sage !
For surely man, at such an age,
Should part from life as from a feast,
Returning decent thanks, at least,
To Him who spread the various cheer,
And unrepining take his bier ;
For shun it long no creature can.
Repinest thou, grey-headed man !
See younger mortals rushing by
To meet their death without a sigh—
Death full of triumph and of fame,
But in its terrors still the same.—
But, ah ! my words are thrown away !
Those men like Death most dread his sway.

II.—THE COBBLER AND THE FINANCIER.

A COBBLER sang from morn till night ;
   'Twas sweet and marvellous to hear,
   His trills and quavers told the ear
Of more contentment and delight,
   Enjoy'd by that laborious wight,

Than e'er enjoy'd the sages seven,
Or any mortals short of heaven.
His neighbour, on the other hand,
With gold in plenty at command,
But little sang, and slumber'd less—
A financier of great success.
If e'er he dozed at break of day,
The cobbler's song drove sleep away;
And much he wish'd that Heaven had made
Sleep a commodity of trade,
In market sold, like food and drink,
So much an hour, so much a wink.
At last, our songster did he call
To meet him in his princely hall.
Said he, Now, honest Gregory,
What may your yearly earnings be?
My yearly earnings! faith, good sir,
I never go, at once, so far,
The cheerful cobbler said,
And queerly scratch'd his head,—
  I never reckon in that way,
  But cobble on from day to day,
Content with daily bread.
Indeed! Well, Gregory, pray,
What may your earnings be per day?
Why, sometimes more and sometimes less.
The worst of all, I must confess,
(And but for which our gains would be
A pretty sight, indeed, to see,)
Is that the days are made so many
In which we cannot earn a penny—
The sorest ill the poor man feels :
They tread upon each other's heels
Those idle days of holy saints!
  And though the year is shingled o'er,
  The parson keeps a-finding more!
With smiles provoked by these complaints,
Replied the lordly financier,
  I'll give you better cause to sing.
These hundred pounds I hand you here
  Will make you happy as a king.
Go, spend them with a frugal heed ;
They'll long supply your every need.
The cobbler thought the silver more
Than he had ever dream'd, before,
The mines for ages could produce,
Or world, with all its people, use.
He took it home, and there did hide,
And with it laid his joy aside.
No more of song, no more of sleep,
  But cares, suspicions in their stead,
  And false alarms, by fancy fed.
His eyes and ears their vigils keep,
And not a cat can tread the floor
But seems a thief slipp'd through the door.
  At last, poor man!
Up to the financier he ran,—
Then in his morning nap profound :
  O, give me back my songs, cried he,
  And sleep, that used so sweet to be,
And take the money, every pound!

III.—THE LION, THE WOLF, AND THE FOX.

A LION, old and impotent with gout,
Would have some cure for age found out.
Impossibilities, on all occasions,
With kings, are rank abominations.

This king, from every species,—
  For each abounds in every sort,—
Call'd to his aid the leeches.
  They came in throngs to court,
From doctors of the highest fee
To nostrum-quacks without degree,—
Advised, prescribed, talk'd learnedly ;
  But with the rest
Came not Sir Cunning Fox, M.D.
Sir Wolf the royal couch attended,
  And his suspicions there express'd.
Forthwith his majesty, offended,
Resolved Sir Cunning Fox should come,
And sent to smoke him from his home.
He came, was duly usher'd in,
And, knowing where Sir Wolf had been,
  Said, Sire, your royal ear
  Has been abused, I fear,
  By rumours false and insincere ;
To wit, that I've been self-exempt
From coming here, through sheer contempt.
But, sire, I've been on pilgrimage,
  By vow expressly made,
  Your royal health to aid,
And, on my way, met doctors sage,
In skill the wonder of the age,
  Whom carefully I did consult
  About that great debility
  Term'd in the books senility,
Of which you fear, with reason, the result.
You lack, they say, the vital heat,
By age extreme become effete.
Drawn from a living wolf, the hide
Should warm and smoking be applied.
The secret's good, beyond a doubt,
For nature's weak, and wearing out.
Sir Wolf, here, won't refuse to give
His hide to cure you, as I live.
The king was pleased with this advice.
Flay'd, jointed, served up in a trice,
Sir Wolf first wrapp'd the monarch up,
Then furnish'd him whereon to sup.

Beware, ye courtiers, lest ye gain,
By slander's arts, less power than pain ;
For in the world where ye are living,
A pardon no one thinks of giving.

IV.—THE POWER OF FABLES.
TO M. DE BARILLON*.

Can diplomatic dignity
  To simple fables condescend?
Can I your famed benignity
  Invoke, my muse an ear to lend?
If once she dares a high intent,
Will you esteem her impudent?
Your cares are weightier, indeed,
  Than listening to the sage debates
  Of rabbit or of weasel states :
So, as it pleases, burn or read ;
But save us from the woful harms
Of Europe roused in hostile arms.
That from a thousand other places
Our enemies should show their faces,
May well be granted with a smile,
But not that England's Isle

* Ambassador to the court of St. James.

Our friendly kings should set
Their fatal blades to whet.
Comes not the time for Louis to repose?
What Hercules, against these hydra foes,
Would not grow weary? Must new heads oppose
His ever-waxing energy of blows?
Now, if your gentle, soul-persuasive powers,
As sweet as mighty in this world of ours,
Can soften hearts, and lull this war to sleep*,
I'll pile your altars with a hundred sheep;
    And this is not a small affair
    For a Parnassian mountaineer.
Meantime, (if you have time to spare,)
Accept a little incense-cheer.
A homely, but an ardent prayer,
    And tale in verse, I give you here.
I'll only say, the theme is fit for you.
    With praise, which envy must confess
To worth like yours is justly due,
No man on earth needs propping less.

In Athens, once, that city fickle,
    An orator†, awake to feel
His country in a dangerous pickle,
    Would sway the proud republic's heart,
    Discoursing of the common weal,
As taught by his tyrannic art.
The people listen'd—not a word.
Meanwhile the orator recurr'd
To bolder tropes—enough to rouse
The dullest blocks that e'er did drowse;
He clothed in life the very dead,
And thunder'd all that could be said.
    The wind received his breath,
    As to the ear of death.
That beast of many heads and light‡,
    The crowd, accustom'd to the sound
Was all intent upon a sight—
A brace of lads in mimic fight.
A new resource the speaker found.
Ceres, in lower tone said he,
Went forth her harvest fields to see:
An eel, as such a fish might be,
And swallow, were her company.
A river check'd the travellers three.
Two cross'd it soon without ado;
The smooth eel swam, the swallow flew.—
    Outcried the crowd,
    With voices loud—
And Ceres—what did she?
Why, what she pleased; but first
Yourselves she justly cursed—
A people puzzling aye your brains
With children's tales and children's play,
While Greece puts on her steel array,
    To save her limbs from tyrant chains!
Why ask you not what Philip does?
At this reproach the idle buzz
Fell to the silence of the grave,
Or moonstruck sea without a wave,
And every eye and ear awoke
To drink the words the patriot spoke.

---

* The parliament of England was determined that, in
case Louis XIV. did not make peace with the allies,
Charles II. should join them to make war on France.
† Demades.
‡ Horace, speaking of the Roman people, said,
    " Bellua multorum est capitum."
                              Epist. I. Book I. 76.

This feather stick in Fable's cap.
We're all Athenians, mayhap;
And I, for one, confess the sin;
    For, while I write this moral here,
    If one should tell that tale so queer
Ycleped, I think, " The Ass's Skin,"
I should not mind my work a pin.
The world is old, they say; I don't deny it;—
    But, infant still
    In taste and will,
Whoe'er would teach, must gratify it.

V.—THE MAN AND THE FLEA.

IMPERTINENT, we tease and weary Heaven
With prayers which would insult mere mortals
    even.
'Twould seem that not a god in all the skies
From our affairs must ever turn his eyes,
And that the smallest of our race
Could hardly eat, or wash his face,
Without, like Greece and Troy for ten years' space,
Embroiling all Olympus in the case.

A flea some blockhead's shoulder bit,
    And then his clothes refused to quit.
O Hercules, he cried, you ought to purge
The world of this far worse than hydra scourge.
O Jupiter, what are your bolts about,
They do not put these foes of mine to rout?

To crush a flea, this fellow's fingers under,
The gods must lend the fool their club and thunder.

VI.—THE WOMEN AND THE SECRET.

THERE's nothing like a secret weighs;
    Too heavy 'tis for women tender;
And, for this matter, in my days,
    I've seen some men of female gender.

To prove his wife, a husband cried,
('The night he knew the truth would hide,)
O Heavens! what's this? O dear—I beg—
I'm torn—O! O! I've laid an egg!
An egg! Why, yes, it's gospel-true.
Look here—see—feel it, fresh and new;
But, wife, don't mention it, lest men
Should laugh at me, and call me hen;
    Indeed, don't say a word about it.
On this, as other matters, green and young,
    The wife, all wonder, did not doubt it,
And pledged herself by Heaven to hold her tongue.
Her oath, however, fled the light
As quick as did the shades of night.
Before Dan Phœbus waked to labour,
The dame was off to see a neighbour.
My friend, she said, half-whispering,
There's come to pass the strangest thing—
If you should tell, 'twould turn me out of door:—
My husband's laid an egg as big as four!
As you would taste of heaven's bliss,
Don't tell a living soul of this.
I tell! why if you knew a thing about me,
You wouldn't for an instant doubt me;

Your confidence I'll ne'er abuse.
The layer's wife went home relieved ;
  The other broil'd to tell the news ;
You need not ask if she believed.
A dame more busy could not be ;
In twenty places, ere her tea,
Instead of one egg, she said three !
  Nor was the story finish'd here :
A gossip, still more keen than she,
  Said four, and spoke it in the ear—
A caution truly little worth,
Applied to all the ears on earth.
Of eggs, the number, thanks to Fame,
  As on from mouth to mouth she sped,
  Had grown a hundred, soothly said,
Ere Sol had quench'd his golden flame !

VII.—THE DOG THAT CARRIED HIS MASTER'S DINNER.

Our eyes are not made proof against the fair,
  Nor hands against the touch of gold.
    Fidelity is sadly rare,
  And has been from the days of old.

Well taught his appetite to check,
  And do full many a handy trick,
  A dog was trotting, light and quick,
His master's dinner on his neck.
A temperate, self-denying dog was he,
More than with such a load he liked to be.
But still he was, while many such as we
Would not have scrupled to make free.
Strange that to dogs a virtue you may teach,
Which, do your best, to men you vainly preach !
This dog of ours, thus richly fitted out,
A mastiff met, who wish'd the meat, no doubt.
To get it was less easy than he thought ;
  The porter laid it down and fought.
Meantime some other dogs arrive :
Such dogs are always thick enough,
And, fearing neither kick nor cuff,
  Upon the public thrive.
Our hero, thus o'ermatch'd and press'd,—
The meat in danger manifest,—
Is fain to share it with the rest ;
And, looking very calm and wise,
No anger, gentlemen, he cries :
My morsel will myself suffice ;
The rest shall be your welcome prize.
With this, the first his charge to violate,
He snaps a mouthful from his freight.
Then follow mastiff, cur, and pup,
Till all is cleanly eaten up.
Not sparingly the party feasted,
And not a dog of all but tasted.

In some such manner men abuse
Of towns and states the revenues.
The sheriffs, aldermen, and mayor,
Come in for each a liberal share.
The strongest gives the rest example :
  'Tis sport to see with what a zest
  They sweep and lick the public chest
Of all its funds, however ample.
If any common weal's defender
  Should dare to say a single word,
  He's shown his scruples are absurd,
And finds it easy to surrender—
Perhaps, to be the first offender.

VIII.—THE JOKER AND THE FISHES.

Some seek for jokers ; I avoid.
A joke must be, to be enjoy'd,
Of wisdom's words, by wit employ'd.
God never meant for men of sense,
The wits that joke to give offence.

Perchance of these I shall be able
To show you one preserved in fable.
A joker at a banker's table,
Most amply spread to satisfy
  The height of epicurean wishes,
  Had nothing near but little fishes.
So, taking several of the fry,
He whisper'd to them very nigh,
And seem'd to listen for reply.
The guests much wonder'd what it meant,
And stared upon him all intent.
The joker, then with sober face,
Politely thus explain'd the case :
A friend of mine, to India bound,
  Has been, I fear,
    Within a year,
By rocks or tempests wreck'd and drown'd.
I ask'd these strangers from the sea
To tell me where my friend might be.
But all replied they were too young
To know the least of such a matter—
The older fish could tell me better.
  Pray, may I hear some older tongue ?
What relish had the gentlefolks
For such a sample of his jokes,
Is more than I can now relate.
They put, I'm sure, upon his plate,
A monster of so old a date,
He must have known the names and fate
Of all the daring voyagers,
Who, following the moon and stars,
Have, by mischances, sunk their bones
Within the realms of Davy Jones ;
And who, for centuries, had seen,
Far down, within the fathomless,
Where whales themselves are sceptreless,
The ancients in their halls of green.

IX.—THE RAT AND THE OYSTER.

A country rat, of little brains,
  Grown weary of inglorious rest,
Left home with all its straws and grains,
  Resolved to know beyond his nest.
When peeping through the nearest fence,
How big the world is, how immense !
He cried ; there rise the Alps, and that
Is doubtless famous Ararat.
His mountains were the works of moles,
Or dirt thrown up in digging holes !
Some days of travel brought him where
The tide had left the oysters bare.
Since here our traveller saw the sea,
He thought these shells the ships must be.
My father was, in truth, said he,
  A coward, and an ignoramus ;
He dared not travel : as for me,
  I've seen the ships and ocean famous ;
Have cross'd the deserts without drinking,
And many dangerous streams unshrinking ;

Such things I know from having seen and felt them.
And, as he went, in tales he proudly dealt them,
Not being of those rats whose knowledge
Comes by their teeth on books in college.
Among the shut-up shell-fish, one
Was gaping widely at the sun;
It breathed, and drank the air's perfume,
Expanding, like a flower in bloom.
Both white and fat, its meat
Appear'd a dainty treat.
Our rat, when he this shell espied,
Thought for his stomach to provide.
If not mistaken in the matter,
Said he, no meat was ever fatter,
Or in its flavour half so fine,
As that on which to-day I dine.
Thus full of hope, the foolish chap
Thrust in his head to taste,
And felt the pinching of a trap—
The oyster closed in haste.

We're first instructed, by this case,
That those to whom the world is new
Are wonder-struck at every view;
And, in the second place,
That the marauder finds his match,
And he is caught who thinks to catch.

X.—THE BEAR AND THE AMATEUR GARDENER.

A CERTAIN mountain bear, unlick'd and rude,
By fate confined within a lonely wood,
A new Bellerophon, whose life,
Knew neither comrade, friend, nor wife,—
Became insane; for reason, as we term it,
Dwells never long with any hermit.
'Tis good to mix in good society,
Obeying rules of due propriety;
And better yet to be alone;
But both are ills when overdone.
No animal had business where
All grimly dwelt our hermit bear;
Hence, bearish as he was, he grew
Heart-sick, and long'd for something new.
While he to sadness was addicted,
An aged man, not far from there,
Was by the same disease afflicted.
A garden was his favourite care,—
Sweet Flora's priesthood, light and fair,
And eke Pomona's—ripe and red
The presents that her fingers shed.
These two employments, true, are sweet
When made so by some friend discreet.
The gardens, gayly as they look,
Talk not, (except in this my book;)
So, tiring of the deaf and dumb,
Our man one morning left his home
Some company to seek,
That had the power to speak.—
The bear, with thoughts the same,
Down from his mountain came;
And in a solitary place,
They met each other, face to face.
It would have made the boldest tremble;
What did our man? To play the Gascon
The safest seem'd. He put the mask on,
His fear contriving to dissemble.

The bear, unused to compliment,
Growl'd bluntly, but with good intent,
Come home with me. The man replied:
Sir Bear, my lodgings, nearer by,
In yonder garden you may spy,
Where, if you'll honour me the while,
We'll break our fast in rural style.
I've fruits and milk,—unworthy fare,
It may be, for a wealthy bear;
But then I offer what I have.
The bear accepts, with visage grave,
But not unpleased; and on their way,
They grow familiar, friendly, gay.
Arrived, you see them side by side,
As if their friendship had been tried.
To a companion so absurd,
Blank solitude were well preferr'd,
Yet, as the bear scarce spoke a word,
The man was left quite at his leisure
To trim his garden at his pleasure.
Sir Bruin hunted—always brought
His friend whatever game he caught;
But chiefly aim'd at driving flies—
Those bold and shameless parasites,
That vex us with their ceaseless bites—
From off our gardener's face and eyes.
One day, while, stretch'd upon the ground
The old man lay, in sleep profound,
A fly that buzz'd around his nose,—
And bit it sometimes, I suppose,—
Put Bruin sadly to his trumps.
At last, determined, up he jumps;
I'll stop thy noisy buzzing now,
Says he; I know precisely how.
No sooner said than done.
He seized a paving-stone;
And by his modus operandi
Did both the fly and man die.

A foolish friend may cause more woe
Than could, indeed, the wisest foe.

XI.—THE TWO FRIENDS.

Two friends, in Monomotapa,
Had all their interests combined.
Their friendship, faithful and refined,
Our country can't exceed, do what it may.
One night, when potent Sleep had laid
All still within our planet's shade,
One of the two gets up alarm'd,
Runs over to the other's palace,
And hastily the servants rallies.
His startled friend, quick arm'd,
With purse and sword his comrade meets,
And thus right kindly greets :—
Thou seldom com'st at such an hour;
I take thee for a man of sounder mind
Than to abuse the time for sleep design'd.
Hast lost thy purse, by Fortune's power?
Here's mine. Hast suffer'd insult, or a blow
I've here my sword—to avenge it let us go.
No, said his friend, no need I feel
Of either silver, gold, or steel;
I thank thee for thy friendly zeal.
In sleep I saw thee rather sad,
And thought the truth might be as bad;

Unable to endure the fear,
That cursed dream has brought me here.

Which think you, reader, loved the most !
If doubtful this, one truth may be proposed :
There's nothing sweeter than a real friend :
        Not only is he prompt to lend—
An angler delicate, he fishes
The very deepest of your wishes,
And spares your modesty the task
His friendly aid to ask.
A dream, a shadow, wakes his fear,
When pointing at the object dear.

XII.—THE HOG, THE GOAT, AND THE SHEEP.

A GOAT, a sheep, and porker fat,
        All to the market rode together.
Their own amusement was not that
        Which caused their journey thither.
Their coachman did not mean to "set them down"
To see the shows and wonders of the town.
The porker cried, in piercing squeals,
As if with butchers at his heels.
The other beasts, of milder mood,
The cause by no means understood.
They saw no harm, and wonder'd why
At such a rate the hog should cry.
Hush there, old piggy ! said the man,
And keep as quiet as you can.
What wrong have you to squeal about,
And raise this devilish, deafening shout ?
These stiller persons at your side
Have manners much more dignified.
        Pray, have you heard
        A single word
Come from that gentleman in wool ?
That proves him wise. That proves him fool,
The testy hog replied ;
        For did he know
        To what we go,
He'd cry almost to split his throat ;
So would her ladyship the goat.
They only think to lose with ease,
The goat her milk, the sheep his fleece :
They're, maybe, right ; but as for me,
This ride is quite another matter.
Of service only on the platter,
My death is quite a certainty.
Adieu, my dear old piggery !
The porker's logic proved at once
Himself a prophet and a dunce.

Hope ever gives a present ease,
But fear beforehand kills :
The wisest he who least foresees
        Inevitable ills.

XIII.—THYRSIS AND AMARANTH.
FOR MADEMOISELLE DE SILLERY.

I HAD the Phrygian quit,
Charm'd with Italian wit * ;
But a divinity
Would on Parnassus see
A fable more from me.

------
* Referring to his Tales, in which he had borrowed
many subjects from Boccaccio.

Such challenge to refuse,
Without a good excuse,
Is not the way to use
Divinity or muse.
        Especially to one
Of those who truly are,
By force of being fair,
Made queens of human will,
        A thing should not be done
In all respects so ill.
For, be it known to all,
From Sillery the call
Has come for bird, and beast,
And insects, to the least,
To clothe their thoughts sublime
In this my simple rhyme.
In saying Sillery,
All's said that need to be.
Her claim to it so good,
Few fail to give her place
Above the human race :
How could they, if they would ?

Now come we to our end :—
        As she opines my tales
Are hard to comprehend ;
        For even genius fails
Some things to understand ;
So let us take in hand
        To make unnecessary,
        For once, a commentary.
Come shepherds now,—and rhyme we afterwards
The talk between the wolves and fleecy herds.

        To Amaranth, the young and fair,
        Said Thyrsis, once, with serious air,—
O, if you knew, like me, a certain ill,
        With which we men are harm'd,
        As well as strangely charm'd,
No boon from Heaven your heart could like it fill !
        Please let me name it in your ear,—
        A harmless word,—you need not fear.
Would I deceive you, you, for whom 1 bear
The tenderest sentiments that ever were ?
        Then Amaranth replied,
        What is its name ? I beg you, do not hide.
'Tis LOVE.—The word is beautiful ! reveal
Its signs and symptoms, how it makes one feel.—
Its pains are ecstacies. So sweet its stings,
The nectar-cups and incense-pots of kings,
Compared, are flat, insipid things.
        One strays all lonely in the wood—
        Leans silent o'er the placid flood,
        And there with great complacency,
        A certain face can see—
'Tis not one's own—but image fair,
                Retreating,
                Fleeting,
                Meeting,
                Greeting,
        Following everywhere.
For all the rest of human kind,
One is as good in short as blind.
There is a shepherd wight, I ween,
Well known upon the village green,
Whose voice, whose name, whose turning of the
        hinge
Excites upon the cheek a richer tinge—
The thought of whom is signal for a sigh—
The breast that heaves it knows not why—

Whose face the maiden fears to see,
Yet none so welcome still as he.—
Here Amaranth cut short his speech:
O ! O ! is that the evil which you preach ?
To me I think it is no stranger ;
I must have felt its power and danger.
Here Thyrsis thought his end was gain'd,
When further thus the maid explain'd :
  'Tis just the very sentiment
  Which I have felt for Clidamant !
  The other, vex'd and mortified,
  Now bit his lips, and nearly died.

Like him are multitudes, who when
Their own advancement they have meant,
Have play'd the game of other men.

———

XIV.—THE FUNERAL OF THE LIONESS.

The lion's consort died :
Crowds, gather'd at his side,
Must needs console the prince,
And thus their loyalty evince
By compliments of course,
Which make affliction worse.
Officially he cites
His realm to funeral rites,
At such a time and place ;
His marshals of the mace
Would order the affair.
Judge you if all came there.
Meantime, the prince gave way
To sorrow night and day.
With cries of wild lament
His cave he well-nigh rent.
And from his courtiers far and near,
Sounds imitative you might hear.

The court a country seems to me,
Whose people are no matter what,—
Sad gay, indifferent, or not,—
As suits the will of majesty ;
Or, if unable so to be,
Their task it is to seem it all—
Chameleons, monkeys, great and small.
'Twould seem one spirit serves a thousand bodies—
A paradise, indeed, for soulless noddies.

  But to our tale again :
The stag graced not the funeral train ;
Of tears his cheeks bore not a stain ;
For how could such a thing have been,
When death avenged him on the queen,
Who, not content with taking one,
Had choked to death his wife and son ?
The tears, in truth, refused to run.
A flatterer, who watch'd the while,
Affirm'd that he had seen him smile.
If, as the wise man somewhere saith,
A king's is like a lion's wrath,
What should King Lion's be but death?
The stag however could not read ;
Hence paid this proverb little heed,
And walk'd, intrepid, towards the throne ;
When thus the king, in fearful tone :
  Thou caitiff of the wood !
  Presum'st to laugh at such a time?
  Joins not thy voice the mournful chime ?
    We suffer not the blood

Of such a wretch profane
Our sacred claws to stain.
Wolves, let a sacrifice be made,
Avenge your mistress' awful shade.
  Sire, did the stag reply,
The time for tears is quite gone by ;
For in the flowers, not far from here,
Your worthy consort did appear ;
Her form, in spite of my surprise,
I could not fail to recognise.
  My friend, said she, beware
Lest funeral pomp about my bier,
  When I shall go with gods to share,
Compel thine eye to drop a tear.
    With kindred saints I rove
    In the Elysian grove,
    And taste a sort of bliss
    Unknown in worlds like this.
Still, let the royal sorrow flow
Its proper season here below ;
  'Tis not unpleasing, I confess.
The king and court scarce hear him out.
Up goes the loud and welcome shout—
A miracle ! an apotheosis !
And such at once the fashion is,
So far from dying in a ditch,
The stag retires with presents rich.

Amuse the ear of royalty
With pleasant dreams, and flattery,—
No matter what you may have done,
Nor yet how high its wrath may run,—
The bait is swallow'd—object won.

———

XV.—THE RAT AND THE ELEPHANT.

One's own importance to enhance,
  Inspirited by self-esteem,
Is quite a common thing in France ;
  A French disease it well might seem.
The strutting cavaliers of Spain
Are in another manner vain.
Their pride has more insanity,
More silliness our vanity.
Let's shadow forth our own disease—
Well worth a hundred tales like these.

A rat, of quite the smallest size,
Fix'd on an elephant his eyes,
And jeer'd the beast of high descent
Because his feet so slowly went.
Upon his back, three stories high,
There sat, beneath a canopy,
A certain sultan of renown,
  His dog, and cat, and concubine,
  His parrot, servant, and his wine,
All pilgrims to a distant town.
The rat profess'd to be amazed
That all the people stood and gazed
With wonder, as he pass'd the road,
Both at the creature and his load.
As if, said he, to occupy
A little more of land or sky
Made one, in view of common sense,
Of greater worth and consequence !
What see ye, men, in this parade,
That food for wonder need be made ?
The bulk which makes a child afraid?

In truth, I take myself to be,
In all respects, as good as he.
And further might have gone his vaunt;
  But, darting down, the cat
  Convinced him that a rat
Is smaller than an elephant.

XVI.—THE HOROSCOPE.

On death we mortals often run,
Just by the roads we take to shun.

A father's only heir, a son,
Was over-loved and doted on
So greatly, that astrology
Was question'd what his fate might be.
The man of stars this caution gave—
  That, until twenty years of age,
  No lion, even in a cage,
The boy should see,—his life to save.
The sire, to silence every fear
About a life so very dear,
Forbade that any one should let
His son beyond his threshold get.
Within his palace walls, the boy
Might all that heart could wish enjoy—
Might with his mates walk, leap, and run,
And frolic in the wildest fun.
When come of age to love the chase,
  That exercise was oft depicted
To him as one that brought disgrace,
  To which but blackguards were addicted.
But neither warning nor derision
Could change his ardent disposition.
The youth, fierce, restless, full of blood,
Was prompted by the boiling flood
To love the dangers of the wood.
The more opposed, the stronger grew
His mad desire. The cause he knew,
For which he was so closely pent ;
  And as, where'er he went,
In that magnificent abode,
Both tapestry and canvas show'd
The feats he did so much admire,
A painted lion roused his ire.
Ah, monster ! cried he, in his rage
'Tis you that keep me in my cage.
  With that, he clinch'd his fist,
  To strike the harmless beast—
  And did his hand impale
  Upon a hidden nail !
  And thus this cherish'd head,
  For which the healing art
  But vainly did its part,
    Was hurried to the dead
By caution blindly meant
To shun that sad event.

The poet Æschylus, 'tis said,
By much the same precaution bled.
  A conjuror foretold
A house would crush him in its fall ;—
  Forth sallied he, though old,
From town and roof-protected hall,
  And took his lodgings, wet or dry,
  Abroad, beneath the open sky.
  An eagle, bearing through the air
  A tortoise for her household fare,

Which first she wish'd to break,
The creature dropp'd, by sad mistake,
  Plump on the poet's forehead bare;
As if it were a naked rock—
To Æschylus a fatal shock !

From these examples, it appears,
This art, if true in any wise,
  Makes men fulfil the very fears
Engender'd by its prophecies.
  But from this charge I justify,
  By branding it a total lie.
  I don't believe that Nature's powers
  Have tied her hands or pinion'd ours,
  By marking on the heavenly vault
  Our fate without mistake or fault.
  That fate depends upon conjunctions
Of places, persons, times, and tracks,
  And not upon the functions
Of more or less of quacks.
A king and clown beneath one planet's nod
Are born ; one wields a sceptre, one a hod.
But it is Jupiter that wills it so !
  And who is he ! A soulless clod.
How can he cause such different powers to flow
  Upon the aforesaid mortals here below ?
  And how, indeed, to this far distant ball ·
  Can he impart his energy at all !—
  How pierce the ether deeps profound,
  The sun and globes that whirl around?
  A mote might turn his potent ray
  For ever from its earthward way.
  Will find it, then, in starry cope,
  The makers of the horoscope ?
The war with which all Europe's now afflicted—
Deserves it not by them to've been predicted ?
  Yet heard we not a whisper of it,
  Before it came, from any prophet.
  The suddenness of passion's gush,
  Of wayward life the headlong rush,—
  Permit they that the feeble ray
  Of twinkling planet, far away,
Should trace our winding, zigzag course ?
And yet this planetary force,
  As steady as it is unknown,
  These fools would make our guide alone—
Of all our varied life the source !
  Such doubtful facts as I relate—
  The petted child's and poet's fate—
  Our argument may well admit.
    The blindest man that lives in France,
    The smallest mark would doubtless hit—
    Once in a thousand times—by chance.

XVII.—THE ASS AND THE DOG.

Dame Nature, our respected mother,
Ordains that we should aid each other.

The ass this ordinance neglected,
Though not a creature ill-affected.
Along the road a dog and he
One master follow'd silently.
Their master slept : meanwhile, the ass
Applied his nippers to the grass,
Much pleased in such a place to stop,
Though there no thistle he could crop.
He would not be too delicate,
Nor spoil a dinner for a plate,

Which, but for that, his favourite dish,
Were all that any ass could wish.
  My dear companion, Towser said,—
'Tis as a starving dog I ask it,—
Pray lower down your loaded basket,
  And let me get a piece of bread.
No answer—not a word !—indeed,
The truth was, our Arcadian steed
Fear'd lest, for every moment's flight,
His nimble teeth should lose a bite.
At last, I counsel you, said he, to wait
  Till master is himself awake,
  Who then, unless I much mistake,
Will give his dog the usual bait.
Meanwhile, there issued from the wood
A creature of the wolfish brood,
Himself by famine sorely pinch'd.
At sight of him the donkey flinch'd,
And begg'd the dog to give him aid.
The dog budged not, but answer made,—
I counsel thee, my friend, to run,
Till master's nap is fairly done ;
There can, indeed, be no mistake,
That he will very soon awake ;
Till then, scud off with all your might ;
And should he snap you in your flight,
This ugly wolf,—why, let him feel
The greeting of your well-shod heel.
I do not doubt, at all, but that
Will be enough to lay him flat.
  But ere he ceased it was too late ;
  The ass had met his cruel fate.

  Thus selfishness we reprobate.

XVIII.—THE PASHAW AND THE MERCHANT.

A TRADING Greek, for want of law,
Protection bought of a pashaw ;
And like a nobleman he paid,
Much rather than a man of trade—
Protection being, Turkish-wise,
A costly sort of merchandise.
So costly was it, in this case,
The Greek complain'd, with tongue and face.
  Three other Turks, of lower rank,
Would guard his substance as their own,
  And all draw less upon his bank,
Than did the great pashaw alone.
The Greek their offer gladly heard,
And closed the bargain with a word.
The said pashaw was made aware,
And counsel'd with a prudent care,
These rivals to anticipate,
By sending them to heaven's gate,
As messengers to Mahomet—
Which measure should he much delay,
Himself might go the self-same way,
By poison offer'd secretly,
Sent on, before his time, to be
Protector to such arts and trades
As flourish in the world of shades.
On this advice, the Turk—no gander—
Behaved himself like Alexander*.

* Who took the medicine presented to him by his phy-
sician Philip, the moment after he had received a letter
announcing that that very man designed to poison him.—
ARRIAN, L. II. Chap. XIV.

Straight to the merchant's, firm and stable,
He went, and took a seat at table.
Such calm assurance there was seen,
Both in his words and in his mien,
That e'en that weasel-sighted Grecian
Could not suspect him of suspicion.
My friend, said he, I know you've quit me,
And some think caution would befit me,
  Lest to despatch me be your plan :
  But, deeming you too good a man
  To injure either friends or foes
  With poison'd cups or secret blows,
I drown the thought, and say no more.
But, as regards the three or four
  Who take my place,
  I crave your grace
To listen to an apologue.

A shepherd, with a single dog,
  Was ask'd the reason why
He kept a dog, whose least supply.
Amounted to a loaf of bread
For every day. The people said
He'd better give the animal
To guard the village senior's hall ;
For him, a shepherd, it would be
A thriftier economy
To keep small curs, say two or three,
That would not cost him half the food,
And yet for watching be as good.
The fools, perhaps, forgot to tell
If they would fight the wolf as well.
The silly shepherd, giving heed,
Cast off his dog of mastiff breed,
And took three dogs to watch his cattle,
Which ate far less, but fled in battle.
His flock such counsel lived to rue,
As doubtlessly, my friend, will you.
If wise, my aid again you'll seek—
And so, persuaded, did the Greek.

Not vain our tale, if it convinces
  Small states that 'tis a wiser thing
  To trust a single powerful king,
Than half a dozen petty princes.

XIX.—THE USE OF KNOWLEDGE.

  BETWEEN two citizens
  A controversy grew.
The one was poor, but much he knew :
The other, rich, with little sense,
Claim'd that, in point of excellence,
The merely wise should bow the knee
To all such money'd men as he.
The merely fools, he should have said ;
For why should wealth hold up its head,
When merit from its side hath fled ?
  My friend, quoth Bloated-purse
  To his reverse,
You think yourself considerable.
Pray, tell me, do you keep a table ?
What comes of this incessant reading,
In point of lodging, clothing, feeding ?
It gives one, true, the highest chamber,
One coat for June and for December,
His shadow for his sole attendant,
And hunger always in th' ascendant.

What profits he his country, too,
 Who scarcely ever spends a sou ?
Will, haply, be a public charge ?
Who profits more the state at large,
Than he whose luxuries dispense
Among the people wealth immense ?
We set the streams of life a flowing ;
We set all sorts of trades a going.
The spinner, weaver, sewer, vender,
And many a wearer, fair and tender,
All live and flourish on the spender—
As do, indeed, the reverend rooks
Who waste their time in making books.
 These words, so full of impudence,
 Received their proper recompense.
The man of letters held his peace,
Though much he might have said with ease.
A war avenged him soon and well ;
In it their common city fell.
Both fled abroad ; the ignorant,
By fortune thus brought down to want,
Was treated everywhere with scorn,
And roamed about, a wretch forlorn ;
Whereas the scholar, everywhere,
Was nourish'd by the public care.

 Let fools the studious despise ;
 There's nothing lost by being wise.

———•———

XX.—JUPITER AND THE THUNDERBOLTS.

———

Said Jupiter, one day,
As on a cloud he lay,
Observing all our crimes,
Come, let us change the times,
By leasing out anew
A world whose wicked crew
Have wearied out our grace,
And cursed us to our face.
Hie hellward, Mercury ;
A Fury bring to me,
The direst of the three.
Race nursed too tenderly !
This day your doom shall be.
E'en while he spoke their fate,
His wrath began to moderate.

O kings, with whom his will
Hath lodged our good and ill,
Your wrath and storm between
One night should intervene.
 The god of rapid wing
And lip unfaltering
To sunless regions sped,
And met the sisters dread.
To grim Tisiphone
And pale Megæra, he
 Preferr'd, as murderess,
Alecto, pitiless.
This choice so roused the fiend,
By Pluto's beard she swore
The human race no more
Should be by handfuls glean'd,
But in one solid mass
Th' infernal gates should pass.
But Jove, displeased with both
The Fury and her oath,

Despatch'd her back to hell.
 And then a bolt he hurl'd,
 Down on a faithless world,
Which in a desert fell.
Aim'd by a father's arm,
It caused more fear than harm.
(All fathers strike aside.)
What did from this betide ?
Our evil race grew bold,
 Resumed their wicked tricks,
Increased them manifold,
Till, all Olympus through,
Indignant murmurs flew.
When, swearing by the Styx,
The sire that rules the air
Storms promised to prepare
More terrible and dark,
Which should not miss their mark.
A father's wrath it is !
The other deities
All in one voice exclaim'd ;
And, might the thing be named,
Some other god would make
Bolts better for our sake.
This Vulcan undertook.
His rumbling forges shook
And glow'd with fervent heat,
While Cyclops blew and beat.
Forth from the plastic flame
Two sorts of bolts there came.
Of these, one misses not :
'Tis by Olympus shot,—
That is, the gods at large.
 The other, bearing wide,
 Hits mountain-top or side,
Or makes a cloud its targe.
And this it is alone
Which leaves the father's throne.

———•———

XXI.—THE FALCON AND THE CAPON.

———

You often hear a sweet seductive call :
If wise, you hasten towards it not at all,—
 And, if you heed my apologue,
 You act like John de Nivelle's dog*.

A capon, citizen of Mans,
Was summon'd from a throng
To answer to the village squire,
Before tribunal call'd the fire.
 The matter to disguise,
 The kitchen sheriff wise
Cried, Biddy—Biddy—Biddy !—
But not a moment did he—
 This Norman and a half†—
 The smooth official trust.
 Your bait, said he, is dust,
And I'm too old for chaff.
Meantime, a falcon, on his perch,
 Observed the flight and search.

———

* A dog which, according to the French proverb, ran
away when his master called him.
 † Though the Normans are proverbial for their shrewd-
ness, the French have, nevertheless, a proverb that they
come to Paris to be hanged. Hence La Fontaine makes
his capon, who knew how to shun a similar fate, *le
Normand et demi*—the Norman and a half.

In man, by instinct or experience,
The capons have so little confidence,
That this was not without much trouble caught,
Though for a splendid supper sought.
    To lie, the morrow night,
    In brilliant candle-light,
    Supinely on a dish
    'Midst viands, fowl, and fish,
With all the ease that heart could wish—
This honour, from his master kind,
The fowl would gladly have declined.
    Outcried the bird of chase,
As in the weeds he eyed the skulker's face,—
Why, what a stupid, blockhead race !—
    Such witless, brainless fools
    Might well defy the schools.
    For me, I understand
      To chase at word
      The swiftest bird,
    Aloft, o'er sea or land ;
      At slightest beck,
      Returning quick
    To perch upon my master's hand.
There, at his window he appears—
He waits thee—hasten—hast no ears ?
Ah ! that I have, the fowl replied ;
But what from master might betide ?
Or cook, with cleaver at his side ?
Return you may for such a call,
But let me fly their fatal hall ;
And spare your mirth at my expense :
Whate'er I lack, 'tis not the sense
To know that all this sweet-toned breath
Is spent to lure me to my death.
    If you had seen upon the spit
      As many of the falcons roast
      As I have of the capon host,
You would not thus reproach my wit.

XXII.—THE CAT AND THE RAT

    Four creatures, wont to prowl,—
      Sly Grab-and-Snatch, the cat,
    Grave Evil-bode, the owl,
      Thief Nibble-stitch, the rat,
And Madam Weasel, prim and fine,—
Inhabited a rotten pine.
A man their home discover'd there,
And set, one night, a cunning snare.
The cat, a noted early-riser,
    Went forth, at break of day,
    To hunt her usual prey.
    Not much the wiser
    For morning's feeble ray,
The noose did suddenly surprise her.
    Waked by her strangling cry,
    Gray Nibble-stitch drew nigh :
    As full of joy was he,
    As of despair was she,
    For in the noose he saw
    His foe of mortal paw.
Dear friend, said Mrs. Grab-and-Snatch,
Do, pray, this cursed cord detach.
    I've always known your skill,
    And often your good-will ;
Now help me from this worst of snares,
In which I fell at unawares.

'Tis by a sacred right,
    You, sole of all your race,
    By special love and grace,
Have been my favourite—
    The darling of my eyes.
'Twas order'd by celestial cares,
No doubt ; I thank the blessed skies,
That, going out to say my prayers,
As cats devout each morning do,
This net has made me pray to you.
Come, fall to work upon the cord.
Replied the rat, And what reward
    Shall pay me, if I dare ?
    Why, said the cat, I swear
    To be your firm ally :
    Henceforth, eternally,
    These powerful claws are yours,
    Which safe your life insures.
I'll guard from quadruped and fowl ;
I'll eat the weasel and the owl.
    Ah, cried the rat, you fool !
I'm quite too wise to be your tool.
He said, and sought his snug retreat,
Close at the rotten pine-tree's feet,
Where plump he did the weasel meet ;
Whom shunning by a happy dodge,
He climb'd the hollow trunk to lodge ;
And there the savage owl he saw.
Necessity became his law,
And down he went, the rope to gnaw
Strand after strand in two he bit,
And freed, at last, the hypocrite.
That moment came the man in sight ;
The new allies took hasty flight.

    A good while after that,
    Our liberated cat
    Espied her favourite rat,
Quite out of reach, and on his guard.
My friend, said she, I take your shyness hard ;
    Your caution wrongs my gratitude ;
    Approach, and greet your staunch ally.
    Do you suppose, dear rat, that I
Forget the solemn oath I mew'd ?
Do I forget, the rat replied,
To what your nature is allied ?
    To thankfulness, or even pity,
    Can cats be ever bound by treaty ?

      Alliance from necessity
      Is safe just while it has to be.

XXIII.—THE TORRENT AND THE RIVER.

    With mighty rush and roar,
    Adown a mountain steep
A torrent tumbled,—swelling o'er
    Its rugged banks,—and bore
    Vast ruin in its sweep.
The traveller were surely rash
To brave its whirling, foaming dash,
But one, by robbers sorely press'd,
Its terrors haply put to test.
They were but threats of foam and sound,
The loudest where the least profound.
With courage from his safe success,
His foes continuing to press,

He met a river in his course:
On stole its waters, calm and deep,
So silently they seem'd asleep,
All sweetly cradled, as I ween,
In sloping banks, and gravel clean,—
They threaten'd neither man nor horse.
Both ventured; but the noble steed,
That saved from robbers by his speed,
From that deep water could not save;
Both went to drink the Stygian wave;
Both went to cross, (but not to swim,)
Where reigns a monarch stern and grim,
　　Far other streams than ours.

Still men are men of dangerous powers;
Elsewhere, 'tis only ignorance that cowers.

XXIV.—EDUCATION.

Lapluck and Cæsar brothers were, descended
From dogs by Fame the most commended,
　　Who falling, in their puppyhood,
　　To different masters anciently,
One dwelt and hunted in the boundless wood;
From thieves the other kept a kitchen free.
　　At first, each had another name;
　　But, by their bringing up, it came,
While one improved upon his nature,
The other grew a sordid creature,
Till, by some scullion called Lapluck,
The name ungracious ever stuck.
　　To high exploits his brother grew,
　　Put many a stag at bay, and tore
Full many a trophy from the boar;
　　In short, him first, of all his crew,
　　The world as Cæsar knew;
And care was had, lest, by a baser mate,
His noble blood should e'er degenerate.
Not so with his neglected brother;
He made whatever came a mother;
And, by the laws of population,
His race became a countless nation—
The common turnspits throughout France:
Where danger is, they don't advance:—
Precisely the antipodes
Of what we call the Cæsars, these!

Oft falls the son below his sire's estate;
Through want of care all things degenerate.
For lack of nursing Nature and her gifts,
What crowds from gods become mere kitchen thrifts!

XXV.—THE TWO DOGS AND THE DEAD ASS.

The Virtues should be sisters, hand in hand,
Since banded brothers all the Vices stand;
　　When one of these our hearts attacks,
　　All come in file; there only lacks,
　　From out the cluster, here and there,
A mate of some antagonising pair,
That can't agree the common roof to share.
But all the Virtues, as a sisterhood,
Have scarcely ever in one subject stood.
　　We find one brave, but passionate;
　　Another prudent, but ingrate.

Of beasts, the dog may claim to be
　　The pattern of fidelity;
　　But, for our teaching little wiser,
　　He's both a fool and gormandiser.
For proof, I cite two mastiffs, that espied
A dead ass floating on a water wide.
The distance growing more and more,
Because the wind the carcass bore,—
My friend, said one, your eyes are best;
Pray let them on the water rest:
What thing is that I seem to see?
An ox, or horse? what can it be?
Hey! cried his mate; what matter which,
Provided we could get a flitch!
It doubtless is our lawful prey:
The puzzle is to find some way
To get the prize; for wide the space
To swim, with wind against your face*.
Let's drink the flood; our thirsty throats
Will gain the end as well as boats.
The water swallow'd, by and bye
We'll have the carcass, high and dry—
Enough to last a week, at least.
Both drank as some do at a feast;
Their breath was quench'd before their thirst,
And presently the creatures burst!

And such is man. Whatever he
May set his soul to do or be,
To him is possibility.
　　How many vows he makes!
　　How many steps he takes!
How does he strive, and pant, and strain,
Fortune's or Glory's prize to gain!
If round my farm off well I must,
Or fill my coffers with the dust,
Or master Hebrew, science, history,—
I make my task to drink the sea.
One spirit's projects to fulfil,
Four bodies would require; and still
　　The work would stop half-done;
The lives of four Methuselahs,
Placed end to end for use, alas!
　　Would not suffice the wants of one.

XXVI.—DEMOCRITUS AND THE PEOPLE OF ABDERA.

How do I hate the tide of vulgar thought!
Profane, unjust, with childish folly fraught,
It breaks and bends the rays of truth divine,
And by its own conceptions measures mine.
　　Famed Epicurus' master tried
　　The power of this unstable tide.
His country said the sage was mad—
　　The simpletons! But why
No prophet ever honour had
　　Beneath his native sky.
Democritus, in truth, was wise;
The mass were mad, with faith in lies.
　　So far this error went,
　　That all Abdera sent
　　To old Hippocrates
　　To cure the sad disease.
Our townsman, said the messengers,
Appropriately shedding tears,

* Did La Fontaine, to enhance the folly of these dogs,
make them bad judges of the course of the wind, or did he
forget what he had said a few lines above?—Translator.

Hath lost his wits ! Democritus,
By study spoil'd, is lost to us.
Were he but fill'd with ignorance,
We should esteem him less a dunce.
He saith that worlds like this exist,
An absolutely endless list,—
And peopled, even, it may be,
With countless hosts as wise as we !
But, not contented with such dreams,
His brain with viewless " atoms" teems,
Instinct with deathless life, it seems.
And, never stirring from the sod below,
  He weighs and measures all the stars ;
  And, while he knows the universe,
    Himself he doth not know.
Though now his lips he strictly bars,
He once delighted to converse.
Come, godlike mortal, try thy art divine
Where traits of worst insanity combine.
  Small faith the great physician lent,
But still, perhaps more readily, he went.
  And mark what meetings strange
Chance causes in this world of change !
  Hippocrates arrived in season,
  Just as his patient (void of reason !)
Was searching whether reason's home,
In talking animals and dumb,
Be in the head, or in the heart,
Or in some other local part.
All calmly seated in the shade,
Where brooks their softest music made,
He traced, with study most insane,
The convolutions of a brain ;
And at his feet lay many a scroll—
The works of sages on the soul.
Indeed, so much absorb'd was he,
His friend, at first, he did not see.
A pair so admirably match'd,
Their compliments erelong despatch'd.
In time and talk, as well as dress,
The wise are frugal, I confess.
Dismissing trifles, they began
At once with eagerness to scan
The life, and soul, and laws of man ;
Nor stopp'd till they had travell'd o'er all
The ground, from physical to moral.
  My time and space would fail
  To give the full detail.

But I have said enough to show
How little 'tis the people know.
How true, then, goes the saw abroad—
Their voice is but the voice of God !

XXVII.—THE WOLF AND THE HUNTER.

THOU lust of gain,—foul fiend, whose evil eyes
Regard as nought the blessings of the skies,
Must I forever battle thee in vain !
  How long demandest thou to gain
  The meaning of my lessons plain ?
  Will constant getting never cloy ?
  Will man ne'er slacken to enjoy ?
Haste, friend ; thou hast not long to live :
  Let me the precious word repeat,
  And listen to it, I entreat ;
  A richer lesson none can give—
The sovereign antidote for sorrow—
ENJOY.—I will.—But when !—To-morrow.—

Ah ! death may take you on the way,
Why not enjoy, I ask, to-day !
Lest envious fate your hopes ingulf,
As once it served the hunter and the wolf.
  The former, with his fatal bow,
  A noble deer had laid full low :
  A fawn approach'd, and quickly lay
    Companion of the dead,
    For side by side they bled.
  Could one have wish'd a richer prey ?
  Such luck had been enough to sate
  A hunter wise and moderate.
Meantime a boar, as big as e'er was taken,
Our archer tempted, proud, and fond of bacon.
  Another candidate for Styx,
  Struck by his arrow, foams and kicks.
  But strangely do the shears of Fate
  To cut his cable hesitate.
  Alive, yet dying, there he lies,
  A glorious and a dangerous prize.
  And was not this enough ? Not quite,
  To fill a conqueror's appetite ;
  For, ere the boar was dead, he spied
  A partridge by a furrow's side—
  A trifle to his other game.
  Once more his bow he drew ;
  The desperate boar upon him came,
  And in his dying vengeance slew :
  The partridge thank'd him as she flew.

  Thus much is to the covetous address'd ;
  The miserly shall have the rest.

A wolf, in passing, saw that woeful sight.
O Fortune, cried the savage, with delight,
  A fane to thee I'll build outright !
  Four carcasses ! how rich ! but spare—
  I'll make them last—such luck is rare,
  (The miser's everlasting plea.)
  They'll last a month, for—let me see—
  One, two, three, four—the weeks are four,
  If I can count—and some days more.
    Well, two days hence
    And I'll commence.
  Meantime, the string upon this bow
  I'll stint myself to eat ;
  For by its mutton-smell I know
  'Tis made of entrails sweet.
His entrails rued the fatal weapon,
Which, while he heedlessly did step on,
The arrow pierced his bowels deep,
And laid him lifeless on the heap.

Hark, stingy souls ! insatiate leeches !
Our text this solemn duty teaches,—
Enjoy the present ; do not wait
To share the wolf's or hunter's fate.

BOOK IX.

I.—THE FAITHLESS DEPOSITARY.

THANKS to Memory's daughters nine,
Animals have graced my line :
  Higher heroes in my story
  Might have won me less of glory.
Wolves, in language of the sky,
  Talk with dogs throughout my verse ;
Beasts with others shrewdly vie,

Representing characters ;
Fools in furs not second-hand,
Sages hoof'd or feather'd, stand :
Fewer truly are the latter,
More the former—ay, and fatter.
  Flourish also in my scene
Tyrants, villains, mountebanks,
Beasts incapable of thanks,
Beasts of rash and reckless pranks,
  Beasts of sly and flattering mien ;
  Troops of liars, too, I ween.
As to men, of every age,
All are liars, saith the sage.
Had he writ but of the low,
One could hardly think it so ;
But that human mortals, all,
Lie like serpents, great and small,
Had another certified it,
I, for one, should have denied it.
He who lies in Æsop's way,
Or like Homer, minstrel gray,
Is no liar, sooth to say.
Charms that bind us like a dream,
  Offspring of their happy art,
Cloak'd in fiction, more than seem
  Truth to offer to the heart.
Both have left us works which I
Think unworthy e'er to die.
Liar call not him who squares
All his ends and aims with theirs ;
  But from sacred truth to vary,
  Like the false depositary,
    Is to be, by every rule
    Both a liar and a fool.
The story goes :
              A man of trade,
In Persia, with his neighbour made
Deposit, as he left the state,
Of iron, say a hundredweight.
Return'd, said he, My iron, neighbour.
Your iron ! you have lost your labour ;
I grieve to say it,—'pon my soul,
A rat has eaten up the whole.
My men were sharply scolded at,
But yet a hole, in spite of that,
  Was left, as one is wont to be
  In every barn or granary,
By which crept in that cursed rat.
Admiring much the novel thief,
The man affected full belief.
  Ere long, his faithless neighbour's child
He stole away,—a heavy lad,—
And then to supper bade the dad,
Who thus plead off in accents sad :—
It was but yesterday I had
  A boy as fine as ever smiled,
An only son, as dear as life,
The darling of myself and wife.
Alas ! we have him now no more,
And every joy with us is o'er.
Replied the merchant, Yesternight,
  By evening's faint and dusky ray,
I saw a monstrous owl alight,
  And bear your darling son away
To yonder tottering ruin gray.
Can I believe you, when you say
An owl bore off so large a prey !
How could it be ! the father cried ;
  The thing is surely quite absurd ;
  My son with ease had kill'd the bird.

The how of it, the man replied,
Is not my province to decide ;
I know I saw your son arise,
Borne through the air before my eyes.
Why should it seem a strange affair,
Moreover, in a country where
A single rat contrives to eat
A hundred pounds of iron meat,
That owls should be of strength to lift yo
A booby boy that weighs but fifty ?
The other plainly saw the trick,
Restored the iron very quick,
And got, with shame as well as joy,
Possession of his kidnapp'd boy.

The like occurr'd two travellers between.
  One was of those
  Who wear a microscope, I ween,
  Each side the nose.
Would you believe their tales romantic,
  Our Europe, in its monsters, beats
The lands that feel the tropic heats,
Surcharged with all that is gigantic.
  This person, feeling free
  To use the trope hyperbole,
  Had seen a cabbage with his eyes
Exceeding any house in size.
And I have seen, the other cries,
Resolved to leave his fellow in the lurch,
A pot that would have held a church.
Why, friend, don't give that doubting look.—
The pot was made your cabbages to cook.
  This pot-discoverer was a wit ;
  The iron-monger, too, was wise.
  To such absurd and ultra lies
  Their answers were exactly fit.
'Twere doing honour overmuch,
To reason or dispute with such.
To overbid them is the shortest path,
And less provocative of wrath.

II.—THE TWO DOVES.

Two doves once cherish'd for each other
The love that brother hath for brother.
But one, of scenes domestic tiring,
To see the foreign world aspiring,
  Was fool enough to undertake
  A journey long, o'er land and lake.
What plan is this ! the other cried ;
Wouldst quit so soon thy brother's side !
This absence is the worst of ills ;
Thy heart may bear, but me it kills.
Pray, let the dangers, toil, and care,
  Of which all travellers tell,
  Your courage somewhat quell.
Still, if the season later were—
O wait the zephyrs !—hasten not—
  Just now the raven, on his oak,
  In hoarser tones than usual spoke.
My heart forebodes the saddest lot,—
The falcons, nets—Alas, it rains !
  My brother, are thy wants supplied—
  Provisions, shelter, pocket-guide,
And all that unto health pertains !
These words occasion'd some demur
In our imprudent traveller.

But restless curiosity
Prevail'd at last ; and so said he,—
The matter is not worth a sigh ;
Three days, at most, will satisfy,
And then, returning, I shall tell
You all the wonders that befell,——
With scenes enchanting and sublime
Shall sweeten all our coming time.
Who seeth nought, hath nought to say.
My travel's course, from day to day,
Will be the source of great delight.
     A store of tales I shall relate,—
     Say there I lodged at such a date,
And saw there such and such a sight.
You'll think it all occurr'd to you.—
On this, both, weeping, bade adieu.
Away the lonely wanderer flew.—
A thunder-cloud began to lower ;
He sought, as shelter from the shower,
The only tree that graced the plain,
Whose leaves ill turn'd the pelting rain.
The sky once more serene above,
On flew our drench'd and dripping dove,
And dried his plumage as he could.
Next, on the borders of a wood,
He spied some scatter'd grains of wheat,
Which one, he thought, might safely eat ;
For there another dove he saw.—
He felt the snare around him draw !
This wheat was but a treacherous bait
To lure poor pigeons to their fate.
The snare had been so long in use,
With beak and wings he struggled loose :
Some feathers perish'd while it stuck ;
But, what was worst in point of luck,
A hawk, the cruellest of foes,
Perceived him clearly as he rose,
Off dragging, like a runaway,
A piece of string.   The bird of prey
Had bound him, in a moment more,
Much faster than he was before,
But from the clouds an eagle came,
And made the hawk himself his game.
By war of robbers profiting,
The dove for safety plied the wing,
And, lighting on a ruin'd wall,
Believed his dangers ended all.
A roguish boy had there a sling,
     (Age pitiless
         We must confess,)
And, by a most unlucky fling,
Half kill'd our hapless dove ;
Who now, no more in love
     With foreign travelling,
     And lame in leg and wing,
Straight homeward urged his crippled flight,
Fatigued, but glad, arrived at night,
In truly sad and piteous plight.
The doves rejoin'd, I leave you all to say,
What pleasure might their pains repay.
Ah, happy lovers, would you roam ?—
Pray, let it not be far from home.
To each the other ought to be
     A world of beauty ever new ;
In each the other ought to see
     The whole of what is good and true.

Myself have loved ; nor would I then,
For all the wealth of crownèd men,

Or arch celestial, paved with gold,
The presence of those woods have sold,
And fields, and banks, and hillocks, which
Were by the joyful steps made rich,
And smiled beneath the charming eyes
Of her who made my heart a prize—
To whom I pledged it, nothing loath,
And seal'd the pledge with virgin oath.
Ah, when will time such moments bring again ?
To me are sweet and charming objects vain—
My soul forsaking to its restless mood ?
O, did my wither'd heart but dare
     To kindle for the bright and good,
Should not I find the charm still there ?
Is love, to me, with things that were ?

III.—THE MONKEY AND THE LEOPARD.

A MONKEY and a leopard were
     The rivals at a country fair.
Each advertised his own attractions.
     Said one, Good sirs, the highest place
     My merit knows ; for, of his grace,
     The king hath seen me face to face ;
And, judging by his looks and actions,
I gave the best of satisfactions.
When I am dead, 'tis plain enough,
My skin will make his royal muff.
So richly is it streak'd and spotted,
So delicately waved and dotted,
Its various beauty cannot fail to please.
And, thus invited, everybody sees ;
But soon they see, and soon depart.
The monkey's show-bill to the mart
His merits thus sets forth the while,
All in his own peculiar style :—
Come, gentlemen, I pray you, come ;
In magic arts I am at home.
The whole variety in which
My neighbour boasts himself so rich,
Is to his simple skin confined,
While mine is living in the mind.
Your humble servant, Monsieur Gille,
The son-in-law to Tickleville,
Pope's monkey, and of great renown,
Is now just freshly come to town,
Arrived in three bateaux, express,
     Your worships to address ;
For he can speak, you understand ;
Can dance, and practise sleight of hand ;
Can jump through hoops, and balance sticks ;
In short, can do a thousand tricks ;
     And all for blancos six—
     Not, messieurs, for a sou.
And, if you think the price won't do,
When you have seen, then he'll restore
Each man his money at the door.

The ape was not to reason blind ;
For who in wealth of dress can find
Such charms as dwell in wealth of mind ?
One meets our ever-new desires,
The other in a moment tires.

Alas ! how many lords there are,
     Of mighty sway and lofty mien,
Who, like this leopard at the fair,
     Show all their talents on the skin !

IV.—THE ACORN AND THE PUMPKIN.

God's works are good. This truth to prove
Around the world I need not move ;
  I do it by the nearest pumpkin.
This fruit so large, on vine so small,
  Surveying once, exclaim'd a bumpkin—
What could He mean who made us all ?
He's left this pumpkin out of place.
If I had order'd in the case,
Upon that oak it should have hung—
A noble fruit as ever swung
To grace a tree so firm and strong.
Indeed, it was a great mistake,
  As this discovery teaches,
That I myself did not partake
His counsels whom my curate preaches.
All things had then in order come ;
  This acorn, for example,
  Not bigger than my thumb,
Had not disgraced a tree so ample.
The more I think, the more I wonder
To see outraged proportion's laws,
And that without the slightest cause ;
God surely made an awkward blunder.
With such reflections proudly fraught,
Our sage grew tired of mighty thought,
And threw himself on Nature's lap,
Beneath an oak, to take his nap.
Plump on his nose, by lucky hap,
An acorn fell : he waked, and in
The matted beard that graced his chin,
He found the cause of such a bruise
As made him different language use.
O ! O ! he cried ; I bleed ! I bleed !
And this is what has done the deed !
But, truly, what had been my fate,
Had this had half a pumpkin's weight !
I see that God had reasons good,
And all his works well understood.
Thus home he went in humbler mood.

V.—THE SCHOOLBOY, THE PEDANT, AND THE OWNER OF A GARDEN.

A boy who savour'd of his school,—
A double rogue and double fool,—
  By youth and by the privilege
Which pedants have, by ancient right,
  To alter reason and abridge,—
A neighbour robb'd, with fingers light,
Of flowers and fruit. This neighbour had,
Of fruits that make the autumn glad,
The very best—and none but he.
Each season brought, from plant and tree,
To him its tribute ; for, in spring,
His was the brightest blossoming.
One day, he saw our hopeful lad
Perch'd on the finest tree he had,
Not only stuffing down the fruit,
But spoiling, like a Vandal brute,
The buds that play advance-courier
Of plenty in the coming year.
The branches, too, he rudely tore,
  And carried things to such a pass,
The owner sent his servant o'er
  To tell the master of his class.

The latter came, and came attended
  By all the urchins of his school,
And thus one plunderer's mischief mended
  By pouring in an orchard-full.
It seems the pedant was intent
  On making public punishment,
To teach his boys the force of law,
And strike their roguish hearts with awe.
The use of which he first must show
  From Virgil and from Cicero,
And many other ancients noted,
From whom, in their own tongues, he quoted.
  So long, indeed, his lecture lasted,
  While not a single urchin fasted,
    That, ere its close, their thievish crimes
    Were multiplied a hundred times.

I hate all eloquence and reason
Expended plainly out of season.
Of all the beasts that earth have cursed
  While they have fed on 't,
The school-boy strikes me as the worst—
  Except the pedant.
The better of these neighbours two
For me, I'm sure, would never do.

VI.—THE SCULPTOR AND THE STATUE OF JUPITER.

A block of marble was so fine,
  To buy it did a sculptor hasten.
What shall my chisel, now 'tis mine—
  A god, a table, or a basin ?

A god, said he, the thing shall be ;
  I'll arm it, too, with thunder.
Let people quake, and bow the knee
  With reverential wonder.

So well the cunning artist wrought
  All things within a mortal's reach,
That soon the marble wanted nought
  Of being Jupiter, but speech.

Indeed, the man whose skill did make
  Had scarcely laid his chisel down,
Before himself began to quake,
  And fear his manufacture's frown.

And even this excess of faith
  The poet once scarce fell behind,
The hatred fearing, and the wrath,
  Of gods the product of his mind.

This trait we see in infancy
  Between the baby and its doll,
Of wax or china, it may be—
  A pocket stuff'd, or folded shawl.

Imagination rules the heart :
  And here we find the fountain head
From whence the pagan errors start,
  That o'er the teeming nations spread.

With violent and flaming zeal,
  Each takes his own chimera's part ;
Pygmalion doth a passion feel
  For Venus chisel'd by his art.

All men, as far as in them lies,
Create realities of dreams.
To truth our nature proves but ice;
To falsehood, fire it seems.

VII.—THE MOUSE METAMORPHOSED INTO A
MAID.

A MOUSE once from an owl's beak fell;
I'd not have pick'd it up, I wis;
A Bramin did it: very well;
Each country has its prejudice.
The mouse, indeed, was sadly bruised.
Although, as neighbours, we are used
To be more kind to many others,
The Bramins treat the mice as brothers.
The notion haunts their heads, that when
The soul goes forth from dying men,
It enters worm, or bird, or beast,
As Providence or Fate is pleased;
And on this mystery rests their law,
Which from Pythagoras they're said to draw.
And hence the Bramin kindly pray'd
To one who knew the wizard's trade,
To give the creature, wounded sore,
The form in which it lodged before.
Forthwith the mouse became a maid,
Of years about fifteen;
A lovelier was never seen.
She would have waked, I ween,
In Priam's son, a fiercer flame
Than did the beauteous Grecian dame.
Surprised at such a novelty,
The Bramin to the damsel cried,
Your choice is free;
For every he
Will seek you for his bride.
Said she, Am I to have a voice?
The strongest, then, shall be my choice.
O sun! the Bramin cried, this maid is thine,
And thou shalt be a son-in-law of mine.
No, said the sun, this murky cloud, it seems,
In strength exceeds me, since he hides my beams;
And him I counsel you to take.
Again the reverend Bramin spake—
O cloud, on-flying with thy stores of water,
Pray wast thou born to wed my daughter?
Ah, no, alas! for, you may see,
The wind is far too strong for me.
My claims with Boreas' to compare,
I must confess, I do not dare.
O wind, then cried the Bramin, vex'd,
And wondering what would hinder next,—
Approach, and, with thy sweetest air,
Embrace—possess—the fairest fair.
The wind, enraptured, thither blew;—
A mountain stopp'd him as he flew,
To him now pass'd the tennis-ball,
And from him to a creature small.
Said he, I'd wed the maid, but that
I've had a quarrel with the rat.
A fool were I to take the bride
From one so sure to pierce my side.
The rat. It thrill'd the damsel's ear;
The name at once seem'd sweet and dear.
The rat! 'Twas one of Cupid's blows;
The like full many a maiden knows;

But all of this beneath the rose.
One smacketh ever of the place
Where first he show'd the world his face.
Thus far the fable's clear as light;
But, if we take a nearer sight,
There lurks within its drapery
Somewhat of graceless sophistry;
For who, that worships e'en the glorious sun,
Would not prefer to wed some cooler one?
And doth a flea's exceed a giant's might,
Because the former can the latter bite?
And, by the rule of strength, the rat
Had sent his bride to wed the cat;
From cat to dog, and onward still
To wolf or tiger, if you will:
Indeed, the fabulist might run
A circle backward to the sun.—
But to the change the tale supposes,—
In learned phrase, metempsychosis.
The very thing the wizard did
Its falsity exposes—
If that indeed were ever hid.
According to the Bramin's plan,
The proud aspiring soul of man,
And souls that dwell in humbler forms
Of rats and mice, and even worms,
All issue from a common source,
And, hence, they are the same of course.—
Unequal but by accident
Of organ and of tenement,
They use one pair of legs, or two,
Or e'en with none contrive to do,
As tyrant matter binds them to.
Why, then, could not so fine a frame
Constrain its heavenly guest
To wed the solar flame?
A rat her love possess'd.

In all respects, compared and weigh'd,
The souls of men and souls of mice
Quite different are made,—
Unlike in sort as well as size.
Each fits and fills its destined part
As Heaven doth well provide;
Nor witch, nor fiend, nor magic art,
Can set their laws aside.

VIII.—THE FOOL WHO SOLD WISDOM.

Of fools come never in the reach:
No rule can I more wisely teach.
Nor can there be a better one
Than this,—distemper'd heads to shun.
We often see them, high and low.
They tickle e'en the royal ear,
As privileged and free from fear
They hurl about them joke and jeer,
At pompous lord or silly beau.

A fool, in town, did wisdom cry;
The people, eager, flock'd to buy.
Each for his money got,
Paid promptly on the spot,
Besides a box upon the head,
Two fathoms' length of thread.
The most were vex'd—but quite in vain;
The public only mock'd their pain.

The wiser they who nothing said,
But pocketed the box and thread.
To search the meaning of the thing
Would only laughs and hisses bring.
Hath reason ever guaranteed
The wit of fools in speech or deed ?
'Tis said of brainless heads in France,
The cause of what they do is chance.
One dupe, however, needs must know
What meant the thread, and what the blow ;
So ask'd a sage, to make it sure.
They're both hieroglyphics pure,
The sage replied without delay ;
All people well advised will stay
From fools this fibre's length away,
Or get—I hold it sure as fate—
The other symbol on the pate.
So far from cheating you of gold,
The fool this wisdom fairly sold.

IX.—THE OYSTER AND THE LITIGANTS.

Two pilgrims on the sand espied
An oyster thrown up by the tide.
In hope, both swallow'd ocean's fruit ;
But ere the fact there came dispute.
While one stoop'd down to take the prey,
The other push'd him quite away.
　　Said he, 'twere rather meet
　　To settle which shall eat.
Why, he who first the oyster saw
Should be its eater, by the law ;
The other should but see him do it.
Replied his mate, if thus you view it,
Thank God the lucky eye is mine.
But I've an eye not worse than thine,
The other cried, and will be cursed,
If, too, I didn't see it first.
You saw it, did you ! Grant it true,
I saw it then, and felt it too.
　　Amidst this sweet affair,
　　Arrived a person very big,
　　Ycleped Sir Nincom Periwig.
They made him judge,—to set the matter square.
Sir Nincom, with a solemn face,
Took up the oyster and the case :
In opening both, the first he swallow'd,
And, in due time, his judgment follow'd.
Attend : the court awards you each a shell
Cost free ; depart in peace, and use them well.
Foot up the cost of suits at law,
The leavings reckon and awards,
The cash you'll see Sir Nincom draw,
And leave the parties—purse and cards.

X.—THE WOLF AND THE LEAN DOG.

　　A TROUTLING, some time since*,
Endeavour'd vainly to convince
　　A hungry fisherman
Of his unfitness for the frying-pan.
That controversy made it plain
That letting go a good secure,
　　In hope of future gain,
　　Is but imprudence pure.

* See Book V. Fable III.

The fisherman had reason good—
The troutling did the best he could—
　　Both argued for their lives.
Now, if my present purpose thrives,
I'll prop my former proposition
By building on a small addition.
A certain wolf, in point of wit
The prudent fisher's opposite,
A dog once finding far astray,
Prepared to take him as his prey.
　　The dog his leanness pled ;
　　Your lordship, sure, he said,
　　Cannot be very eager
　　To eat a dog so meagre.
To wait a little do not grudge :
The wedding of my master's only daughter
Will cause of fatted calves and fowls a slaughter ;
　　And then, as you yourself can judge,
　　I cannot help becoming fatter.
The wolf, believing, waived the matter,
And so, some days therefrom,
　　Return'd with sole design to see
If fat enough his dog might be.
The rogue was now at home :
He saw the hunter through the fence.
　　My friend, said he, please wait ;
I'll be with you a moment hence,
And fetch our porter of the gate.
This porter was a dog immense,
That left to wolves no future tense.
　　Suspicion gave our wolf a jog,—
It might not be so safely tamper'd.
　　My service to your porter dog,
Was his reply, as off he scamper'd.
His legs proved better than his head,
And saved him life to learn his trade.

XI.—NOTHING TOO MUCH.

Look where we will throughout creation,
We look in vain for moderation.
There is a certain golden mean,
Which Nature's sovereign Lord, I ween,
Design'd the path of all forever.
Doth one pursue it ! Never.
E'en things which by their nature bless,
Are turn'd to curses by excess.

The grain, best gift of Ceres fair,
Green waving in the genial air,
By overgrowth exhausts the soil ;
　　By superfluity of leaves
　　Defrauds the treasure of its sheaves,
And mocks the busy farmer's toil.
Not less redundant is the tree,
So sweet a thing is luxury.
The grain within due bounds to keep,
Their Maker licenses the sheep
The leaves excessive to retrench.
　　In troops they spread across the plain,
　　And, nibbling down the hapless grain,
Contrive to spoil it, root and branch.

So, then, with licence from on high,
The wolves are sent on sheep to prey ;
The whole the greedy gluttons slay ;
　　Or, if they don't, they try.

Next, men are sent on wolves to take
The vengeance now condign:
In turn the same abuse they make
Of this behest divine.

Of animals, the human kind
Are to excess the most inclined.
On low and high we make the charge,—
Indeed, upon the race at large.
There liveth not the soul select
That sinneth not in this respect.
Of " Nought too much," the fact is,
All preach the truth,—none practise.

XII.—THE WAX-CANDLE.

FROM bowers of gods the bees came down to man.
On Mount Hymettus, first, they say,
They made their home, and stored away
The treasures which the zephyrs fan.
When men had robb'd these daughters of the sky,
And left their palaces of nectar dry,—
Or, as in French the thing's explain'd
When hives were of their honey drain'd,—
The spoilers 'gan the wax to handle,
And fashion'd from it many a candle.
Of these, one, seeing clay, made brick by fire,
Remain uninjured by the teeth of time,
Was kindled into great desire
For immortality sublime.
And so this new Empedocles
Upon the blazing pile one sees,
Self-doom'd by purest folly
To fate so melancholy.
The candle lack'd philosophy :
All things are made diverse to be.
To wander from our destined tracks—
There cannot be a vainer wish ;
But this Empedocles of wax,
That melted in the chafing-dish,
Was truly not a greater fool
Than he of whom we read at school.

XIII.—JUPITER AND THE PASSENGER.

How danger would the gods enrich,
If we the vows remember'd which
It drives us to ! But, danger past,
Kind Providence is paid the last.
No earthly debt is treated so.
Now, Jove, the wretch exclaims, will wait ;
He sends no sheriff to one's gate,
Like creditors below;
But let me ask the dolt
What means the thunderbolt !

A passenger, endanger'd by the sea,
Had vow'd a hundred oxen good
To him who quell'd of old Terra's brood.
He had not one : as well might he
Have vow'd a hundred elephants.
Arrived on shore, his good intents
Were dwindled to the smoke which rose
An offering merely for the nose,

From half a dozen beefless bones.
Great Jove, said he, behold my vow !
The fumes of beef thou breathest now
. Are all thy godship ever owns :
From debt I therefore stand acquitted.
With seeming smile, the god submitted,
But not long after caught him well,
By sending him a dream, to tell
Of treasure hid. Off ran the liar,
As if to quench a house on fire,
And on a band of robbers fell.
As but a crown he had that day,
He promised them of sterling gold
A hundred talents truly told ;
Directing where conceal'd they lay,
In such a village on their way.
The rogues so much the tale suspected,
Said one, If we should suffer you to,
You'd cheaply get us all detected ;
Go, then, and bear your gold to Pluto.

XIV.—THE CAT AND THE FOX.

THE cat and fox, when saints were all the rage,
Together went on pilgrimage.
Arch hypocrites and swindlers, they,
By sleight of face and sleight of paw,
Regardless both of right and law,
Contrived expenses to repay,
By eating many a fowl and cheese,
And other tricks as bad as these.
Disputing served them to beguile
The road of many a weary mile.
Disputing ! but for this resort,
The world would go to sleep, in short.
Our pilgrims, as a thing of course,
Disputed till their throats were hoarse.
Then, dropping to a lower tone,
They talk'd of this, and talk'd of that,
Till Renard whisper'd to the cat,
You think yourself a knowing one :
How many cunning tricks have you !
For I've a hundred old and new,
All ready in my haversack.
The cat replied, I do not lack,
Though with but one provided ;
And, truth to honour, for that matter,
I hold it than a thousand better.
In fresh dispute they sided ;
And loudly were they at it, when
Approach'd a mob of dogs and men.
Now, said the cat, your tricks ransack,
And put your cunning brains to rack,
One life to save ; I'll show you mine—
A trick, you see, for saving nine.
With that, she climb'd a lofty pine.
The fox his hundred ruses tried,
And yet no safety found.
A hundred times he falsified
The nose of every hound.—
. Was here, and there, and everywhere,
Above, and under ground ;
But yet to stop he did not dare.
Pent in a hole, it was no joke
To meet the terriers or the smoke.
So, leaping into upper air,
He met two dogs, that choked him there.

Expedients may be too many,
Consuming time to choose and try.
On one, but that as good as any,
'Tis best in danger to rely.

XV.—THE HUSBAND, THE WIFE, AND THE THIEF.

A MAN that loved,—and loved his wife,—
Still led an almost joyless life.
No tender look, nor gracious word,
Nor smile, that, coming from a bride,
Its object would have deified,
E'er told her doting lord
The love with which he burn'd
Was in its kind return'd.
Still unrepining at his lot,
This man, thus tied in Hymen's knot,
Thank'd God for all the good he got.
But why ! If love doth fail to season
Whatever pleasures Hymen gives,
I'm sure I cannot see the reason
Why one for him the happier lives.
However, since his wife
Had ne'er caress'd him in her life,
He made complaint of it one night.
The entrance of a thief
Cut short his tale of grief,
And gave the lady such a fright,
She shrunk from dreaded harms
Within her husband's arms.
Good thief, cried he,
This joy so sweet, I owe to thee :
Now take, as thy reward,
Of all that owns me lord,
Whatever suits thee save my spouse ;
Ay, if thou pleasest, take the house.
As thieves are not remarkably
O'erstock'd with modesty,
This fellow made quite free.

From this account it doth appear,
The passions all are ruled by fear.
Aversion may be conquer'd by it,
And even love may not defy it.
But still some cases there have been
Where love hath ruled the roast, I ween.
That lover witness, highly bred,
Who burnt his house above his head,
And all to clasp a certain dame,
And bear her harmless through the flame.
This transport through the fire,
I own, I much admire ;
And for a Spanish soul reputed coolish,
I think it grander even than 'twas foolish *.

XVI.—THE TREASURE AND THE TWO MEN.

A MAN whose credit fail'd, and what was worse,
Who lodged the devil in his purse,—
That is to say, lodged nothing there,—
By self-suspension in the air

* La Fontaine here refers to the adventure of the Spanish Count Villa Medina with Elizabeth of France, wife of Philip IV. of Spain. The former, having invited the Spanish court to a splendid entertainment in his palace, had it set on fire, that he might personally rescue the said lady from its flames.

Concluded his accounts to square,
Since, should he not, he understood,
From various tokens, famine would—
A death for which no mortal wight
Had ever any appetite.
A ruin, crown'd with ivy green,
Was of his tragedy the scene.
His hangman's noose he duly tied,
And then to drive a nail he tried ;—
But by his blows the wall gave way,
Now tremulous and old,
Disclosing to the light of day
A sum of hidden gold.
He clutch'd it up, and left Despair
To struggle with his halter there.
Nor did the much delighted man
E'en stop to count it as he ran.
But, while he went, the owner came,
Who loved it with a secret flame,
Too much indeed for kissing,—
And found his money—missing !
O Heavens ! he cried, shall I
Such riches lose, and still not die ?
Shall I not hang !—as I, in fact,
Might justly do if cord I lack'd ;
But now, without expense I can ;
This cord here only lacks a man.
The saving was no saving clause ;
It suffer'd not his heart to falter,
Until it reach'd his final pause
As full possessor of the halter.—
'Tis thus the miser often grieves,
Who e'er the benefit receives
Of what he owns, he never must—
Mere treasurer for thieves,
Or relatives, or dust.
But what say we about the trade
In this affair by Fortune made ?
Why, what but that it was just like her !
In freaks like this delighteth she.
The shorter any turn may be,
The better it is sure to strike her.
It fills that goddess full of glee
A self-suspended man to see ;
And that it does especially,
When made so unexpectedly.

XVII.—THE MONKEY AND THE CAT.

SLY Bertrand and Ratto in company sat,
(The one was a monkey, the other a cat,)
Co-servants and lodgers :
More mischievous codgers
Ne'er mess'd from a platter, since platters were flat.
Was any thing wrong in the house or about it,
The neighbours were blameless,—no mortal could
doubt it ;
For Bertrand was thievish, and Ratto so nice,
More attentive to cheese than he was to the mice.
One day the two plunderers sat by the fire,
Where chestnuts were roasting, with looks of desire.
To steal them would be a right noble affair.
A double inducement our heroes drew there—
'Twould benefit them, could they swallow their fill,
And then 'twould occasion to somebody ill.
Said Bertrand to Ratto, My brother, to-day
Exhibit your powers in a masterly way,
And take me these chestnuts, I pray.

Which were I but otherwise fitted
(As I am ingeniously witted)
For pulling things out of the flame,
Would stand but a pitiful game.
'Tis done, replied Ratto, all prompt to obey;
And thrust out his paw in a delicate way.
First giving the ashes a scratch,
He open'd the coveted batch;
Then lightly and quickly impinging,
He drew out, in spite of the singeing,
One after another, the chestnuts at last,—
While Bertrand contrived to devour them as fast.
A servant girl enters.   Adieu to the fun.
Our Ratto was hardly contented, says one.—

No more are the princes, by flattery paid
For furnishing help in a different trade,
And burning their fingers to bring
More power to some mightier king.

XVIII.—THE KITE AND THE NIGHTINGALE.

A NOTED thief, the kite,
Had set a neighbourhood in fright,
And raised the clamorous noise
Of all the village boys,
When, by misfortune,—sad to say,—
A nightingale fell in his way.
Spring's herald begg'd him not to eat
A bird for music—not for meat.
O spare ! cried she, and I'll relate
The crime of Tereus and his fate.—
What's Tereus ? Is it food for kites?—
No, but a king, of female rights
The villain spoiler, whom I taught
A lesson with repentance fraught ;
And, should it please you not to kill,
  My song about his fall
Your very heart shall thrill,
  As it, indeed, does all.—
Replied the kite, Pretty thing,
When I am faint and famishing,
To let you go, and hear you sing ?—
Ah, but I entertain the king !—
Well, when he takes you, let him hear
  Your tale, full wonderful, no doubt ;
  For me, a kite, I'll go without,
An empty stomach hath no ear.

XIX.—THE SHEPHERD AND HIS FLOCK.

WHAT ! shall I lose them one by one,
  This stupid coward throng ?
And never shall the wolf have done?
They were at least a thousand strong,
But still they've let poor Robin fall a prey !
  Ah, woe's the day !
Poor Robin Wether lying dead !
He follow'd for a bit of bread
His master through the crowded city,
  And would have follow'd, had he led,
Around the world.   O ! what a pity !
My pipe, and even step, he knew ;
To meet me when I came, he flew ;
In hedge-row shade we napp'd together ;
Alas, alas, my Robin Wether !

When Willy thus had duly said
His eulogy upon the dead,
And unto everlasting fame
Consign'd poor Robin Wether's name,
He then harangued the flock at large,
  From proud old chieftain rams
  Down to the smallest lambs,
Addressing them this weighty charge,—
Against the wolf, as one, to stand,
In firm, united, fearless band,
By which they might expel him from their land.
  Upon their faith, they would not flinch,
  They promised him, a single inch.
We'll choke, said they, the murderous glutton
Who robb'd us of our Robin Mutton.
  Their lives they pledged against the beast,
  And Willy gave them all a feast.
But evil Fate, than Phœbus faster,
Ere night had brought a new disaster :
A wolf there came.   By nature's law,
  The total flock were prompt to run ;
And yet 'twas not the wolf they saw,
But shadow of him from the setting sun.

Harangue a craven soldiery,
What heroes they will seem to be !
But let them snuff the smoke of battle,
Or even hear the ramrods rattle,
Adieu to all their spunk and mettle :
Your own example will be vain,
And exhortations, to retain
  The timid cattle.

~~~~~~~~~~

BOOK X.

I.—THE TWO RATS, THE FOX, AND THE EGG.

ADDRESS TO MADAME DE LA SABLIÈRE.

You, Iris, 'twere an easy task to praise ;
But you refuse the incense of my lays.
In this you are unlike all other mortals,
Who welcome all the praise that seeks their
    portals ;
Not one who is not soothed by sound so sweet.
For me to blame this humour were not meet,
  By gods and mortals shared in common,
  And, in the main, by lovely woman.
That drink, so vaunted by the rhyming trade
That cheers the god who deals the thunder-blow,
And oft intoxicates the gods below,—
The nectar, Iris, is of praises made.
  You taste it not.   But, in its place,
  Wit, science, even trifles grace
Your bill of fare ; but, for that matter,
The world will not believe the latter.
  Well, leave the world in unbelief.
Still science, trifles, fancies light as air,
I hold, should mingle in a bill of fare,
  Each giving each its due relief ;
  As, where the gifts of Flora fall,
    On different flowers we see
    Alight the busy bee,
  Educing sweet from all.
Thus much premised, don't think it strange,
Or aught beyond my muse's range,

If e'en my fables should infold,
　Among their nameless trumpery,
　The traits of a philosophy
Far-famed as subtle, charming, bold.
They call it new— the men of wit ;
Perhaps you have not heard of it* ?
My verse will tell you what it means :—
They say that beasts are mere machines ;
That, in their doings, everything
　Is done by virtue of a spring—
　No sense, no soul, nor notion ;
But matter merely,—set in motion,
　Just such the watch in kind,
　Which joggeth on, to purpose blind.
Now ope, and read within its breast—
The place of soul is by its wheels possess'd.
One moves a second, that a third,
　Till finally its sound is heard.
　And now the beast, our sages say,
　Is moved precisely in this way.
An object strikes it in a certain place :
The spot thus struck, without a moment's space,
　To neighbouring parts the news conveys ;
Thus sense receives it through the chain,
And takes impression.—How ? Explain.—
Not I. They say, by sheer necessity,
　From will as well as passion free,
　The animal is found the thrall
　Of movements which the vulgar call
Joy, sadness, pleasure, pain, and love—
　The cause extrinsic and above.—
Believe it not. What's this I hold ?
Why, sooth, it is a watch of gold.
Its life, the mere unbending of a spring.
And we ?—are quite a different thing.
Hear how Descartes—Descartes, whom all applaud,
　Whom pagans would have made a god,
　Who holds, in fact, the middle place
　'Twixt ours and the celestial race,
About as does the plodding ass
From man to oyster as you pass—
Hear how this author states the case :
　Of all the tribes to being brought
　By our Creator out of nought,
　I only have the gift of thought.
　Now, Iris, you will recollect
　We were by older science taught
That when brutes think, they don't reflect.
Descartes proceeds beyond the wall,
And says they do not think at all.
　This you believe with ease ;
And so could I, if I should please.
Still, in the forest, when, from morn
Till midday, sounds of dog and horn
　Have terrified the stag forlorn ;
When he has doubled forth and back,
And labour'd to confound his track,
Till tired and spent with efforts vain--
　An ancient stag, of antlers ten;—
　He puts a younger in his place,
　All fresh, to weary out the chase.—
What thoughts for one that merely grazes !
The doublings, turnings, windings, mazes,

The substituting fresher bait,
Were worthy of a man of state—
And worthy of a better fate !
To yield to rascal dogs his breath
Is all the honour of his death.
And when the partridge danger spies,
Before her brood have strength to rise,
　She wisely counterfeits a wound,
　And drags her wing upon the ground—
Thus, from her home, beside some ancient log,
Safe drawing off the sportsman and his dog ;
And while the latter seems to seize her,
　The victim of an easy chase—
Your teeth are not for such as me, sir,
　　　She cries,
　　　And flies,
And laughs the former in his face.

Far north, 'tis said, the people live
In customs nearly primitive ;
　That is to say, are bound
　In ignorance profound :—
I mean the people human ;
For animals are dwelling there
With skill such buildings to prepare
As could on earth but few men.
Firm laid across the torrent's course,
Their work withstands its mighty force,
So damming it from shore to shore,
　That, gliding smoothly o'er,
　In even sheets the waters pour.
Their work, as it proceeds, they grade and bevel,
　Or bring it up to plumb or level ;
First lay their logs, and then with mortar smear,
As if directed by an engineer.
　Each labours for the public good ;
　The old command, the youthful brood
Cut down, and shape, and place the wood.
Compared with theirs, e'en Plato's model state
Were but the work of some apprentice pate.
Such are the beaver folks, who know
Enough to house themselves from snow,
And bridge, though they can swim, the pools.
Meanwhile, our kinsmen are such fools,
　In spite of their example,
　They dwell in huts less ample,
　And cross the streams by swimming,
　However cold and brimming!
　Now that the skilful beaver,
　Is but a body void of spirit,
From whomsoever I might hear it,
　I would believe it never.

But I go farther in the case.
　Pray listen while I tell
　A thing which lately fell
From one of truly royal race†.
A prince beloved by Victory,
　The north's defender here shall be
My voucher and your guaranty ;
　　Whose mighty name alone
　　Commands the sultan's throne,
The king whom Poland calls her own.
This king declares (kings cannot lie, we hear)
　　That, on his own frontier,
　　Some animals there are
　　Engaged in ceaseless war ;
From age to age the quarrel runs,
Transmitted down from sires to sons ;

† John Sobieski.

(These beasts, he says, are to the fox akin ;)
And with more skill no war hath been,
By highest military powers,
Conducted in this age of ours.
Guards, piquets, scouts, and spies,
And ambuscade that hidden lies,
The foe to capture by surprise,
And many a shrewd appliance
Of that pernicious, cursed science,
The daughter of the Stygian wave,
And mother harsh of heroes brave,
Those military creatures have.
To chant their feats a bard we lack,
Till Death shall give us Homer back.
   And should he such a wonder do,
And, while his hand was in, release
   Old Epicurus' rival * too,
What would the latter say to facts like these?
Why, as I've said, that nature does such things
   In animals by means of springs ;
   That Memory is but corporeal ;
   And that to do the things array'd
So proudly in my story all,
   The animal but needs her aid.
At each return, the object, so to speak,
   Proceeds directly to her store
With keenest optics—there to seek
The image it had traced before,
Which, found, proceeds forthwith to act
Just as at first it did, in fact,
By neither thought nor reason back'd.
Not so with us, beasts perpendicular ;
With us kind Heaven is more particular.
   Self-ruled by independent mind,
   We're not the sport of objects blind,
   Nor e'en to instinct are consign'd.
I walk ; I talk ; I feel the sway
     Of power within
     This nice machine
    It cannot but obey.
This power, although with matter link'd,
Is comprehended as distinct.
Indeed 'tis comprehended better,
In truth and essence than is matter.
O'er all our arts it is supreme.
   But how doth matter understand
Or hear its sovereign lord's command ?
Here doth a difficulty seem :
   I see the tool obey the hand ;
But then the hand who guideth it ;
Who guides the stars in order fit ?
   Perhaps each mighty world,
   Since from its Maker hurl'd,
Some angel may have kept in custody.
   However that may be,
A spirit dwells in such as we ;
It moves our limbs ; we feel its mandates now ;
We see and know it rules, but know not how :
   Nor shall we know, indeed,
   Till in the breast of God we read.
And, speaking in all verity,
Descartes is just as ignorant as we ;
   In things beyond a mortal's ken,
He knows no more than other men.
But, Iris, I confess to this,
   That in the beasts of which I speak
   Such spirit it were vain to seek,
For man its only temple is.

* Descartes.

   Yet beasts must have a place
   Beneath our godlike race,
   Which no mere plant requires
   Although the plant respires.

   But what shall one reply
   To what I next shall certify?
Two rats in foraging fell on an egg,—
   For gentry such as they
   A genteel dinner every way ;
They needed not to find an ox's leg.
Brimful of joy and appetite,
   They were about to sack the box,
   So tight without the aid of locks,
When suddenly there came in sight
   A personage—Sir Pullet Fox.
Sure, luck was never more untoward
Since Fortune was a vixen froward !
How should they save their egg and bacon !
   Their plunder couldn't then be bagg'd ;
Should it in forward paws be taken,
   Or roll'd along, or dragg'd ?
   Each method seem'd impossible,
   And each was then of danger full.
Necessity, ingenious mother,
Brought forth what help'd them from their
     pother.
As still there was a chance to save their prey,—
The spunger yet some hundred yards away,—
One seized the egg, and turn'd upon his back,
And then, in spite of many a thump and thwack,
That would have torn, perhaps, a coat of mail,
   The other dragg'd him by the tail.
   Who dares the inference to blink,
   That beasts possess wherewith to think ?

   Were I commission'd to bestow
   This power on creatures here below,
   The beasts should have as much of mind
   As infants of the human kind.
Think not the latter, from their birth ?
It hence appears there are on earth
That have the simple power of thought
Where reason hath no knowledge wrought.
And on this wise an equal power I'd yield
To all the various tenants of the field ;
Not reason such as in ourselves we find,
But something more than any mainspring blind.
A speck of matter I would subtilise
Almost beyond the reach of mental eyes ;—
   An atom's essence, one might say,
   An extract of a solar ray,
More quick and pungent than a flame of fire,—
   For if of flame the wood is sire,
   Cannot the flame, itself refined,
   Give some idea of the mind !
     Comes not the purest gold
     From lead, as we are told ?
To feel and choose, my work should soar—
Unthinking judgment—nothing more.
No monkey of my manufacture
Should argue from his sense or fact, sure :
   But my allotment to mankind
   Should be of very different mind.
We men should share in double measure,
Or rather have a twofold treasure ;
   The one the soul, the same in all
   That bear the name of animal—
   The sages, dunces, great and small,
   That tenant this our teeming ball ;—

The other still another soul,
Which should to mortals here belong
In common with the angel throng ;
  Which, made an independent whole,
Could pierce the skies to worlds of light,
Within a point have room to be,—
Its life a morn, sans noon or night.
Exempt from all destructive change—
A thing as real as 'tis strange.
In infancy this child of day
Should glimmer but a feeble ray.
Its earthly organs stronger grown,
The beam of reason, brightly thrown,
Should pierce the darkness, thick and gross,
That holds the other prison'd close.

II.—THE MAN AND THE ADDER.

You villain ! cried a man who found
An adder coil'd upon the ground,
To do a very grateful deed
For all the world, I shall proceed.
  On this the animal perverse
    (I mean the snake ;
    Pray don't mistake
  The human for the worse)
Was caught and bagg'd, and, worst of all,
His blood was by his captor to be spilt
Without regard to innocence or guilt.
Howe'er, to show the why, these words let fall
His judge and jailor, proud and tall :—
Thou type of all ingratitude !
All charity to hearts like thine
Is folly, certain to be rued.
    Die, then,
    Thou foe of men !
Thy temper and thy teeth malign
Shall never hurt a hair of mine.
The muffled serpent, on his side,
The best a serpent could, replied,—
If all this world's ingrates
  Must meet with such a death,
Who from this worst of fates
  Could save his breath !
Upon thyself thy law recoils ;
I throw myself upon thy broils,
Thy graceless revelling on spoils ;
If thou but homeward cast an eye,
Thy deeds all mine will justify.
But strike : my life is in thy hand ;
Thy justice, all may understand,
Is but thy interest, pleasure, or caprice :—
Pronounce my sentence on such laws as these.
But give me leave to tell thee, while I can,
The type of all ingratitude is man.
By such a lecture somewhat foil'd,
The other back a step recoil'd,
  And finally replied,—
    Thy reasons are abusive,
    And wholly inconclusive.
  I might the case decide
Because to me such right belongs ;
But let 's refer the case of wrongs.
The snake agreed ; they to a cow referr'd it,
Who, being called, came graciously and heard it.
  Then, summing up, What need, said she,
  In such a case, to call on me !

The adder 's right, plain truth to bellow ;
For years I've nursed this haughty fellow,
Who, but for me, had long ago
Been lodging with the shades below.
For him my milk has had to flow,
  My calves at tender age, to die.
And for this best of wealth,
And often reëstablish'd health,
  What pay, or even thanks, have I !
Here, feeble, old, and worn, alas !
I'm left without a bite of grass.
Were I but left, it might be weather'd,
But, shame to say it, I am tether'd.
And now my fate is surely sadder
Than if my master were an adder,
  With brains within the latitude
  Of such immense ingratitude.
This, gentles, is my honest view ;
And so I bid you both adieu.
The man, confounded and astonish'd
To be so faithfully admonish'd,
Replied, What fools to listen, now,
To this old, silly, dotard cow !
Let 's trust the ox. Let 's trust, replied
The crawling beast, well gratified.
    So said, so done ;
The ox, with tardy pace, came on,
And, ruminating o'er the case,
Declared, with very serious face,
That years of his most painful toil
Had clothed with Ceres' gifts our soil—
Her gifts to men—but always sold
To beasts for higher cost than gold ;
And that for this, for his reward,
More blows than thanks return'd his lord ;
And then, when age had chill'd his blood,
  And men would quell the wrath of Heaven,
Out must be pour'd the vital flood,
  For others' sins, all thankless given.
So spake the ox ; and then the man :—
  Away with such a dull declaimer !
Instead of judge, it is his plan
  To play accuser and defamer.
A tree was next the arbitrator,
And made the wrong of man still greater.
It served as refuge from the heat,
The showers, and storms which madly beat ;
It grew our gardens' greatest pride,
Its shadow spreading far and wide,
And bow'd itself with fruit beside :
But yet a mercenary clown
With cruel iron chopp'd it down.
Behold the recompense for which,
Year after year, I did enrich,
With spring's sweet flowers, and autumn's fruits,
And summer's shade, both men and brutes,
  And warm'd the hearth with many a limb
Which winter from its top did trim !
Why could not man have pruned and spared,
And with itself for ages shared !
Much scorning thus to be convinced,
  The man resolved his cause to gain.
Quoth he, My goodness is evinced
  By hearing this, 'tis very plain ;
Then flung the serpent bag and all,
With fatal force, against a wall.

So ever is it with the great,
With whom the whim doth always run
  That Heaven all creatures doth create
For their behoof, beneath the sun—

Count they four feet, or two, or none.
If one should dare the fact dispute,
He's straight set down a stupid brute.
Now, grant it so,—such lords among,
What should be done, or said, or sung?
At distance speak, or hold your tongue.

III.—THE TORTOISE AND THE TWO DUCKS.

A LIGHT-BRAIN'D tortoise, anciently,
Tired of her hole, the world would see.
Prone are all such, self-banished, to roam—
Prone are all cripples to abhor their home.
Two ducks, to whom the gossip told
The secret of her purpose bold,
    Profess'd to have the means whereby
    They could her wishes gratify.
Our boundless road, said they, behold!
        It is the open air;
        And through it we will bear
      You safe o'er land and ocean.
Republics, kingdoms, you will view,
And famous cities, old and new;
    And get of customs, laws, a notion,—
Of various wisdom various pieces,
As did, indeed, the sage Ulysses.
The eager tortoise waited not
To question what Ulysses got,
But closed the bargain on the spot.
A nice machine the birds devise
To bear their pilgrim through the skies.
Athwart her mouth a stick they throw:
Now bite it hard, and don't let go,
They say, and seize each duck an end,
And, swiftly flying, upward tend.
It made the people gape and stare
    Beyond the expressive power of words,
To see a tortoise cut the air,
    Exactly poised between two birds.
A miracle, they cried, is seen!
There goes the flying tortoise queen!
The queen! ('twas thus the tortoise spoke;)
I'm truly that, without a joke.
Much better had she held her tongue;
For, opening that whereby she clung,
Before the gazing crowd she fell,
And dash'd to bits her brittle shell.

    Imprudence, vanity, and babble,
        And idle curiosity,
    An ever-undivided rabble,
        Have all the same paternity.

IV.—THE FISHES AND THE CORMORANT.

No pond nor pool within his haunt
But paid a certain cormorant
Its contribution from its fishes,
And stock'd his kitchen with good dishes.
Yet, when old age the bird had chill'd,
His kitchen was less amply fill'd.
All cormorants, however grey,
Must die, or for themselves purvey.
But ours had now become so blind,
His finny prey he could not find;
And, having neither hook nor net,
His appetite was poorly met.

What hope, with famine thus infested!
    Necessity whom history mentions
    A famous mother of inventions,
The following stratagem suggested:
    He found upon the water's brink
    A crab, to which said he, My friend,
    A weighty errand let me send;
        Go quicker than a wink—
    Down to the fishes sink,
And tell them they are doom'd to die;
For, ere eight days have hasten'd by,
Its lord will fish this water dry.
The crab, as fast as she could scrabble,
Went down, and told the scaly rabble.
What bustling, gathering, agitation!
Straight up they send a deputation
    To wait upon the ancient bird.
Sir Cormorant, whence hast thou heard
    This dreadful news? And what
Assurance of it hast thou got?
How such a danger can we shun!
Pray tell us, what is to be done!
Why, change your dwelling-place, said he,
What, change our dwelling! How can we?
O, by your leave, I'll take that care,
And, one by one, in safety bear
        You all to my retreat:
        The path's unknown
            To any feet,
        Except my own.
A pool, scoop'd out by Nature's hands,
Amidst the desert rocks and sands,
Where human traitors never come,
Shall save your people from their doom.
The fish republic swallow'd all,
And, coming at the fellow's call,
Were singly borne away to stock
A pond beneath a lonely rock;
And there good prophet cormorant,
    Proprietor and bailiff sole,
    From narrow water, clear and shoal,
With ease supplied his daily want,
And taught them, at their own expense,
That heads well stored with common sense
Give no devourers confidence.—
Still did the change not hurt their case,
Since, had they staid, the human race,
Successful by pernicious art,
Would have consumed as large a part.
What matters who your flesh devours,
Of human or of bestial powers?
In this respect, or wild or tame,
All stomachs seem to me the same:
The odds is small, in point of sorrow,
Of death to-day, or death to-morrow.

V.—THE BURIER AND HIS COMRADE.

A CLOSE-FIST had his money hoarded
Beyond the room his till afforded.
His avarice aye growing ranker,
(Whereby his mind of course grew blanker,)
He was perplex'd to choose a banker:
    For banker he must have, he thought,
    Or all his heap would come to nought.
I fear, said he, if kept at home,
And other robbers should not come,

It might be equal cause of grief
That I had proved myself the thief.
The thief! Is to enjoy one's pelf
To rob or steal it from one's self?
My friend, could but my pity reach you,
This lesson I would gladly teach you,
That wealth is weal no longer than
Diffuse and part with it you can:
Without that power, it is a woe.
Would you for age keep back its flow?
Age buried 'neath its joyless snow?
With pains of getting, care of got
Consumes the value, every jot,
Of gold that one can never spare.
To take the load of such a care,
Assistants were not very rare.
The earth was that which pleased him best.
Dismissing thought of all the rest,
He with his friend, his trustiest,—
  A sort of shovel-secretary,—
  Went forth his hoard to bury.
Safe done, a few days afterward,
The man must look beneath the sward—
When, what a mystery! behold
The mine exhausted of its gold!
Suspecting, with the best of cause,
His friend was privy to his loss,
He bade him, in a cautious mood,
To come as soon as well he could,
For still some other coins he had,
Which to the rest he wish'd to add.
Expecting thus to get the whole,
The friend put back the sum he stole,
Then came with all despatch.
The other proved an overmatch:
Resolved at length to save by spending,
His practice thus most wisely mending,
The total treasure home he carried—
No longer hoarded it or buried.
  Chapfallen was the thief, when gone
He saw his prospects and his pawn.

From this it may be stated,
That knaves with ease are cheated.

VI.—THE WOLF AND THE SHEPHERDS.

  A WOLF, replete
  With humanity sweet,
(A trait not much suspected,)
  On his cruel deeds,
  The fruit of his needs,
Profoundly thus reflected.

  I'm hated, said he
  As joint enemy,
By hunters, dogs, and clowns.
  They swear I shall die,
  And their hue and cry
The very thunder drowns.

  My brethren have fled,
  With price on the head,
From England's merry land.
  King Edgar came out,
  And put them to rout,
With many a deadly band.

  And there's not a squire
  But blows up the fire
By hostile proclamation;
  Nor a human brat
  Dares cry, but that
Its mother mocks my nation.

  And all for what?
  For a sheep with the rot,
  Or scabby, mangy ass,
  Or some snarling cur,
  With less meat than fur,
On which I've broken fast!

  Well, henceforth I'll strive
  That nothing alive
Shall die to quench my thirst;
  No lambkin shall fall,
  Nor puppy, at all,
To glut my maw accurst.
  With grass I'll appease,
  Or browse on the trees,
Or die of famine first.

  What of carcass warm?
  Is it worth the storm
Of universal hate?
  As he spoke these words,
  The lords of the herds,
All seated at their bait,
  He saw; and observed
  The meat which was served
Was nought but roasted lamb!
  O! O! said the beast,
  Repent of my feast—
All butcher as I am—
  On these vermin mean,
  Whose guardians e'en
Eat at a rate quadruple!—
  Themselves and their dogs,
  As greedy as hogs,
And I, a wolf, to scruple!

  Look out for your wool!
  I'll not be a fool,
The very pet I'll eat;
  The lamb the best-looking,
  Without any cooking,
I'll strangle from the teat;
  And swallow the dam,
  As well as the lamb,
And stop her foolish bleat.
  Old Hornie, too,—rot him,—
  The sire that begot him
Shall be among my meat!

  Well-reasoning beast!
  Were we sent to feast
On creatures wild and tame?
  And shall we reduce
  The beasts to the use
Of vegetable game?

  Shall animals not
  Have flesh-hook or pot,
As in the age of gold?
  And we claim the right,
  In the pride of our might,
Themselves to have and hold?

O shepherds, that keep
Your folds full of sheep,
The wolf was only wrong
Because, so to speak,
His jaws were too weak
To break your palings strong.

VII.—THE SPIDER AND THE SWALLOW.

O JUPITER, whose fruitful brain,
By odd obstetrics freed from pain,
Bore Pallas, erst my mortal foe,
Pray listen to my tale of woe.
This Progne takes my lawful prey.
As through the air she cuts her way,
And skims the waves in seeming play,
My flies she catches from my door,—
    Yes, *mine*—I emphasize the word,—
    And, but for this accursed bird,
My net would hold an ample store :
For I have woven it of stuff
To hold the strongest strong enough.—
'Twas thus, in terms of insolence,
Complain'd the fretful spider, once
Of palace-tapestry a weaver,
    But then a spinster and deceiver,
That hoped within her toils to bring
Of insects all that ply the wing.
The sister swift of Philomel,
Intent on business, prosper'd well ;
In spite of the complaining pest,
The insects carried to her nest—
Nest pitiless to suffering flies—
Mouths gaping aye, to gormandise,
    Of young ones clamouring,
        And stammering,
With unintelligible cries.
The spider, with but head and feet,
    And powerless to compete
    With wings so fleet,
Soon saw herself a prey.
    The swallow, passing swiftly by,
    Bore web and all away,
The spinster dangling in the sky !

Two tables hath our Maker set
For all that in this world are met.
    To seats around the first
The skilful, vigilant, and strong are beckon'd :
    Their hunger and their thirst
The rest must quell with leavings at the second.

VIII.—THE PARTRIDGE AND THE COCKS.

WITH a set of uncivil and turbulent cocks,
That deserved for their noise to be put in the stocks,
    A partridge was placed to be rear'd.
    Her sex, by politeness revered,
Made her hope, from a gentry devoted to love,
For the courtesy due to the tenderest dove ;
Nay, protection chivalric from knights of the yard.
That gentry, however, with little regard
For the honours and knighthood wherewith they
        were deck'd,
And for the strange lady as little respect,
Her ladyship often most horribly peck'd.

At first, she was greatly afflicted therefor,
But when she had noticed these madcaps at war
With each other, and dealing far bloodier blows,
Consoling her own individual woes,—
Entail'd by their customs, said she, is the shame ;
Let us pity the simpletons rather than blame.
Our Maker creates not all spirits the same ;
The cocks and the partridges certainly differ,
By a nature than laws of civility stiffer,
Were the choice to be mine, I would finish my life
In society freer from riot and strife.
    But the lord of this soil has a different plan ;
His tunnel our race to captivity brings,
He throws us with cocks, after clipping our wings.
'Tis little we have to complain of but man.

IX.—THE DOG WHOSE EARS WERE CROPPED.

WHAT have I done, I'd like to know,
    To make my master maim me so !
        A pretty figure I shall cut !
From other dogs I'll keep, in kennel shut.
Ye kings of beasts, or rather tyrants, ho !
    Would any beast have served you so !
    Thus Growler cried, a mastiff young ;—
    The man, whom pity never stung,
    Went on to prune him of his ears.
Though Growler whined about his losses,
    He found, before the lapse of years,
Himself a gainer by the process ;
    For, being by his nature prone
    To fight his brethren for a bone,
    He'd oft come back from sad reverse
    With those appendages the worse.
    All snarling dogs have ragged ears.

The less of hold for teeth of foe,
The better will the battle go.
    When, in a certain place, one fears
The chance of being hurt or beat,
He fortifies it from defeat.
    Besides the shortness of his ears,
See Growler arm'd against his likes
With gorget full of ugly spikes.
A wolf would find it quite a puzzle
To get a hold about his muzzle.

X.—THE SHEPHERD AND THE KING.

Two demons at their pleasure share our being—
The cause of Reason from her homestead fleeing ;
No heart but on their altars kindleth flames.
If you demand their purposes and names,
The one is Love, the other is Ambition.
Of far the greater share this takes possession,
    For even into love it enters,
Which I might prove ; but now my story centres
Upon a shepherd clothed with lofty powers :
The tale belongs to older times than ours.

A king observed a flock, wide spread
Upon the plains, most admirably fed,
O'erpaying largely, as return'd the years,
Their shepherd's care, by harvests for his shears.
Such pleasure in this man the monarch took,—
Thou meritest, said he, to wield a crook

O'er higher flock than this ; and my esteem
    'er men now makes thee judge supreme.
Behold our shepherd, scales in hand,
Although a hermit and a wolf or two,
Besides his flock and dogs, were all he knew !
Well stock'd with sense, all else upon demand
Would come of course, and did, we understand.
His neighbour hermit came to him to say,
Am I awake ? Is this no dream, I pray ?
You favourite ! you great ! beware of kings
Their favours are but slippery things,
Dear-bought ; to mount the heights to which they call
Is but to court a more illustrious fall.
You little know to what this lure beguiles
My friend, I say, Beware. The other smiles.
    The hermit adds, See how
The court has marr'd your wisdom even now !
    That purblind traveller I seem to see,
Who, having lost his whip, by strange mistake,
    Took for a better one a snake ;
But, while he thank'd his stars, brimful of glee,
Outcried a passenger, God shield your breast !
Why, man, for life, throw down that treacherous pest,
That snake !—It is my whip.—A snake, I say :
What selfish end could prompt my warning, pray ?
Think you to keep your prize ?—And wherefore not !
My whip was worn ; I've found another new :
This counsel grave from envy springs in you.—
The stubborn wight would not believe a jot,
    Till warm and lithe the serpent grew,
    And, striking with his venom, slew
The man almost upon the spot.
And as to you, I dare predict
That something worse will soon afflict.
Indeed ! What worse than death, prophetic hermit ?
Perhaps the compound heartache I may term it.
    And never was there truer prophecy.
Full many a courtier pest, by many a lie,
    Contrived, and many a cruel slander,
To make the king suspect the judge awry
    In both ability and candour.
Cabals were raised, and dark conspiracies,
Of men that felt aggrieved by his decrees.
With wealth of ours he hath a palace built,
Said they. The king, astonish'd at his guilt,
    His ill-got riches ask'd to see.
    He found but mediocrity,
    Bespeaking strictest honesty.
    So much for his magnificence.
Anon, his plunder was a hoard immense
Of precious stones that fill'd an iron box,
All fast secured by half a score of locks.
Himself the coffer oped, and sad surprise
Befell those manufacturers of lies.
The open'd lid disclosed no other matters
Than, first, a shepherd's suit in tatters,
And then a cap and jacket, pipe and crook,
And scrip, mayhap with pebbles from the brook.
O treasure sweet, said he, that never drew
The viper brood of envy's lies on you !
I take you back, and leave this palace splendid,
As some roused sleeper doth a dream that's ended.
    Forgive me, sire, this exclamation.
In mounting up, my fall I had foreseen,
Yet loved the height too well ; for who hath been,
Of mortal race, devoid of all ambition !

XI.—THE FISHES AND THE SHEPHERD WHO PLAYED THE FLUTE.

THYRSIS—who for his Annette dear
    Made music with his flute and voice,
Which might have roused the dead to hear,
    And in their silent graves rejoice—
        Sang once the livelong day,
        In the flowery month of May,
    Up and down a meadow brook,
While Annette fish'd with line and hook.
    But ne'er a fish would bite ;
        So the shepherdess's bait
        Drew not a fish to its fate,
    From morning dawn till night.
The shepherd, who, by his charming songs,
Had drawn savage beasts to him in throngs,
    And done with them as he pleased to,
    Thought that he could serve the fish so.
O citizens, he sang, of this water,
Leave your Naiad in her grot profound ;
Come and see the blue sky's lovely daughter,
    Who a thousand times more will charm you ;
    Fear not that her prison will harm you,
Though there you should chance to get bound.
    'Tis only to us men she is cruel :
        You she will treat kindly ;
    A snug little pond she'll find ye,
Clearer than a crystal jewel,
Where you may all live and do well ;
        Or, if by chance some few
            Should find their fate
            Conceal'd in the bait,
        The happier still are you ;
For envied is the death that's met
At the hands of sweet Annette.
    This eloquence not effecting
        The object of his wishes,
    Since it failed in collecting
        The deaf and dumb fishes,—
        His sweet preaching wasted,
        His honey'd talk untasted,
A net the shepherd seized, and, pouncing
With a fell scoop at the scaly fry,
He caught them ; and now, madly flouncing,
At the feet of his Annette they lie !

O ye shepherds, whose sheep men are,
To trust in reason never dare.
The arts of eloquence sublime
Are not within your calling ;
Your fish were caught, from oldest time,
    By dint of nets and hauling.

XII.—THE TWO PARROTS, THE KING, AND HIS SON.

Two parrots lived, a sire and son,
    On roastings from a royal fire.
Two demigods, a son and sire,
These parrots pension'd for their fun.
Time tied the knot of love sincere :
    The sires grew to each other dear ;
The sons, in spite of their frivolity,
Grew comrades boon, in joke and jollity ;
    At mess they mated, hot or cool ;
    Were fellow-scholars at a school,

Which did the bird no little honour, since
The boy, by king begotten, was a prince.
By nature fond of birds, the prince, too, petted
A sparrow, which delightfully coquetted.
　　These rivals, both of unripe feather,
　　One day were frolicking together :
　　As oft befalls such little folks,
　　A quarrel follow'd from their jokes.
　　The sparrow, quite uncircumspect,
　　Was by the parrot sadly peck'd ;
　　With drooping wing and bloody head,
　　His master pick'd him up for dead,
And, being quite too wroth to bear it,
In heat of passion kill'd his parrot.
　　When this sad piece of news he heard,
　　Distracted was the parent bird.
　　His piercing cries bespoke his pain ;
　　But cries and tears were all in vain.
　　The talking bird had left the shore* ;
　　In short, he, talking now no more,
　　Caused such a rage to seize his sire,
　　That, lighting on the prince in ire,
　　He put out both his eyes,
　　And fled for safety as was wise.
　　　The bird a pine for refuge chose,
　　　And to its lofty summit rose ;
　　There, in the bosom of the skies,
　　　Enjoy'd his vengeance sweet,
　　And scorn'd the wrath beneath his feet.
Out ran the king, and cried, in soothing tone,
Return, dear friend ; what serves it to bemoan ?
Hate, vengeance, mourning, let us both omit.
　　For me, it is no more than fit
　　To own, though with an aching heart,
　　The wrong is wholly on our part.
　　Th' aggressor truly was my son—
My son ? no ; but by Fate the deed was done.
Ere birth of Time, stern Destiny
Had written down the sad decree,
That by this sad calamity
Your child should cease to live, and mine to see.

　　Let both, then, cease to mourn ;
　And you, back to your cage return.
Sire king, replied the bird,
Think you that, after such a deed,
　　I ought to trust your word ?
You speak of Fate ; by such a heathen creed
Hope you that I shall be enticed to bleed !
But whether Fate or Providence divine
　　Gives law to things below,
'Tis writ on high, that on this waving pine,
　　Or where wild forests grow,
　My days I finish, safely, far
From that which ought your love to mar,
　　And turn it all to hate.
Revenge, I know,'s a kingly morsel,
And ever hath been part and parcel
　Of this your godlike state.
You would forget the cause of grief ;
　Suppose I grant you my belief,—
　'Tis better still to make it true,
　By keeping out of sight of you.
Sire king, my friend, no longer wait
　For friendship to be heal'd ; . . . . .
But absence is the cure of hate,
　As 'tis from love the shield.

* " Stygia natabat jam frigida cymba."—VIRG.

THE lioness had lost her young ;
　　A hunter stole it from the vale ;
The forests and the mountains rung
　　Responsive to her hideous wail.
Nor night, nor charms of sweet repose,
Could still the loud lament that rose
　　From that grim forest queen.
No animal, as you might think,
With such a noise could sleep a wink.
　　A bear presumed to intervene.
　　One word, sweet friend, quoth she,
　　And that is all, from me.
The young that through your teeth have pass'd,
　In file unbroken by a fast,
　　Had they nor dam nor sire ?
　They had them both.   Then I desire,
Since all their deaths caused no such grievous riot,
While mothers died of grief beneath your fiat,
To know why you yourself cannot be quiet ?
　I quiet !—I !—a wretch bereaved !
　My only son !—such anguish be relieved !
　No, never ! All for me below
　Is but a life of tears and woe !____
But say, why doom yourself to sorrow so ?____
Alas ! 'tis Destiny that is my foe.

　　Such language, since the mortal fall,
　Has fallen from the lips of all.
　Ye human wretches, give your heed ;
　For your complaints there's little need.
Let him who thinks his own the hardest case,
　Some widow'd, childless Hecuba behold,
　Herself to toil and shame of slavery sold,
And he will own the wealth of heavenly grace.

———◆———

No flowery path to glory leads.
This truth no better voucher needs
Than Hercules, of mighty deeds.
Few demigods, the tomes of fable
Reveal to us as being able
Such weight of task-work to endure :
In history, I find still fewer.
One such, however, here behold—
A knight by talisman made bold,
Within the regions of romance,
To seek adventures with the lance.
There rode a comrade at his side,
And as they rode they both espied
　This writing on a post :—
" Wouldst see, sir valiant knight,
A thing whereof the sight
　No errant yet can boast ?
Thou hast this torrent but to ford,
　And, lifting up alone
　The elephant of stone
　Upon its margin shored,
Upbear it to the mountain's brow,
Round which, aloft before thee now,
　The misty chaplets wreathe—
　Not stopping once to breathe."
One knight, whose nostrils bled,
Betokening courage fled,

Cried out, What if that current's sweep
Not only rapid be, but deep !
And grant it cross'd,—pray, why encumber
One's arms with that unwieldy lumber,
   An elephant of stone?
Perhaps the artist may have done
His work in such a way, that one
   Might lug it twice its length ;
But then to reach yon mountain top,
And that without a breathing stop,
Were surely past a mortal's strength—
Unless, indeed, it be no bigger
Than some wee, pigmy, dwarfish figure,
Which one would head a cane withal ;—
And if to this the case should fall,
The adventurer's honour would be small !
This posting seems to me a trap,
Or riddle for some greenish chap ;
   I therefore leave the whole to you.
The doubtful reasoner onward hies.
With heart resolved, in spite of eyes,
   The other boldly dashes through ;
   Nor depth of flood nor force
   Can stop his onward course.
He finds the elephant of stone ;
   He lifts it all alone ;
   Without a breathing stop,
   He bears it to the top
Of that steep mount, and seeth there
A high-wall'd city, great and fair.
Out-cried the elephant—and hush'd ;
But forth in arms the people rush'd.
A knight less bold had surely fled ;
But he, so far from turning back,
His course right onward sped,
   Resolved himself to make attack,
And die but with the bravest dead.
Amazed was he to hear that band
Proclaim him monarch of their land,
And welcome him, in place of one
Whose death had left a vacant throne !
In sooth, he lent a gracious ear,
Meanwhile expressing modest fear,
Lest such a load of royal care
Should be too great for him to bear.
And so, exactly, Sixtus said,
When first the pope's tiara press'd his head ;
(Though, is it such a grievous thing
To be a pope, or be a king ?)
But days were few before they read it
That with but little truth he said it.

Blind Fortune follows daring blind,
Oft executes the wisest man,
Ere yet the wisdom of his mind
Is task'd his means or end to scan.

* * *

XV.—THE RABBITS.
AN ADDRESS TO THE DUKE DE LA ROCHEFOUCAULD.

WHILE watching man in all his phases,
And seeing that, in many cases,
   He acts just like the brute creation,—
I've thought the lord of all these races
Of no less failings show'd the traces
   Than do his lieges in relation ;
And that, in making it, Dame Nature
Hath put a spice in every creature

From off the self-same spirit-stuff—
Not from the immaterial,
But what we call ethereal,
   Refined from matter rough.
An illustration please to hear.
   Just on the still frontier
   Of either day or night,—
   Or when the lord of light
   Reclines his radiant head
   Upon his watery bed,
   Or when he dons the gear,
   To drive a new career,—
   While yet with doubtful sway
The hour is ruled 'twixt night and day,—
Some border forest-tree I climb ;
And, acting Jove, from height sublime
   My fatal bolt at will directing,
   I kill some rabbit unsuspecting.
The rest that frolick'd on the heath,
Or browsed the thyme with dainty teeth,
   With open eye and watchful ear,
Behold, all scampering from beneath,
   Instinct with mortal fear.
All, frighten'd simply by the sound,
Hie to their city underground.
But soon the danger is forgot,
And just as soon the fear lives not :
The rabbits, gayer than before,
I see beneath my hand once more !

Are not mankind well pictured here ?
   By storms asunder driven,
   They scarcely reach their haven,
   And cast their anchor, ere
   They tempt the same dread shocks
   Of tempests, waves, and rocks.
True rabbits, back they frisk
To meet the self-same risk !

I add another common case.
   When dogs pass through a place
   Beyond their customary bounds,
And meet with others, curs or hounds,
   Imagine what a holiday !
The native dogs, whose interests centre
In one great organ, term'd the venter,
   The strangers rush at, bite, and bay ;
With cynic pertness tease and worry,
And chase them off their territory.
So, too, do men. Wealth, grandeur, glory,
   To men of office or profession,
   Of every sort, in every nation,
   As tempting are, and sweet,
As is to dogs the refuse meat.
With us, it is a general fact,
One sees the latest-come attack'd,
   And plunder'd to the skin.
Coquettes and authors we may view,
   As samples of the sin ;
For woe to belle or writer new !
The fewer eaters round the cake,
The fewer players for the stake,
The surer each one's self to take.
A hundred facts my truth might test ;
But shortest works are always best.
In this I but pursue the chart
Laid down by masters of the art ;
And, on the best of themes, I hold,
The truth should never all be told.

Hence, here my sermon ought to close.
O thou, to whom my fable owes
Whate'er it has of solid worth,—
Who, great by modesty as well as birth,
Hast ever counted praise a pain,—
Whose leave I could so ill obtain
That here your name, receiving homage,
Should save from every sort of damage
My slender works—which name, well known
To nations, and to ancient Time,
All France delights to own,
Herself more rich in names sublime
Than any other earthly clime ;—
Permit me here the world to teach
That you have given my simple rhyme
The text from which it dares to preach.

XVI.—THE MERCHANT, THE NOBLE, THE SHEPHERD, AND THE KING'S SON.

Four voyagers to parts unknown,
On shore, not far from naked, thrown
By furious waves,—a merchant now undone,
A noble, shepherd, and a monarch's son,—
Brought to the lot of Belisarius*,
Their wants supplied on alms precarious.
To tell what fates, and winds, and weather,
Had brought these mortals all together,
Though from far distant points abscinded,
Would make my tale long-winded.
Suffice to say, that, by a fountain met
In council grave, these outcasts held debate.
The prince enlarged, in an oration set,
Upon the miseries that befall the great.
The shepherd deem'd it best to cast
Off thought of all misfortune past,
And each to do the best he could,
In efforts for the common weal.
Did ever a repining mood,
He added, a misfortune heal!
Toil, friends, will take us back to Rome,
Or make us here as good a home.
A shepherd so to speak ! a shepherd ? What !
As though crown'd heads were not,
By Heaven's appointment fit,
The sole receptacles of wit !
As though a shepherd could be deeper,
In thought or knowledge, than his sheep are !
The three, howe'er, at once approved his plan,
Wreck'd as they were on shores American.
I'll teach arithmetic, the merchant said,—
Its rules, of course, well seated in his head,—
For monthly pay.   The prince replied, And I
Will teach political economy.
And I, the noble said, in heraldry
Well versed, will open for that branch a school—
As if, beyond a thousand leagues of sea,
That senseless jargon could befool !
My friends, you talk like men,
The shepherd cried, but then

---

* Belisarius was a great general, who, having commanded the armies of the emperor, and lost the favour of his master, fell to such a point of destitution that he asked alms upon the highways.—NOTE OF LA FONTAINE.
The touching story of the fall of Belisarius, of which painters and poets have made so much, is entirely false, as may be seen by consulting Gibbon's " Decline and Fall of the Roman Empire," chap. xliii.—TRANSLATOR.

The month has thirty days ; till they are spent,
Are we upon your faith to keep full Lent !
The hope you give is truly good ;
But, ere it comes, we starve for food !
Pray tell me, if you can divine,
On what, to-morrow, we shall dine ;
Or tell me, rather, whence we may
Obtain a supper for to-day.
This point, if truth should be confess'd,
Is first, and vital to the rest.
Your science short in this respect,
My hands shall cover the defect.—
This said, the nearest woods he sought,
And thence for market fagots brought,
Whose price that day, and eke the next,
Relieved the company perplex'd—
Forbidding that, by fasting, they should go
To use their talents in the world below.

We learn, from this adventure's course,
There needs but little skill to get a living.
Thanks to the gifts of Nature's giving,
Our hands are much the readiest resource.

BOOK XI.

I.—THE LION.

Some time ago, a sultan Leopard,
By means of many a rich escheat,
Had many an ox in meadow, sweet,
And many a stag in forest, fleet,
And (what a savage sort of shepherd !)
Full many a sheep upon the plains,
That lay within his wide domains.
Not far away, one morn,
There was a lion born.
Exchanged high compliments of state,
As is the custom with the great,
The sultan call'd his vizier Fox,
Who had a deeper knowledge-box,
And said to him, This lion's whelp you dread ;
What can he do, his father being dead ?
Our pity rather let him share,
An orphan so beset with care.
The luckiest lion ever known,
If, letting conquest quite alone,
He should have power to keep his own.
Sir Renard said,
And shook his head,
Such orphans, please your majesty,
Will get no pity out of me.
We ought to keep within his favour,
Or else with all our might endeavour
To thrust him out of life and throne,
Ere yet his claws and teeth are grown.
There's not a moment to be lost.
His horoscope I've cast ;
He'll never quarrel to his cost ;
But then his friendship fast
Will be to friends of greater worth
Than any lion's e'er on earth.
Try then, my liege, to make it ours,
Or else to check his rising powers.
The warning fell in vain.
The sultan slept ; and beasts and men
Did so, throughout his whole domain,

Till lion's whelp became a lion.
Then came at once the tocsin cry on,
Alarm and fluttering consternation.
The vizier call'd to consultation,
    A sigh escaped him as he said,
    Why all this mad excitement now,
    When hope is fled, no matter how ?
A thousand men were useless aid,—
The more, the worse,—since all their power
Would be our mutton to devour.
Appease this lion ; sole he doth exceed
The helpers all that on us feed.
And three hath he, that cost him nought,—
His courage, strength, and watchful thought.
Quick send a wether for his use :
    If not contented, send him more;
Yes, add an ox, and see you choose
    The best our pastures ever bore.
Thus save the rest.—But such advice
The sultan spurn'd, as cowardice.
And his, and many states beside,
Did ills, in consequence, betide.
However fought this world allied,
The beast maintain'd his power and pride.
If you must let the lion grow,
Don't let him live to be your foe.

II.—THE GODS WISHING TO INSTRUCT A SON OF JUPITER.

FOR MONSEIGNEUR THE DUKE DU MAINE.

To Jupiter was born a son,
    Who, conscious of his origin,
    A godlike spirit had within.
To love, such age is little prone ;
    Yet this celestial boy
    Made love his chief employ,
And was beloved wherever known.
    In him both love and reason
    Sprang up before their season.
With charming smiles and manners winning,
Had Flora deck'd his life's beginning,
    As an Olympian became :
    Whatever lights the tender flame,—
    A heart to take and render bliss,—
Tears, sighs, in short the whole were his.
Jove's son, he should of course inherit
A higher and a nobler spirit
Than sons of other deities.
It seem'd as if by Memory's aid—
As if a previous life had made
    Experiment and hid it—
He plied the lover's hard-learn'd trade,
    So perfectly he did it.
Still Jupiter would educate
In manner fitting to his state.
The gods, obedient to his call,
Assemble in their council-hall ;
When thus the sire : Companionless and sole,
Thus far the boundless universe I roll ;
But numerous other offices there are,
Of which I give to younger gods the care.
I'm now forecasting for this cherish'd child,
Whose countless altars are already piled ;
To merit such regard from all below,
All things the young immortal ought to know
    No sooner had the Thunderer ended,
    Than each his godlike plan commended ;

Nor did the boy too little yearn
His lesson infinite to learn.
Said fiery Mars, I take the part
To make him master of the art
Whereby so many heroes high
Have won the honours of the sky.
To teach him music be my care,
Apollo said, the wise and fair ;
And mine, that mighty god replied,
In the Nemæan lion's hide,
To teach him to subdue
The vices, an envenom'd crew,
Like Hydras springing ever new.
The foe of weakening luxury,
The boy divine will learn from me
Those rugged paths, so little trod,
That lead to glory man and god.
Said Cupid, when it came his turn,
All things from me the boy may learn.

    Well spoke the god of love.
    What feat of Mars, or Hercules,
        Or bright Apollo, lies above
    Wit, wing'd by a desire to please ?

III.—THE FARMER, THE DOG, AND THE FOX

The wolf and fox are neighbours strange :
I would not build within their range.
The fox once eyed with strict regard
From day to day, a poultry-yard ;
But though a most accomplish'd cheat,
He could not get a fowl to eat.
Between the risk and appetite,
His rogueship's trouble was not slight.
Alas ! quoth he, this stupid rabble
But mock me with their constant gabble ;
I go and come, and rack my brains,
And get my labour for my pains.
Your rustic owner, safe at home,
Takes all the profits as they come :
He sells his capons and his chicks,
    Or keeps them hanging on his hook,
    All dress'd and ready for his cook ;
But I, adept in art and tricks,
Should I but catch the toughest crower,
Should be brimful of joy, and more.
O Jove supreme, why was I made
A master of the fox's trade ?
By all the higher powers and lower,
I swear to rob this chicken-grower !
Revolving such revenge within,
When night had still'd the various din,
And poppies seem'd to bear full sway
O'er man and dog, as lock'd they lay
Alike secure in slumber deep,
And cocks and hens were fast asleep,
Upon the populous roost he stole.
    By negligence,—a common sin,—
The farmer left unclosed the hole,
    And, stooping down, the fox went in.
The blood of every fowl was spill'd,
The citadel with murder fill'd.
The dawn disclosed sad sights, I ween,
When heaps on slaughter'd heaps were seen,
All weltering in their mingled gore.
With horror stricken, as of yore,

The sun well nigh shrunk back again,
To hide beneath the liquid main.
Such sight once saw the Trojan plain,
When on the fierce Atrides' head
    Apollo's awful anger fell,
And strew'd the crimson field with dead :
    Of Greeks, scarce one was left to tell
The carnage of that night so dread.
Such slaughter, too, around his tent,
    The furious Ajax made, one night,
Of sheep and goats, in easy fight ;
In anger blindly confident
That by his well-directed blows
Ulysses fell, or some of those
By whose iniquity and lies
That wily rival took the prize.
The fox, thus having Ajax play'd,
    Bore off the nicest of the brood,—
    As many pullets as he could,—
And left the rest, all prostrate laid.
The owner found his sole resource
His servants and his dog to curse.
You useless puppy, better drown'd !
Why did you not your 'larum sound ?
Why did you not the evil shun,
Quoth Towser, as you might have done ?
If you, whose interest was more,
Could sleep and leave an open door,
Think you that I, a dog at best,
Would watch, and lose my precious rest ?
This pithy speech had been, in truth,
Good logic in a master's mouth ;
But, coming from a menial's lip,
It even lack'd the lawyership
To save poor Towser from the whip.

O thou who head'st a family,
(An honour never grudged by me,)
Thou art a patriarch unwise,
To sleep, and trust another's eyes.
Thyself shouldst go to bed the last,
Thy doors all seen to, shut and fast.
I charge you never let a fox see
Your special business done by proxy.

IV.—THE MOGUL'S DREAM.

Long since, a Mogul saw, in dream,
    A vizier in Elysian bliss ;
No higher joy could be or seem,
    Or purer, than was ever his.
Elsewhere was dream'd of by the same
A wretched hermit wrapp'd in flame,
Whose lot e'en touch'd, so pain'd was he,
The partners of his misery.
Was Minos mock'd ? or had these ghosts,
By some mistake, exchanged their posts ?
Surprise at this the vision broke ;
The dreamer suddenly awoke.
    Some mystery suspecting in it,
    He got a wise one to explain it.
Replied the sage interpreter, ·
Let not the thing a marvel seem :
There is a meaning in your dream :
    If I have aught of knowledge, sir,
It covers counsel from the gods.
While tenanting these clay abodes,

This vizier sometimes gladly sought
The solitude that favours thought ;
Whereas, the hermit, in his cot,
Had longings for a vizier's lot.
To this interpretation dared I add,
    The love of solitude I would inspire.
    It satisfies the heart's desire
With unencumber'd gifts and glad—
Heaven-planted joys, of stingless sweet,
Aye springing up beneath our feet.
O Solitude, whose secret charms I know—
Retreats that I have loved—when shall I go
To taste, far from a world of din and noise,
Your shades so fresh, where silence has a voice ?
When shall their soothing gloom my refuge be ?
    When shall the sacred Nine, from courts afar,
    And cities with all solitude at war,
Engross entire, and teach their votary
The stealthy movements of the spangled nights,
The names and virtues of those errant lights
Which rule o'er human character and fate ?
Or, if not born to purposes so great,
The streams, at least, shall win my heartfelt thanks,
While, in my verse, I paint their flowery banks.
Fate shall not weave my life with golden thread,
Nor, 'neath rich fret-work, on a purple bed,
Shall I repose, full late, my care-worn head.
    But will my sleep be less a treasure ?
    Less deep, thereby, and full of pleasure ?
I vow it, sweet and gentle as the dew,
Within those deserts sacrifices new ;
And when the time shall come to yield my breath,
Without remorse I'll join the ranks of Death.

V.—THE LION, THE MONKEY, AND THE TWO ASSES.

The lion, for his kingdom's sake,
In morals would some lessons take,
And therefore call'd, one summer's day,
The monkey, master of the arts,
An animal of brilliant parts,
    To hear what he could say.
Great king, the monkey thus began,
To reign upon the wisest plan
Requires a prince to set his zeal,
And passion for the public weal,
Distinctly and quite high above
A certain feeling call'd self-love,
    The parent of all vices,
    In creatures of all sizes.
To will this feeling from one's breast away,
Is not the easy labour of a day ;
'Tis much to moderate its tyrant sway.
By that your majesty august
Will execute your royal trust
From folly free and aught unjust.
    Give me, replied the king,
    Example of each thing.
    Each species, said the sage,—
    And I begin with ours,—
Exalts its own peculiar powers
Above sound reason's gauge.
Meanwhile, all other kinds and tribes
As fools and blockheads it describes,
    With other compliments as cheap.
But, on the other hand, the same
    Self-love inspires a beast to heap
The highest pyramid of fame

For every one that bears his name ;
Because he justly deems such praise
The easiest way himself to raise.
'Tis my conclusion in the case,
That many a talent here below
Is but cabal, or sheer grimace,—
The art of seeming things to know—
An art in which perfection lies
More with the ignorant than wise.

Two asses tracking, t'other day,
  Of which each in his turn
Did incense to the other burn,
  Quite in the usual way,—
I heard one to his comrade say,
  My lord, do you not find
The prince of knaves and fools
To be this man, who boasts of mind
Instructed in his schools !
  With wit unseemly and profane,
  He mocks our venerable race—
On each of his who lacketh brain
  Bestows our ancient surname, ass !
And, with abusive tongue portraying,
Describes our laugh and talk as braying !
These bipeds of their folly tell us,
While thus pretending to excel us.
No, 'tis for you to speak, my friend,
And let their orators attend.
The braying is their own, but let them be :
We understand each other, and agree,
And that's enough. As for your song,
Such wonders to its notes belong,
The nightingale is put to shame,
And Lambert loses half his fame.
My lord, the other ass replied,
Such talents in yourself reside,
Of asses all, the joy and pride.
These donkeys, not quite satisfied
With scratching thus each other's hide,
  Must needs the cities visit,
  Their fortunes there to raise,
  By sounding forth the praise,
Each, of the other's skill exquisite.
Full many, in this age of ours,—
  Not only among asses,
  But in the higher classes,
Whom Heaven hath clothed with higher powers,—
Dared they but do it, would exalt
A simple innocence from fault,
  Or virtue common and domestic,
  To excellence majestic.
I've said too much, perhaps ; but I suppose
Your majesty the secret won't disclose,
  Since 'twas your majesty's request that I
  This matter should exemplify.
How love of self gives food to ridicule,
I've shown. To prove the balance of my rule,
That justice is a sufferer thereby,
  A longer time will take.—

    'Twas thus the monkey spake.
But my informant does not state,
That e'er the sage did demonstrate
The other point, more delicate.
Perhaps he thought none but a fool
A lion would too strictly school.

VI.—THE WOLF AND THE FOX.

Why Æsop gave the palm of cunning,
O'er flying animals and running,
  To Renard Fox, I cannot tell,
Though I have search'd the subject well.
Hath not Sir Wolf an equal skill
  In tricks and artifices shown,
When he would do some life an ill,
  Or from his foes defend his own ?
I think he hath ; and, void of disrespect,
I might, perhaps, my master contradict :
Yet here 's a case, in which the burrow-lodger
Was palpably, I own, the brightest dodger.
  One night he spied within a well,
Wherein the fullest moonlight fell,
  What seem'd to him an ample cheese.
Two balanced buckets took their turns
When drawers thence would fill their urns.
  Our fox went down in one of these,
By hunger greatly press'd to sup,
And drew the other empty up.
Convinced at once of his mistake,
And anxious for his safety's sake,
He saw his death was near and sure,
  Unless some other wretch in need
The same moon's image should allure
  To take a bucket and succeed
  To his predicament, indeed.
Two days pass'd by, and none approach'd the well ;
Unhalting Time, as is his wont,
Was scooping from the moon's full front,
And as he scoop'd Sir Renard's courage fell.
His crony wolf, of clamorous maw,
  Poor fox at last above him saw,
And cried, My comrade, look you here !
See what abundance of good cheer !
  A cheese of most delicious zest !
Which Faunus must himself have press'd,
  Of milk by heifer Io given.
If Jupiter were sick in heaven,
The taste would bring his appetite.
I've taken, as you see, a bite ;
But still for both there is a plenty.
Pray take the bucket that I've sent ye ;
Come down, and get your share.
Although, to make the story fair,
The fox had used his utmost care,
The wolf (a fool to give him credit)
Went down because his stomach bid it—
  And by his weight pull'd up
  Sir Renard to the top.

We need not mock this simpleton,
For we ourselves such deeds have done.
Our faith is prone to lend its ear
To aught which we desire or fear.

√ VII.—THE PEASANT OF THE DANUBE.

To judge no man by outside view,
Is good advice, though not quite new.
Some time ago, a mouse's fright
Upon this moral shed some light.
  I have for proof at present,
  With Æsop and good Socrates,
Of Danube's banks a certain peasant,
  Whose portrait drawn to life one sees,
By Marc Aurelius, if you please.

The first are well known, far and near :
I briefly sketch the other here.
The crop upon his fertile chin
Was anything but soft or thin ;
Indeed, his person, clothed in hair,
Might personate an unlick'd bear.
Beneath his matted brow there lay
An eye that squinted every way ;
A crooked nose and monstrous lips he bore,
    And goat-skin round his trunk he wore,
With bulrush belt.   And such a man as this is
Was delegate from towns the Danube kisses,
When not a nook on earth there linger'd
By Roman avarice not finger'd.
    Before the senate thus he spoke :—
    Romans and senators who hear
I, first of all, the gods invoke,
    The powers whom mortals justly fear,
That from my tongue there may not fall
A word which I may need recall.
Without their aid there enters nought
    To human hearts of good or just :
Whoever leaves the same unsought,
    Is prone to violate his trust ;
The prey of Roman avarice,
Ourselves are witnesses of this.
Rome, by our crimes, our scourge has grown,
More than by valour of our own.
Romans, beware lest Heaven, some day,
Exact for all our groans the pay,
And, arming us, by just reverse,
    To do its vengeance, stern, but meet,
Shall pour on you the vassal's curse,
    And place your necks beneath our feet !
And wherefore not ?   For are you better
Than hundreds of the tribes diverse
Who clank the galling Roman fetter ?
    What right gives you the universe ?
Why come and mar our quiet life ?
We till'd our acres free from strife ;
In arts our hands were skill'd to toil,
As well as o'er the generous soil.
What have you taught the Germans brave ?
    Apt scholars, had but they
    Your appetite for sway,
They might, instead of you, enslave,
    Without your inhumanity.
That which your prætors perpetrate
On us, as subjects of your state,
My powers would fail me to relate.
Profaned their altars and their rites,
The pity of your gods our lot excites.
Thanks to your representatives,
In you they see but shameless thieves,
Who plunder gods as well as men.
By sateless avarice insane,
The men that rule our land from this
Are like the bottomless abyss.
To satisfy their lust of gain,
Both man and nature toil in vain.
Recall them ; for indeed we will
Our fields for such no longer till.
From all our towns and plains we fly
For refuge to our mountains high.
We quit our homes and tender wives,
To lead with savage beasts our lives—
No more to welcome into day
A progeny for Rome a prey.
And as to those already born—
    Poor helpless babes forlorn !—

We wish them short career in time :
Your prætors force us to the crime.
Are they our teachers ?   Call them home,—
    They teach but luxury and vice,—
Lest Germans should their likes become,
    In fell remorseless avarice.
Have we a remedy at Rome ?
I'll tell you here how matters go.
Hath one no present to bestow,
    No purple for a judge or so,
The laws for him are deaf and dumb ;
    Their minister has aye in store
A thousand hindrances or more.
I'm sensible that truths like these
    Are not the things to please.
I've done.   Let death avenge you here
Of my complaint, a little too sincere.

He said no more ; but all admired
The thought with which his speech was fired ;
The eloquence and heart of oak
With which the prostrate savage spoke.
Indeed, so much were all delighted,
As due revenge, the man was knighted.
    The prætors were at once displaced,
    And better men the office graced.
The senate, also, by decree,
    Besought a copy of the speech,
Which might to future speakers be
    A model for the use of each.
Not long, howe'er, had Rome the sense
To entertain such eloquence.

—————

VIII.—THE OLD MAN AND THE THREE YOUNG
                    ONES.
    ———

A MAN was planting at fourscore.
Three striplings, who their satchels wore,
    In building, cried, the sense were more ;
But then to plant young trees at that age !
The man is surely in his dotage.
    Pray, in the name of common sense,
What fruit can he expect to gather
Of all this labour and expense ?
Why, he must live like Lamech's father !
    What use for thee, grey-headed man,
    To load the remnant of thy span
With care for days that never can be thine ?
Thyself to thought of errors past resign.
    Long-growing hope, and lofty plan,
Leave thou to us, to whom such things belong.
To you ! replied the old man hale and strong ;
I dare pronounce you altogether wrong.
    The settled part of man's estate
    Is very brief, and comes full late.
    To those pale, gaming sisters trine,
    Your lives are stakes as well as mine.
    While so uncertain is the sequel,
    Our terms of future life are equal ;
For none can tell who last shall close his eyes
Upon the glories of these azure skies ;
Nor any moment give us, ere it flies,
Assurance that another such shall rise.
But my descendants, whosoe'er they be,
Shall owe these cooling fruits and shades to me.
Do you acquit yourselves, in wisdom's sight,
From ministering to other hearts' delight ?

212

Why, boys, this is the fruit I gather now ;
And sweeter never blush'd on bended bough.
Of this, to-morrow, I may take my fill ;
Indeed, I may enjoy its sweetness till
I see full many mornings chase the glooms
From off the marble of your youthful tombs.
The grey-beard man was right. One of the three,
　　Embarking foreign lands to see,
　　Was drown'd within the very port.
　　In quest of dignity at court,
　　Another met his country's foe,
　　And perish'd by a random blow.
The third was kill'd by falling from a tree
Which he himself would graft. The three
Were mourn'd by him of hoary head,
　　Who chisel'd on each monument—
　　　On doing good intent—
　　　The things which we have said.

IX.—THE MICE AND THE OWL.

　　Beware of saying, Lend an ear
To something marvellous or witty.
　To disappoint your friends who hear,
Is possible, and were a pity.
　　But now a clear exception see,
　　Which I maintain a prodigy—
A thing which with the air of fable,
Is true as is the interest-table.
　　A pine was by a woodman fell'd,
　　　Which ancient, huge, and hollow tree
　An owl had for his palace held—
　　A bird the Fates had kept in fee,
　　Interpreter to such as we.
Within the caverns of the pine,
With other tenants of that mine,
Were found full many footless mice,
But well provision'd, fat, and nice.
The bird had bit off all their feet,
And fed them there with heaps of wheat.
That this owl reason'd who can doubt ?
When to the chase he first went out,
And home alive the vermin brought,
Which in his talons he had caught,
　The nimble creatures ran away.
Next time resolved to make them stay,
He cropp'd their legs, and found, with pleasure,
That he could eat them at his leisure ;
　　It were impossible to eat
　　Them all at once, did health permit.
His foresight equal to our own,
In furnishing their food was shown.
Now, let Cartesians, if they can,
Pronounce this owl a mere machine.
Could springs originate the plan
　　Of maiming mice when taken lean,
　　To fatten for his soup-tureen ?
If reason did no service there,
I do not know it anywhere.
　Observe the course of argument:
These vermin are no sooner caught than gone :
They must be used as soon, 'tis evident ;
　　But this to all cannot be done.
　　　And then, for future need,
　　I might as well take heed.
　Hence, while their ribs I lard,
　I must from their elopement guard.

But how !—A plan complete !—
　I'll clip them of their feet !
Now, find me, in your human schools,
　A better use of logic's tools !
Upon your faith, what different art of thought
Has Aristotle or his followers taught* !

EPILOGUE.

'Tis thus, by crystal fount, my muse hath sung,
　Translating into heavenly tongue
　Whatever came within my reach,
From hosts of beings borrowing nature's speech.
　　Interpreter of tribes diverse,
I've made them actors on my motley stage ;
　　For in this boundless universe
There's none that talketh, simpleton or sage,
More eloquent at home than in my verse.
If some should find themselves by me the worse,
And this my work prove not a model true,
　To that which I at least rough-hew
Succeeding hands will give the finish due.
Ye pets of those sweet sisters nine,
　Complete the task that I resign ;
　The lessons give, which doubtless I've omitted,
　With wings by these inventions nicely fitted.
But you're already more than occupied ;
For while my muse her harmless work hath plied,
　All Europe to our sovereign yields,
　And learns, upon her battle-fields,
　　To bow before the noblest plan
　　That ever monarch form'd, or man.
　Thence draw those sisters themes sublime,
　With power to conquer Fate and Time.

BOOK XII.

I.—THE COMPANIONS OF ULYSSES.

TO MONSEIGNEUR THE DUKE DE BOURGOGNE.

Dear prince, a special favourite of the skies,
Pray let my incense from your altars rise.
With these her gifts if rather late my muse,
My age and labours must her fault excuse.
My spirit wanes, while yours beams on the sight
At every moment with augmented light :
It does not go—it runs,—it seems to fly ;
And he from whom it draws its traits so high,
In war a hero burns to do the same.
　No lack of his that, with victorious force,
　His giant strides mark not his glory's course :
Some god retains : our sovereign I might name ;
Himself no less than conqueror divine,
Whom one short month made master of the Rhine.
It needed then upon the foe to dash ;
Perhaps, to-day, such generalship were rash.
But hush,—they say the Loves and Smiles
Abhor a speech spun out in miles ;
　　And of such deities your court
　　Is constantly composed, in short.

* La Fontaine, in a note, asserts that the subject of this
fable, however marvellous, was a fact which was actually
observed. His commentators, however, think the observers
must have been in some measure mistaken, and I agree
with them.—ED.

Not but that other gods, as meet,
    There hold the highest seat :
For, free and lawless as the rest may seem,
Good Sense and Reason bear a sway supreme.
    Consult these last about the case
    Of certain men of Grecian race,
    Who, most unwise and indiscreet,
    Imbibed such draughts of poison sweet,
    As changed their form, and brutified.
Ten years the heroes at Ulysses' side
    Had been the sport of wind and tide.
      At last those powers of water
      The sea-worn wanderers bore
      To that enchanted shore
Where Circe reign'd, Apollo's daughter.
    She press'd upon their thirsty lips
Delicious drink, but full of bane:
    Their reason, at the first light sips,
Laid down the sceptre of its reign.
Then took their forms and features
The lineaments of various creatures.
To bears and lions some did pass,
Or elephants of ponderous mass;
    While not a few, I ween,
    In smaller forms were seen,—
In such, for instance, as the mole.
Of all, the sage Ulysses sole
Had wit to shun that treacherous bowl.
With wisdom and heroic mien,
And fine address, he caused the queen
To swallow, on her wizard throne,
    A poison somewhat like her own.
A goddess, she to speak her wishes dared,
    And hence, at once, her love declared.
      Ulysses, truly too judicious
      To lose a moment so propitious,
Besought that Circe would restore
His Greeks the shapes that first they wore.
Replied the nymph, But will they take them back !
Go make the proffer to the motley pack.
Ulysses ran, both glad and sure :
That poisonous cup, cried he, hath yet its cure ;
And here I bring what ends your shame and
      pain.
    Will you, dear friends, be men again ?
    Pray speak, for speech is now restored.
    No, said the lion,—and he roar'd,—
    My head is not so void of brains !
    Renounce shall I my royal gains ?
I've claws and teeth to tear my foes to bits,
    And, more than that, I'm king.
    Am I such gifts away to fling,
To be but one of Ithaca's mere cits ?
    In rank and file perhaps I might bear arms.
    In such a change I see no charms.—
Ulysses passes to the bear :—
How changed, my friend, from what you were !
    How sightly once, how ugly now !
    Humph ! truly how ?—
    Growl'd Bruin in his way—
How else than as a bear should be, I pray ?
Who taught your stilted highness to prefer
    One form to every other, sir ?
    Doth yours possess peculiar powers
    The merits to decide, of ours ?
With all respect, I shall appeal my case
To some sweet beauty of the bearish race.
Please pass it by, if you dislike my face.
    I live content, and free from care ;
    And, well remembering what we were,

I say it, plain and flat,
I'll change to no such state as that.
Next to the wolf the princely Greek
With flattering hope began to speak :—
    Comrade, I blush, I must confess,
    To hear a gentle shepherdess
    Complaining to the echoing rocks
Of that outrageous appetite
    Which drives you, night by night,
    To prey upon her flocks.
You had been proud to guard her fold
In your more honest life of old.
Pray quit this wolfship, now you can,
And leave the woods an honest man.
But is there one ? the wolf replied:
Such man, I own, I never spied.
You treat me as a ravenous beast,
But what are you ? To say the least,
You would yourself have eat the sheep,
Which, eat by me, the village weep.
Now, truly, on your faith confess,
Should I, as man, love flesh the less ?
Why, man, not seldom, kills his very brother ;
What, then, are you but wolves to one another ?
    Now, everything with care to scan,
    And rogue with rogue to rate,
    I'd better be a wolf than man,
    And need not change my state.
Thus all did wise Ulysses try,
And got from all the same reply,
As well from great as small.
Wild liberty was dear to all ;
To follow lawless appetite
They counted their supreme delight.
All banish'd from their thought and care
The glorious praise of actions fair.
Where passion led, they thought their course was
    free ;
Self-bound, their chains they could not see.

Prince, I had wish'd for you a theme to choose,
Where I might mingle pleasantry with use ;
    And I should meet with your approving voice.
    No doubt, if I could make such choice.
      At last, Ulysses' crew
      Were offer'd to my view.
    And there are like them not a few,
    Who may for penalty await
    Your censure and your hate.

———◆———

II.—THE CAT AND THE TWO SPARROWS
TO MONSEIGNEUR THE DUKE DE BOURGOGNE.

CONTEMPORARY with a sparrow tame
There lived a cat ; from tenderest age,
Of both, the basket and the cage
    Had household gods the same.
The bird's sharp beak full oft provoked the cat,
Who play'd in turn, but with a gentle pat,
His wee friend sparing with a merry laugh,
Not punishing his faults by half.
In short, he scrupled much the harm,
Should he with points his ferule arm.
The sparrow, less discreet than he,
With dagger beak made very free.
Sir Cat, a person wise and staid,
Excused the warmth with which he play'd :

For 'tis full half of friendship's art
To take no joke in serious part.
Familiar since they saw the light,
  Mere habit kept their friendship good ;
Fair play had never turn'd to fight,
  Till, of their neighbourhood,
Another sparrow came to greet
Old Ratto grave and saucy Pete.
Between the birds a quarrel rose,
  And Ratto took his side.
A pretty stranger, with such blows
  To beat our friend ! he cried.
A neighbour's sparrow eating ours !
Not so, by all the feline powers.
And quick the stranger he devours.
  Now, truly, saith Sir Cat,
I know how sparrows taste by that.
Exquisite, tender, delicate!
This thought soon seal'd the other's fate.—
But hence what moral can I bring ?
For, lacking that important thing,
A fable lacks its finishing :
I seem to see of one some trace,
But still its shadow mocks my chase.
Yours, prince, it will not thus abuse :
For you such sports, and not my muse.
In wit, she and her sisters eight
Would fail to match you with a mate.

III.—THE MISER AND THE MONKEY.

A MAN amass'd. The thing, we know,
  Doth often to a frenzy grow.
No thought had he but of his minted gold—
Stuff void of worth when unemploy'd, I hold.
Now, that this treasure might the safer be,
  Our miser's dwelling had the sea
As guard on every side from every thief.
  With pleasure very small in my belief,
  But very great in his, he there
Upon his hoard bestow'd his care.
  No respite came of everlasting
  Recounting, calculating, casting ;
For some mistake would always come
To mar and spoil the total sum.
A monkey there, of goodly size,—
And than his lord, I think, more wise,—
Some doubloons from the window threw,
And render'd thus the count untrue.
  The padlock'd room permitted
  Its owner, when he quitted,
To leave his money on the table.
One day, bethought this monkey wise
To make the whole a sacrifice
To Neptune on his throne unstable.
I could not well award the prize
Between the monkey's and the miser's pleasure
  Derived from that devoted treasure.
With some, Don Bertrand would he honour gain,
For reasons it were tedious to explain.
  One day, then, left alone,
  That animal, to mischief prone,
    Coin after coin detach'd,
    A gold jacobus snatch'd,
  Or Portuguese doubloon,
  Or silver ducatoon,
Or noble, of the English rose,
And flung with all his might

Those discs, which oft excite
The strongest wishes mortal ever knows.
  Had he not heard, at last,
  The turning of his master's key,
  The money all had pass'd
  The same short road to sea ;
And not a single coin but had been pitch'd
Into the gulf by many a wreck enrich'd.
Now, God preserve full many a financier
Whose use of wealth may find its likeness here.

IV.—THE TWO GOATS.

SINCE goats have browsed, by freedom fired,
To follow fortune they've aspired.
To pasturage they're wont to roam
Where men are least disposed to come.
If any pathless place there be,
  Or cliff, or pendent precipice,
'Tis there they cut their capers free :
There's nought can stop these dames, I wis.
  Two goats, thus self-emancipated,—
The white that on their feet they wore
Look'd back to noble blood of yore,—
  Once quit the lowly meadows, sated,
And sought the hills, as it would seem :
  In search of luck, by luck they met
Each other at a mountain stream.
As bridge a narrow plank was set,
On which, if truth must be confest,
Two weasels scarce could go abreast.
And then the torrent, foaming white,
As down it tumbled from the height,
Might well those Amazons affright.
But maugre such a fearful rapid,
Both took the bridge, the goats intrepid !
I seem to see our Louis Grand
  And Philip IV. advance
  To the Isle of Conference,
That lies 'twixt Spain and France,
Each sturdy for his glorious land.
Thus each of our adventurers goes,
Till foot to foot, and nose to nose,
Somewhere about the midst they meet,
  And neither will an inch retreat.
For why ? they both enjoy'd the glory
Of ancestors in ancient story.
The one, a goat of peerless rank
Which, browsing on Sicilian bank,
The Cyclop gave to Galatæa ;
The other famous Amalthæa,
The goat that suckled Jupiter,
  As some historians aver.
For want of giving back, in troth,
A common fall involved them both—
  A common accident, no doubt,
  On Fortune's changeful route.

TO MONSEIGNEUR THE DUKE DE BURGOGNE,

WHO HAD REQUESTED OF M. DE LA FONTAINE A FABLE
WHICH SHOULD BE CALLED "THE CAT AND THE MOUSE."

To please a youthful prince, whom Fame
  A temple in my writings vows,
What fable answers to the name,
  "The Cat and Mouse ?"

Shall I in verse the fair present,
With softest look but hard intent,
Who serves the hearts her charms entice
As does the cat its captive mice ?
Or make my subject Fortune's sport ?
She treats the friends that make her court,
And follow closest her advice,
As treats the cat the silly mice.

Shall I for theme a king select
Who sole, of all her favourites,
Commands the goddess's respect ?
For whom she from her wheel alights ?
Who, never stay'd by foes a trice,
Whene'er they block his way,
Can with the strongest play
As doth the cat with mice ?

Insensibly, while casting thus about,
Quite anxious for my subject's sake,
A theme I meet, and, if I don't mistake,
Shall spoil it, too, by spinning out.
The prince will treat my muse, for that,
As mice are treated by the cat.

V.—THE OLD CAT AND THE YOUNG MOUSE.

A YOUNG and inexperienced mouse
Had faith to try a veteran cat,—
Raminagrobis, death to rat,
And scourge of vermin through the house,—
Appealing to his clemency
With reasons sound and fair.
Pray let me live ; a mouse like me
It were not much to spare.
Am I, in such a family,
A burden ? Would my largest wish
Our wealthy host impoverish ?
A grain of wheat will make my meal ;
A nut will fat me like a seal.
I'm lean at present ; please to wait,
And for your heirs reserve my fate.
The captive mouse thus spake.
Replied the captor, You mistake ;
To me shall such a thing be said ?
Address the deaf ! address the dead !
A cat to pardon !—old one too !
Why, such a thing I never knew.
Thou victim of my paw,
By well-establish'd law,
Die as a mousling should,
And beg the sisterhood
Who ply the thread and shears,
To lend thy speech their ears.
Some other like repast
My heirs may find, or fast.
He ceased. The moral's plain.
Youth always hopes its ends to gain,
Believes all spirits like its own :
Old age is not to mercy prone.

VI.—THE SICK STAG.

A STAG, where stags abounded,
Fell sick, and was surrounded
Forthwith by comrades kind,
All pressing to assist,

Or see, their friend, at least,
And ease his anxious mind—
An irksome multitude.
Ah, sirs ! the sick was fain to cry,
Pray leave me here to die,
As others do, in solitude.
Pray, let your kind attentions cease,
Till death my spirit shall release.
But comforters are not so sent :
On duty sad full long intent,
When Heaven pleased, they went,
But not without a friendly glass ;
That is to say, they cropp'd the grass
And leaves which in that quarter grew,
From which the sick his pittance drew.
By kindness thus compell'd to fast,
He died for want of food at last.
The men take off no trifling dole
Who heal the body or the soul.
Alas the times ! do what we will,
They have their payment, cure or kill.

VII.—THE BAT, THE BUSH, AND THE DUCK.

A BUSH, duck, and bat, having found that in trade
Confined to their country small profits were made,
Into partnership enter'd to traffic abroad, [fraud.
Their purse, held in common, well guarded from
Their factors and agents, those trading allies
Employ'd where they needed, as cautious as wise :
Their journals and ledgers, exact and discreet,
Recorded by items expense and receipt.
All throve, till an argosy, on its way home,
With a cargo worth more than their capital sum,
In attempting to pass through a dangerous strait,
Went down with its passengers, sailors, and freight,
To enrich those enormous and miserly stores,
From Tartarus distant but very few doors.
Regret was a thing which the firm could but feel ;
Regret was the thing they were slow to reveal ;
For the least of a merchant well knows that the weal
Of his credit requires him his loss to conceal.
But that which our trio unluckily suffer'd
Allow'd no repair, and of course was discover'd.
No money nor credit, 'twas plain to be seen
Their heads were now threaten'd with bonnets of
    green * ;
And, the facts of the case being everywhere known,
No mortal would open his purse with a loan.
Debts, bailiffs, and lawsuits, and creditors gruff,
    At the crack of day knocking,
    (Importunity shocking !)
    Our trio kept busy enough.
The bush, ever ready and on the alert,
Now caught all the people it could by the skirt :—
Pray, sir, be so good as to tell, if you please,
If you know whereabout the old villanous seas
Have hid all our goods which they stole t'other night.
The diver, to seek them, went down out of sight.
The bat didn't venture abroad in the day,
And thus of the bailiffs kept out of the way.

Full many insolvents, not bats, to hide so,
Nor bushes, nor divers, I happen to know,
But even grand seigniors, quite free from all cares,
By virtue of brass, and of private backstairs.

---

* Such as insolvent debtors were anciently required to
wear, in France, after making cession of their effects, in
order to escape imprisonment.—ED.

VIII.—THE QUARREL OF THE DOGS AND CATS, AND THAT OF THE CATS AND MICE.

ENTHRONED by an eternal law,
Hath discord reign'd throughout the universe.
In proof, I might from this our planet draw
	A thousand instances diverse.
	Within the circle of our view,
	This queen hath subjects not a few.
	Beginning with the elements,
		It is astonishing to see
	How they have stood, to all intents,
		As wrestlers from eternity.
	Besides these four great potentates,
		Old stubborn earth, fire, flood, and air,
	How many other smaller states
		Are waging everlasting war!
In mansion deck'd with frieze and column,
	Dwelt dogs and cats in multitudes;
Decrees, promulged in manner solemn,
	Had pacified their ancient feuds.
Their lord had so arranged their meals and
		labours,
And threaten'd quarrels with the whip,
That, living in sweet cousinship,
They edified their wondering neighbours.
	At last, some dainty plate to lick,
	Or profitable bone to pick,
	Bestow'd by some partiality,
	Broke up the smooth equality.
	The side neglected were indignant
	At such a slight malignant.
Some writers make the whole dispute begin
With favours to a bitch while lying in.
	Whate'er the cause, the altercation
	Soon grew a perfect conflagration.
In hall and kitchen, dog and cat
Took sides with zeal for this or that.
	New rules upon the cat side falling
	Produced tremendous caterwauling.
Their advocate, against such rules as these,
Advised recurrence to the old decrees.
They search'd in vain, for, hidden in a nook,
The thievish mice had eaten up the book.
	Another quarrel, in a trice,
	Made many sufferers with the mice;
	For many a veteran whisker'd-face,
With craft and cunning richly stored,
	And grudges old against the race,
Now watch'd to put them to the sword;
Nor mourn'd for this that mansion's lord.

Resuming our discourse, we see
No creature from opponents free.
'Tis nature's law for earth and sky;
'Twere vain to ask the reason why;
God's works are good,—I cannot doubt it,—
And that is all I know about it.
	I know, however, that the cause
	Which hath our human quarrels brought,
	Three quarters of the time, is nought
	That will be, is, or ever was.
Ye veterans, in state and church,
	At threescore years, indeed,
	It seems there still is need
To give you lessons with the birch!

IX.—THE WOLF AND THE FOX.

WHENCE comes it that there liveth not
A man contented with his lot!
Here's one who would a soldier be,
Whom soldiers all with envy see.

A fox to be a wolf once sigh'd.
With disappointments mortified,
Who knows but that, his wolfship cheap,
The wolf himself would be a sheep!

I marvel that a prince is able,
At eight, to put the thing in fable;
While I, beneath my seventy snows,
	Forge out, with toil and time,
	The same in labour'd rhyme,
Less striking than his prose.

The traits which in his work we meet,
	A poet, it must be confess'd,
	Could not have half so well express'd:
He bears the palm as more complete.
'Tis mine to sing it to the pipe;
	But I expect that when the sands
Of Time have made my hero ripe,
	He'll put a trumpet in my hands.

My mind but little doth aspire
	To prophecy; but yet it reads
On high, that soon his glorious deeds
Full many Homers will require—
Of which this age produces few.
But, bidding mysteries adieu,
I try my powers upon this fable new.

Dear wolf, complain'd a hungry fox,
A lean chick's meat, or veteran cock's,
Is all I get by toil or trick:
Of such a living I am sick.
With far less risk, you've better cheer;
A house you need not venture near,
But I must do it, spite of fear.
Pray, make me master of your trade,
And let me by that means be made
The first of all my race that took
Fat mutton to his larder's hook:
Your kindness shall not be repented.
The wolf quite readily consented.
I have a brother, lately dead;
Go fit his skin to yours, he said.
'Twas done; and then the wolf proceeded:
Now mark you well what must be done,
The dogs that guard the flock to shun.
The fox the lessons strictly heeded.
At first, he boggled in his dress;
But awkwardness grew less and less,
Till perseverance gave success.
His education scarce complete,
A flock, his scholarship to greet,
	Came rambling out that way.
The new-made wolf his work began,
Amidst the heedless nibblers ran,
	And spread a sore dismay.
Such terror did Patroclus spread,
	When on the Trojan camp and town,
Clad in Achilles' armour dread,
	He valiantly came down.

The matrons, maids, and aged men
All hurried to the temples then.—
The bleating host now surely thought
That fifty wolves were on the spot :
    Dog, shepherd, sheep, all homeward fled,
And left a single sheep in pawn,
Which Renard seized when they were gone.
    But, ere upon his prize he fed,
There crow'd a cock near by, and down
The scholar threw his prey and gown,
That he might run that way the faster—
Forgetting lessons, prize and master.
    How useless is the art of seeming !
    Reality, in every station,
    Is through its cloak at all times gleaming,
    And bursting out on fit occasion.

Young prince, to your unrivall'd wit
My muse gives credit, as is fit,
For what she here hath labour'd with—
The subject, characters, and pith.

———

X.—THE LOBSTER AND HER DAUGHTER.

The wise, sometimes, as lobsters do,
To gain their ends back foremost go.
It is the rower's art; and those
Commanders who mislead their foes,
Do often seem to aim their sight
Just where they don't intend to smite.
My theme, so low, may yet apply
To one whose fame is very high,
    Who finds it not the hardest matter
    A hundred-headed league to scatter.
What he will do, what leave undone,
    Are secrets with unbroken seals,
    Till victory the truth reveals.
Whatever he would have unknown
Is sought in vain.   Decrees of Fate
Forbid to check, at first, the course
Which sweeps at last with torrent force.
One Jove, as ancient fables state,
Exceeds a hundred gods in weight.
So Fate and Louis would seem able
    The universe to draw,
    Bound captive to their law.—
But come we to our fable.
A mother lobster did her daughter chide :
For shame, my daughter ! can't you go ahead ?
    And how go you yourself ? the child replied ;
Can I be but by your example led !
Head foremost should I, singularly, wend,
While all my race pursue the other end !
She spoke with sense : for better or for worse,
Example has a universal force.
    To some it opens wisdom's door,
    But leads to folly many more.
    Yet, as for backing to one's aim,
      When properly pursued
      The art is doubtless good,
    At least in grim Bellona's game.

———

XI.—THE EAGLE AND THE MAGPIE.

———

The eagle, through the air a queen,
And one far different, I ween,
In temper, language, thought, and mien,—
The magpie,—once a prairie cross'd.

The by-path where they met was drear,
And Madge gave up herself for lost ;
    But having dined on ample cheer,
    The eagle bade her, Never fear ;
You're welcome to my company ;
For if the king of gods can be
    Full oft in need of recreation,—
Who rules the world,—right well may I,
    Who serve him in that high relation :
Amuse me, then, before you fly.
Our cackler, pleased, at quickest rate
Of this and that began to prate.
Not he of whom old Flaccus writes,
The most impertinent of wights,
    Or any babbler, for that matter,
    Could more incontinently chatter.
At last she offer'd to make known—
A better spy had never flown—
All things, whatever she might see,
In travelling from tree to tree.
But, with her offer little pleased—
Nay, gathering wrath at being teased,—
For such a purpose never rove,
Replied th' impatient bird of Jove.
Adieu, my cackling friend, adieu ;
My court is not the place for you :
Heaven keep it free from such a bore !
Madge flapp'd her wings, and said no more.

'Tis far less easy than it seems
    An entrance to the great to gain.
The honour oft hath cost extremes
    Of mortal pain.
The craft of spies, the tattling art,
And looks more gracious than the heart,
    Are odious there ;
But still, if one would meet success,
Of different parishes the dress
    He, like the pie, must wear.

———

XII.—THE KING, THE KITE, AND THE
FALCONER.

TO HIS AUGUST HIGHNESS, MONSEIGNEUR THE PRINCE
DE CONTI.

The gods, for that themselves are good,
The like in mortal monarchs would.
The prime of royal rights is grace ;
To this e'en sweet revenge gives place.
So thinks your highness, while your wrath
Its cradle for its coffin hath.
Achilles no such conquest knew—
In this a hero less than you.
That name indeed belongs to none,
Save those who have, beneath the sun,
Their hundred generous actions done.
The golden age produced such powers,
But truly few this age of ours.
The men who now the topmost sit,
Are thank'd for crimes which they omit.
For you, unharm'd by such examples,
A thousand noble deeds are winning temples,
Wherein Apollo, by the altar-fire,
Shall strike your name upon his golden lyre.
The gods await you in their azure dome :
One age must serve for this your lower home.
One age entire with you would Hymen dwell :
    O that his sweetest spell

For you a destiny may bind
By such a period scarce confined!
The princess and yourself no less deserve.
Her charms as witnesses shall serve ;
As witnesses, those talents high
Pour'd on you by the lavish sky,
Outshining all pretence of peers
    Throughout your youthful years.
A Bourbon seasons grace with wit :
To that which gains esteem in mixture fit,
  He adds a portion from above
    Wherewith to waken love.
To paint your joy—my task is less sublime :
  I therefore turn aside to rhyme
  What did a certain bird of prey.

A kite, possessor of a nest antique,
    Was caught alive one day.
    It was the captor's freak
    That this so rare a bird
Should on his sovereign be conferr'd.
The kite, presented by the man of chase,
With due respect, before the monarch's face,
    If our account is true,
    Immediately flew
And perch'd upon the royal nose.
What ! on the nose of majesty ?
Ay, on the consecrated nose did he.
Had not the king his sceptre and his crown ?
  Why, if he had, or had not, 'twere all one :
The royal nose, as if it graced a clown,
  Was seized. The things by courtiers done,
And said, and shriek'd, 'twere hopeless to relate.
    The king in silence sate ;
    An outcry for a sovereign king,
    Were quite an unbecoming thing.
The bird retain'd the post where he had fasten'd ;
No cries nor efforts his departure hasten'd.
His master call'd, as in an agony of pain,
Presented lure and fist, but all in vain.
    It seem'd as if the cursed bird,
    With instinct most absurd,
    In spite of all the noise and blows,
    Would roost upon that sacred nose !
The urging off of courtiers, pages, master,
But roused his will to cling the faster.
At last he quit, as thus the monarch spoke :
Give egress hence, imprimis, to this kite,
And, next, to him who aim'd at our delight.
    From each his office we revoke.
    The one as kite we now discharge ;
    The other, as a forester at large.
    As in our station it is fit,
    We do all punishment remit.
The court admired. The courtiers praised the
        deed
In which themselves did but so ill succeed.—
    Few kings had taken such a course.
  The fowler might have fared far worse ;
    His only crime, as of his kite,
    Consisted in his want of light
  About the danger there might be
  In coming near to royalty.
Forsooth, their scope had wholly been
  Within the woods. Was that a sin ?—
By Pilpay this remarkable affair
  Is placed beside the Ganges' flood.
  No human creature ventures, there,
    To shed of animals the blood :
The deed not even royalty would dare.

Know we, they say,—both lord and liege,—
This bird saw not the Trojan siege ?
Perhaps a hero's part he bore,
And there the highest helmet wore.
What once he was, he yet may be.
Taught by Pythagoras are we,
That we our forms with animals exchange ;
We're kites or pigeons for a while,
Then biped plodders on the soil ;
    And then
    As volatile, again
    The liquid air we range.—
Now since two versions of this tale exist,
I'll give the other if you list.
A certain falconer had caught
A kite, and for his sovereign thought
The bird a present rich and rare.
    It may be once a century
Such game is taken from the air ;
  For 'tis the pink of falconry.
The captor pierced the courtier crowd,
  With zeal and sweat, as if for life ;
Of such a princely present proud,
  His hopes of fortune sprang full rife ;
When, slap, the savage made him feel
His talons newly arm'd with steel,
By perching on his nasal member,
As if it had been senseless timber.
Outshriek'd the wight ; but peals of laughter,
Which threaten'd cieling, roof, and rafter,
From courtier, page, and monarch broke :
Who had not laugh'd at such a joke ?
From me, so prone am I to such a sin,
  An empire had not held me in.
I dare not say, that, had the pope been there,
He would have join'd the laugh sonorous ;
But sad the king, I hold, who should not dare
To lead for such a cause in such a chorus.
The gods are laughers. Spite of ebon brows,
Jove joins the laugh which he allows.
As history saith, the thunderer's laugh went up
When limping Vulcan served the nectar cup.
Whether or not immortals here are wise,
Good sense, I think, in my digression lies.
For, since the moral 's what we have in view,
What could the falconer's fate have taught us new ?
Who does not notice, in the course of things,
More foolish falconers than indulgent kings ?

XIII.—THE FOX, THE FLIES, AND THE
HEDGEHOG.

A FOX, old, subtle, vigilant, and sly,—
By hunters wounded, fallen in the mud,—
Attracted, by the traces of his blood,
    That buzzing parasite, the fly.
He blamed the gods, and wonder'd why
The Fates so cruelly should wish
To feast the fly on such a costly dish.
What ! light on me ! make me its food !
Me, me, the nimblest of the wood !
How long has fox-meat been so good ?
What serves my tail ? Is it a useless weight ?
Go,—Heaven confound thee, greedy reprobate !—
And suck thy fill from some more vulgar veins !
A hedgehog, witnessing his pains,
    (This fretful personage
    Here graces first my page,)

Desired to set him free
From such cupidity.
My neighbour fox, said he,
My quills these rascals shall empale,
And ease thy torments without fail.
Not for the world, my friend! the fox replied.
Pray let them finish their repast.
These flies are full. Should they be set aside,
New hungrier swarms would finish me at last.
Consumers are too common here below,
In court and camp, in church and state, we know.
Old Aristotle's penetration
Remark'd our fable's application ;
It might more clearly in our nation.
The fuller certain men are fed,
The less the public will be bled.

- - -

XIV.—LOVE AND FOLLY.

Love bears a world of mystery—
His arrows, quiver, torch, and infancy :
'Tis not a trifling work to sound
A sea of science so profound :
And, hence, t' explain it all to-day
Is not my aim, but, in my simple way,
To show how that blind archer lad
(And he a god !) came by the loss of sight,
And eke what consequence the evil had,
Or good, perhaps, if named aright—
A point I leave the lover to decide,
As fittest judge, who hath the matter tried.
Together, on a certain day,
Said Love and Folly were at play :
The former yet enjoy'd his eyes.
Dispute arose. Love thought it wise
Before the council of the gods to go,
Where both of them by birth held stations ;
But Folly, in her lack of patience,
Dealt on his forehead such a blow
As seal'd his orbs to all the light of heaven.
Now Venus claim'd that vengeance should be given.
And by what force of tears yourselves may guess
The woman and the mother sought redress.
The gods were deafen'd with her cries—
Jove, Nemesis, the stern assize
Of Orcus,—all the gods, in short,
From whom she might the boon extort.
The enormous wrong she well portray'd—
Her son a wretched groper made,
An ugly staff his steps to aid !
For such a crime, it would appear,
No punishment could be severe :
The damage, too, must be repair'd.
The case maturely weigh'd and cast,
The public weal with private squared :
Poor Folly was condemn'd at last,
By judgment of the court above,
To serve for aye as guide to Love.

- - -

XV.—THE RAVEN, THE GAZELLE, THE TOR-
TOISE, AND THE RAT.

TO MADAME DE LA SABLIÈRE.

A temple I reserved you in my rhyme :
It might not be completed but with time.
Already its endurance I had grounded
Upon this charming art, divinely founded ;

And on the name of that divinity
For whom its adoration was to be
These words I should have written o'er its gate—
To Iris is this palace consecrate ;
Not her who served the queen divine ;
For Juno's self, and he who crown'd her bliss,
Had thought it for their dignity, I wis,
To bear the messages of mine.
Within the dome the apotheosis
Should greet th' enraptured sight—
All heaven, in pomp and order meet,
Conducting Iris to her seat
Beneath a canopy of light !
The walls would amply serve to paint her life,—
A matter sweet, indeed, but little rife
In those events, which, order'd by the Fates,
Cause birth, or change, or overthrow of states.
The innermost should hold her image,—
Her features, smiles, attractions there,—
Her art of pleasing without care,—
Her loveliness, that's sure of homage.
Some mortals, kneeling at her feet,—
Earth's noblest heroes,—should be seen ;
Ay, demigods, and even gods, I ween :
(The worshipp'd of the world thinks meet,
Sometimes her altar to perfume.)
Her eyes, so far as that might be,
Her soul's rich jewel should allume ;
Alas ! but how imperfectly !
For could a heart that throbb'd to bless
Its friends with boundless tenderness,—
Or could that heaven-descended mind
Which, in its matchless beauty, join'd
The strength of man with woman's grace,—
Be given to sculptor to express ?
O Iris, who canst charm the soul—
Nay, bind it with supreme control,—
Whom as myself I can but love,—
(Nay, not that word : as I'm a man,
Your court has placed it under ban,
And we'll dismiss it,) pray approve
My filling up this hasty plan !
This sketch has here received a place,
A simple anecdote to grace,
Where friendship shows so sweet a face,
That in its features you may find
Somewhat accordant to your mind.
Not that the tale may kings beseem ;
But he who winneth your esteem
Is not a monarch placed above
The need and influence of love,
But simple mortal, void of crown,
That would for friends his life lay down—
Than which I know no friendlier act.
Four animals, in league compact,
Are now to give our noble race
A useful lesson in the case.
Rat, raven, tortoise, and gazelle,
Once into firmest friendship fell.
'Twas in a home unknown to man
That they their happiness began.
But safe from man there's no retreat :
Pierce you the loneliest wood,
Or dive beneath the deepest flood,
Or mount you where the eagles brood,—
His secret ambuscade you meet.
The light gazelle, in harmless play,
Amused herself abroad one day,
When, by mischance, her track was found
And follow'd by the baying hound—

220

That barbarous tool of barbarous man —
From which far, far away she ran.
    At meal-time to the others
    The rat observed,—My brothers,
    How happens it that we
    Are met to-day but three ?
Is Miss Gazelle so little steady ?
Hath she forgotten us already ?
Out cried the tortoise at the word,—
    Were I, as Raven is, a bird,
    I'd fly this instant from my seat,
And learn what accident, and where,
Hath kept away our sister fair,—
    Our sister of the flying feet ;
    For of her heart, dear rat,
    It were a shame to doubt of that.
        The raven flew ;
He spied afar,—the face he knew,—
The poor gazelle entangled in a snare,
In anguish vainly floundering there.
Straight back he turn'd, and gave the alarm ;
For to have ask'd the sufferer now,
The why and wherefore, when and how,
She had incurr'd so great a harm,—
        And lose in vain debate
        The turning-point of fate,
As would the master of a school,—
He was by no means such a fool.
On tidings of so sad a pith,
The three their council held forthwith.
        By two it was the vote
        To hasten to the spot
    Where lay the poor gazelle.
    Our friend here in his shell,
    I think, will do as well
To guard the house, the raven said ;
    For, with his creeping pace,
    When would he reach the place ?
    Not till the deer was dead.
    Eschewing more debate,
    They flew to aid their mate,
    That luckless mountain roe.
The tortoise, too, resolved to go.
Behold him plodding on behind,
And plainly cursing in his mind,
The fate that left his legs to lack,
And glued his dwelling to his back.
The snare was cut by Rongemail,
(For so the rat they rightly hail.)
Conceive their joy yourself you may.
Just then the hunter came that way,
And, Who hath filch'd my prey ?
    Cried he, upon the spot
    Where now his prey was not.—
    A hole hid Rongemail ;
    A tree the bird as well ;
    The woods, the free gazelle.
The hunter, well nigh mad,
To find no inkling could be had,
Espied the tortoise in his path,
And straightway check'd his wrath.
    Why let my courage fag ?
Because my snare has chanced to miss ?
I'll have a supper out of this.
He said, and put it in his bag.
And it had paid the forfeit so,
Had not the raven told the roe,
    Who from her covert came,
    Pretending to be lame.
The man, right eager to pursue,

Aside his wallet threw,
    Which Rongemail took care
To serve as he had done the snare ;
    Thus putting to an end
The hunter's supper on his friend.
'Tis thus sage Pilpay's tale I follow.
Were I the ward of golden-hair'd Apollo,
It were, by favour of that god, easy—
    And surely for your sake—
    As long a tale to make
    As is the Iliad or Odyssey.
Grey Rongemail the hero's part should play,
Though each would be as needful in his way.
He of the mansion portable awoke
    Sir Raven by the words he spoke,
To act the spy, and then the swift express.
The light gazelle alone had had th' address
The hunter to engage, and furnish time
For Rongemail to do his deed sublime.
Thus each his part perform'd. Which wins the prize ?
The heart, so far as in my judgment lies.

XVI.—THE WOODS AND THE WOODMAN.

A CERTAIN wood-chopper lost or broke
From his axe's eye a bit of oak.
The forest must needs be somewhat spared
While such a loss was being repair'd.
Came the man at last, and humbly pray'd
    That the woods would kindly lend to him—
    A moderate loan—a single limb,
Whereof might another helve be made,
And his axe should elsewhere drive its trade.
O, the oaks and firs that then might stand,
A pride and a joy throughout the land,
For their ancientness and glorious charms !
The innocent Forest lent him arms ;
But bitter indeed was her regret ;
For the wretch, his axe new-helved and whet,
Did nought but his benefactress spoil
Of the finest trees that graced her soil ;
And ceaselessly was she made to groan,
Doing penance for that fatal loan.

Behold the world-stage and its actors,
Where benefits hurt benefactors !—
    A weary theme, and full of pain ;
For where 's the shade so cool and sweet,
Protecting strangers from the heat,
    But might of such a wrong complain ?
        Alas ! I vex myself in vain :
        Ingratitude, do what I will,
        Is sure to be the fashion still

XVII.—THE FOX, THE WOLF, AND THE HORSE.

A FOX, though young, by no means raw,
Had seen a horse—the first he ever saw :
Ho ! neighbour wolf, said he to one quite green,
A creature in our meadow I have seen,—
    Sleek, grand ! I seem to see him yet,—
    The finest beast I ever met.
    Is he a stouter one than we ?
    The wolf demanded, eagerly.
    Some picture of him let me see.
If I could paint, said fox, I should delight
T' anticipate your pleasure at the sight ;

But come ; who knows ? perhaps it is a prey
  By fortune offer'd in our way.
They went. The horse, turn'd loose to graze,
Not liking much their looks or ways,
    Was just about to gallop off.
Sir, said the fox, your humble servants, we
Make bold to ask you what your name may be.
The horse, an animal with brains enough,
Replied, Sirs, you yourselves may read my name ;
My shoer round my heel hath writ the same.
The fox excused himself for want of knowledge :
Me, sir, my parents did not educate,—
So poor, a hole was their entire estate.
My friend, the wolf, however, taught at college,
    Could read it were it even Greek.
    The wolf, to flattery weak,
    Approach'd, to verify the boast ;
    For which, four teeth he lost.
The high-raised hoof came down with such a blow,
As laid him bleeding on the ground full low.
My brother, said the fox, this shows how just
  What once was taught me by a fox of wit,—
  Which on thy jaws this animal hath writ,—
" All unknown things the wise mistrust."

XVIII.—THE FOX AND THE TURKEYS.

AGAINST a robber fox, a tree
  Some turkeys served as citadel.
  That villain, much provoked to see
  Each standing there as sentinel,
    Cried out, Such witless birds
At me stretch out their necks, and gobble !
No, by the powers ! I'll give them trouble.
    He verified his words.
The moon, that shined full on the oak,
Seem'd then to help the turkey folk.
But fox, in arts of siege well versed,
Ransack'd his bag of tricks accursed.
He feign'd himself about to climb ;
Walk'd on his hinder legs sublime ;
Then death most aptly counterfeited,
And seem'd anon resuscitated.
    A practiser of wizard arts
    Could not have fill'd so many parts.
    In moonlight he contrived to raise
His tail, and make it seem a blaze :
And countless other tricks like that.
Meanwhile, no turkey slept or sat.
Their constant vigilance at length,
As hoped the fox, wore out their strength.
Bewilder'd by the rigs he run,
They lost their balance one by one.
As Renard slew, he laid aside,
Till nearly half of them had died ;
Then proudly to his larder bore,
And laid them up, an ample store.

A foe, by being over-heeded,
Has often in his plan succeeded.

XIX.—THE APE.

THERE is an ape in Paris,
  To which was given a wife :
Like many a one that marries,
  This ape, in brutal strife,
Soon beat her out of life.

Their infant cries,—perhaps not fed,—
    But cries, I ween, in vain ;
The father laughs : his wife is dead,
  And he has other loves again,
Which he will also beat, I think,—
Return'd from tavern drown'd in drink.

For aught that's good, you need not look
    Among the imitative tribe ;
A monkey be it, or what makes a book—
  The worse, I deem—the aping scribe.

XX.—THE SCYTHIAN PHILOSOPHER.

A SCYTHIAN philosopher austere,
Resolved his rigid life somewhat to cheer,
Perform'd the tour of Greece, saw many things,
But, best, a sage,—one such as Virgil sings,—
A simple, rustic man, that equal'd kings ;
From whom the gods would hardly bear the palm,
  Like them unawed, content, and calm.
His fortune was a little nook of land ;
And there the Scythian found him, hook in hand,
His fruit-trees pruning.   Here he cropp'd
A barren branch, there slash'd and lopp'd,
    Correcting Nature everywhere,
    Who paid with usury his care.
    Pray, why this wasteful havoc, sir ?—
    So spoke the wondering traveller ;
    Can I, I ask, in reason's name,
    Be wise these harmless trees to maim ?
    Fling down that instrument of crime,
    And leave them to the scythe of Time.
    Full soon, unhasten'd, they will go
    To deck the banks of streams below.
    Replied the tranquil gardener,
    I humbly crave your pardon, sir ;
    Excess is all my hook removes,
    By which the rest more fruitful proves.
    The philosophic traveller,—
    Once more within his country cold,—
    Himself of pruning-hook laid hold,
    And made a use most free and bold ;
Prescribed to friends, and counsel'd neighbours,
To imitate his pruning labours.
The finest limbs he did not spare,
But pruned his orchard past all reason,
Regarding neither time nor season,
  Nor taking of the moon a care.
    All wither'd, droop'd, and died.
    This Scythian I set beside
The indiscriminating Stoic.
The latter, with a blade heroic,
Retrenches, from his spirit sad,
Desires and passions, good and bad,
Not sparing e'en a harmless wish.
Against a tribe so Vandalish
With earnestness I here protest.
    They maim our hearts, they stupefy
    Their strongest springs, if not their best ;
They make us cease to live before we die.

XXI.—THE ELEPHANT AND THE APE OF
JUPITER.

'TWIXT elephant and beast of horned nose
About precedence a dispute arose,
Which they determined to decide by blows.
The day was fix'd, when came a messenger

To say the ape of Jupiter
Was swiftly earthward seen to bear
His bright caduceus through the air.
This monkey, named in history Gill,
The elephant at once believed
A high commission had received
To witness, by his sovereign's will,
The aforesaid battle fought.
Uplifted by the glorious thought,
The beast was prompt on Monsieur Gill to wait,
But found him slow, in usual forms of state,
His high credentials to present.
The ape, however, ere he went,
Bestow'd a passing salutation.
His excellency would have heard
The subject matter of legation :
          But not a word !
His fight, so far from stirring heaven,—
The news was not received there, even !
What difference sees the impartial sky
Between an elephant and fly ?
Our monarch, doting on his object,
Was forced himself to break the subject.
My cousin Jupiter, said he,
Will shortly, from his throne supreme,
A most important combat see,
For all his court a thrilling theme.
What combat? said the ape, with serious face.
Is't possible you should not know the case !—
The elephant exclaim'd—not know, dear sir,
That Lord Rhinoceros disputes
With me precedence of the brutes ?
    That Elephantis is at war
    With savage hosts of Rhinoccr ?
You know these realms, not void of fame !
I joy to learn them now by name,
Return'd Sir Gill, for, first or last,
No lisp of them has ever pass'd
Throughout our dome so blue and vast.
Abash'd, the elephant replied,
    What came you, then, to do ?—
Between two emmets to divide
    A spire of grass in two.
    We take of all a care ;
    And, as to your affair,
Before the gods, who view with equal eyes
The small and great, it hath not chanced to rise.

———◆———

XXII.—THE FOOL AND THE SAGE.

A FOOL pursued, with club and stone,
A sage, who said, My friend, well done !
Receive this guinea for your pains ;
They well deserve far higher gains.
The workman 's worthy of his hire,
'Tis said.   There comes a wealthy squire,
Who hath wherewith thy works to pay ;
To him direct thy gifts, and they
Shall gain their proper recompense.
    Urged by the hope of gain,
    Upon the wealthy citizen
The fool repeated the offence.
His pay this time was not in gold.
    Upon the witless man
A score of ready footmen ran,
And on his back, in full, his wages told.
In courts, such fools afflict the wise ;

They raise the laugh at your expense.
To check their babble, were it sense
Their folly meetly to chastise ?
Perhaps 'twill take a stronger man.
Then make them worry one who can.

———◆———

XXIII.—THE ENGLISH FOX.
TO MADAM HARVEY.

SOUND reason and a tender heart
With thee are friends that never part.
A hundred traits might swell the roll ;—
Suffice to name thy nobleness of soul ;
Thy power to guide both men and things ;
Thy temper open, bland and free,
A gift that draweth friends to thee,
To which thy firm affection clings,
Unmarr'd by age or change of clime,
Or tempests of this stormy time ;—
All which deserve, in highest lyric,
A rich and lofty panegyric :
But no such thing wouldst thou desire,
Whom pomp displeases, praises tire.
Hence mine is simple, short, and plain ;
    Yet, madam, I would fain
    Tack on a word or two
Of homage to your country due,—
    A country well beloved by you.

With mind to match the outward case,
The English are a thinking race.
They pierce all subjects through and through ;
Well arm'd with facts, they hew their way,
And give to science boundless sway.
Quite free from flattery, I say,
Your countrymen, for penetration,
Must bear the palm from every nation ;
For e'en the dogs they breed excel
Our own in nicety of smell.
Your foxes, too, are cunninger,
As readily we may infer
From one that practised, 'tis believed,
A stratagem the best conceived.
The wretch, once, in the utmost strait
By dogs of nose so delicate,
Approach'd a gallows, where,
A lesson to like passengers,
Or clothed in feathers or in furs,
Some badgers, owls, and foxes, pendent were.
Their comrade, in his pressing need,
Arranged himself among the dead.
I seem to see old Hannibal
Outwit some Roman general,
And sit securely in his tent,
The legions on some other scent.
But certain dogs, kept back
To tell the errors of the pack,
Arriving where the traitor hung,
A fault in fullest chorus sung.
Though by their bark the welkin rung,
Their master made them hold the tongue.
Suspecting not a trick so odd.
Said he, the rogue 's beneath the sod.
My dogs, that never saw such jokes,
Won't bark beyond these honest folks.

The rogue would try the trick again.
He did so to his cost and pain.
Again with dogs the welkin rings ;
Again our fox from gallows swings ;

But though he hangs with greater faith,
This time, he does it to his death.
    So uniformly is it true,
    A stratagem is best when new.
The hunter, had himself been hunted,
So apt a trick had not invented,
Not that his wit had been deficient ;—
    With that, it cannot be denied,
Your English folks are well-provision'd ;—
    But wanting love of life sufficient,
    Full many an Englishman has died.

One word to you, and I must quit
    My much-inviting subject :
    A long eulogium is a project
For which my lyre is all unfit.
The song or verse is truly rare,
Which can its meed of incense bear,
And yet amuse the general ear,
Or wing its way to lands afar.
Your prince once told you, I have heard,
    (An able judge, as rumour says,)
That he one dash of love preferr'd
    To all a sheet could hold of praise.
Accept—'tis all I crave—the offering
Which here my muse has dared to bring—
    Her last, perhaps, of earthly acts ;
    She blushes at its sad defects.
    Still, by your favour of my rhyme,
Might not the self-same homage please, the while,
    The dame who fills your northern clime
    With wingéd emigrants sublime
        From Cytherea's isle ?
By this, you understand, I mean
Love's guardian goddess, Mazarin.

<hr/>

XXIV.—THE SUN AND THE FROGS.

Long from the monarch of the stars
    The daughters of the mud received
Support and aid ; nor dearth nor wars,
    Meanwhile, their teeming nation grieved.
They spread their empire far and wide
Through every marsh, by every tide.
The queens of swamps—I mean no more
    Than simply frogs (great names are cheap)—
Caball'd together on the shore,
    And cursed their patron from the deep,
And came to be a perfect bore.
Pride, rashness, and ingratitude,
The progeny of fortune good,
Soon brought them to a bitter cry,—
The end of sleep for earth and sky.
Their clamours, if they did not craze,
Would truly seem enough to raise
All living things to mutiny
Against the power of Nature's eye.
The sun, according to their croak,
Was turning all the world to smoke.
It now behoved to take alarm,
And promptly powerful troops to arm.
    Forthwith in haste they sent
    Their croaking embassies ;
To all their states they went,
    And all their colonies.
To hear them talk, the all
That rides upon this whirling ball,
Of men and things, was left at stake
Upon the mud that skirts a lake !

The same complaint, in fens and bogs,
    Still ever strains their lungs ;
And yet these much-complaining frogs
    Had better hold their tongues ;
For, should the sun in anger rise,
And hurl his vengeance from the skies,
That kingless, half-aquatic crew
Their impudence would sorely rue.

<hr/>

XXV.—THE LEAGUE OF THE RATS.

A mouse was once in mortal fear
Of a cat that watch'd her portal near.
What could be done in such a case ?
With prudent care she left the catship,
And courted, with a humble grace,
A neighbour of a higher race,
Whose lordship—I should say his ratship—
Lay in a great hotel ;
And who had boasted oft, 'tis said,
Of living wholly without dread.
    Well, said this braggart, well,
    Dame Mouse, what should I do ?
    Alone I cannot rout
    The foe that threatens you.
I'll rally all the rats about,
And then I'll play him such a trick !
    The mouse her courtesy dropp'd,
And off the hero scamper'd quick,
Nor till he reach'd the buttery stopp'd,
Where scores of rats were clustered,
    In riotous extravagance,
All feasting at the host's expense.
To him, arriving there much flustered,
    Indeed, quite out of breath,
A rat among the feasters saith,
What news ? what news ? I pray you, speak.
The rat, recovering breath to squeak,
Replied, To tell the matter in a trice,
It is, that we must promptly aid the mice ;
For old Raminagrab is making
Among their ranks a dreadful quaking.
This cat, of cats the very devil,
When mice are gone, will do us evil.
    True, true, said each and all ;
    To arms ! to arms ! they cry and call.
    Some ratties by their fears
    Were melted e'en to tears.
    It matter'd not a whisk,
    Nor check'd the valour brisk.
        Each took upon his back
        Some cheese in havresack,
    And roundly swore to risk
        His carcass in the cause.
    They march'd as to a feast,
    Not flinching in the least,—
But quite too late, for in his jaws
The cat already held the mouse.
They rapidly approach'd the house—
To save their friend, beyond a doubt.
Just then the cat came growling out,
The mouse beneath his whisker'd nose,
And march'd along before his foes.
At such a voice, our rats discreet,
    Foreboding a defeat,
    Effected, in a style most fleet,
        A fortunate retreat.
Back hurried to his hole each rat,
And afterwards took care to shun the cat.

XXVI.—DAPHNIS AND ALCIMADURE.

AN IMITATION OF THEOCRITUS.

TO MADAME DE LA MÉSANGÈRE.

OFFSPRING of her to whom, to-day,
While from thy lovely self away,
A thousand hearts their homage pay*,
Besides the throngs whom friendship binds to please,
And some whom love presents thee on their knees!
A mandate which I cannot thrust aside
Between you both impels me to divide
Some of the incense which the dews distil
Upon the roses of a sacred hill,
And which, by secret of my trade,
Is sweet and most delicious made.
To you, I say, ... but all to say
Would task me far beyond my day ;
I need judiciously to choose ;
Thus husbanding my voice and muse,
Whose strength and leisure soon will fail.
I'll only praise your tender heart, and hale,
Exalted feelings, wit, and grace,
In which there's none can claim a higher place,
Excepting her whose praise is your entail.
Let not too many thorns forbid to touch
These roses—I may call them such—
If Love should ever say as much.
By him it will be better said, indeed ;
And them who his advices will not heed,
    Scourge fearfully will he,
    As you shall shortly see.

A blooming miracle of yore
Despised his godship's sovereign power ;
They call'd her name Alcimadure.
A haughty creature, fierce and wild,
She sported, Nature's tameless child.
Rough paths her wayward feet would lead
To darkest glens of mossy trees ;
Or she would dance on daisied mead,
    With nought of law but her caprice.
    A fairer could not be,
    Nor crueller, than she.
Still charming in her sternest mien,—
    E'en when her haughty look debarr'd,—
What had she been to lover, in
The fortress of her kind regard !
Daphnis, a high-born shepherd swain,
Had loved this maiden to his bane.
Not one regardful look or smile,
Nor e'en a gracious word, the while,
Relieved the fierceness of his pain.
O'erwearied with a suit so vain,
    His hope was but to die ;
    No power had he to fly.
He sought, impell'd by dark despair,
The portals of the cruel fair.
Alas ! the winds his only listeners were !
The mistress gave no entrance there—
No entrance to the palace where,
Ingrate, against her natal day,
She join'd the treasures sweet and gay
In garden or in wild-wood grown,
To blooming beauty all her own.
    I hoped, he cried,
Before your eyes I should have died ;

* Madame de la Mésangère was the daughter of Madame
de la Sabliere.

But, ah ! too deeply I have won your hate ;
Nor should it be surprising news
To me, that you should now refuse
    To lighten thus my cruel fate.
My sire, when I shall be no more,
Is charged to lay your feet before
The heritage your heart neglected.
With this my pasturage shall be connected,
My trusty dog, and all that he protected ;
    And, of my goods which then remain,
    My mourning friends shall rear a fanc.
There shall your image stand, midst rosy bowers,
Reviving through the ceaseless hours
An altar built of living flowers.
Near by, my simple monument
Shall this short epitaph present :
" Here Daphnis died of love. Stop, passenger,
    And say thou, with a falling tear,
This youth here fell, unable to endure
    The ban of proud Alcimadure."

He would have added, but his heart
Now felt the last, the fatal dart.
Forth march'd the maid, in triumph deck'd,
And of his murder little reck'd.
In vain her steps her own attendants check'd,
    And plead
    That she, at least, should shed,
    Upon her lover dead,
    Some tears of due respect.
The rosy god, of Cytherea born,
She ever treated with the deepest scorn :
Contemning him, his laws, and means of damage,
She drew her train to dance around his image,
    When, woful to relate,
The statue fell, and crush'd her with its weight !
    A voice forth issued from a cloud,—
    And echo bore the words aloud
    Throughout the air wide spread,—
" Let all now love—the insensible is dead."
Meanwhile, down to the Stygian tide
    The shade of Daphnis hied,
And quaked and wonder'd there to meet
The maid, a ghostess, at his feet.
All Erebus awaken'd wide,
To hear that beauteous homicide
Beg pardon of the swain who died,
For being deaf to love confess'd,
    As was Ulysses to the prayer
    Of Ajax, begging him to spare,
Or as was Dido's faithless guest.

XXVII.—THE ARBITER, THE ALMONER, AND THE HERMIT.

THREE saints, for their salvation jealous,
Pursued, with hearts alike most zealous,
By routes diverse, their common aim.
All highways lead to Rome : the same
Of heaven our rivals deeming true,
Each chose alone his pathway to pursue.
Moved by the cares, delays, and crosses
Attach'd to suits by legal process,
One gave himself as judge, without reward,
For earthly fortune having small regard.
Since there are laws, to legal strife
Man damns himself for half his life.

For half !—Three-fourths !—perhaps the whole !
  The hope possess'd our umpire's soul,
That on his plan he should be able
To cure this vice detestable.—
The second chose the hospitals.
  I give him praise : to solace pain
  Is charity not spent in vain,
While men in part are animals.
The sick—for things went then as now they go—
Gave trouble to the almoner, I trow.
  Impatient, sour, complaining ever,
As rack'd by rheum, or parch'd with fever,—
  His favourites are such and such ;
  With them he watches over-much,
    And lets us die, they say,—
  Such sore complaints from day to day
  Were nought to those that did await
  The reconciler of debate.
  His judgments suited neither side ;
    Forsooth, in either party's view,
    He never held the balance true.
  But swerved in every cause he tried.

Discouraged by such speech, the arbiter
Betook himself to see the almoner.
As both received but murmurs for their fees,
  They both retired, in not the best of moods,
  To break their troubles to the silent woods,
And hold communion with the ancient trees.
  There, underneath a rugged mountain,
  Beside a clear and silent fountain,
A place revered by winds, to sun unknown,
They found the other saint, who lived alone.
  Forthwith they ask'd his sage advice.
  Your own, he answer'd, must suffice ;

Who but yourselves your wants should know ?
  To know one's self, is, here below,
  The first command of the Supreme.
Have you obey'd, among the bustling throngs ?
Such knowledge to tranquillity belongs ;
  Elsewhere to seek were fallacy extreme.
Disturb the water—do you see your face ?
  See we ourselves within a troubled breast ?
    A murky cloud in such a case,
    Though once it were a crystal vase !
    But, brothers, let it simply rest,
And each shall see his features there impress'd.
For inward thought a desert home is best.

  Such was the hermit's answer brief ;
  And, happily, it gain'd belief.

But business, still, from life must not be stricken.
Since men will doubtless sue at law, and sicken,
Physicians there must be, and advocates,—
Whereof, thank God, no lack the world awaits,
While wealth and honours are the well-known baits.
Yet, in the stream of common wants when thrown,
What busy mortal but forgets his own ?
O, you who give the public all your care,
  Be it as judge, or prince, or minister,
  Disturb'd by countless accidents most sinister,
By adverse gales abased, debased by fair,—
Yourself you never see, nor *see* you aught.
Comes there a moment's rest for serious thought,
There comes a flatterer too, and brings it all to
  This lesson seals our varied page :   [nought.
  O, may it teach from age to age !
  To kings I give it, to the wise propose.
Where could my labours better close ?

INDEX.

THE END.

THE UNIVERSAL LIBRARY

OF THE

BEST WORKS OF THE BEST AUTHORS OF ALL NATIONS,

IN ALL DEPARTMENTS OF LITERATURE,

BEAUTIFULLY AND UNIFORMLY PRINTED IN ROYAL OCTAVO, WITH TWO OR MORE FIRST-CLASS ILLUSTRATIONS
TO EACH NUMBER, AND A HANDSOME COVER.

/0 4 0

PROSPECTUS

IN adding to the number of cheap popular Libraries now in course of publication, it is necessary
briefly to describe the characteristic features of the present undertaking. These may be stated as

1. The Standard Excellence of the Works selected.
2. The Variety and Number of Subjects and Authors.
3. The Excellence of the Type, the Printing, and the Paper.
4. The Beauty of the Illustrations.
5. The Cheapness of the Price.
6. The Convenience of the mode of Publication.

1. *The Standard Excellence of the Works selected.*—No work will be included in this Library which has not already
so completely gained universal approbation as to have become an indispensable part of the world's literature;
such works as ought to be found in every public library, and which the present undertaking will place within the
reach of the inmates of every house where the English language is spoken.

2. *The Variety and Number of Subjects and Authors.*—The Library will embrace works in

I.—HISTORY AND BIOGRAPHY.	IV.—FICTION.
II.—VOYAGES AND TRAVELS.	V.—ESSAYS AND CRITICISM.
III.—POETRY.	VI.—MISCELLANEOUS WORKS.

The authors from whose works selections will be made, will include the best writers of all countries, as the
following selection from the list will show :—

ENGLISH.			ITALIAN.	GERMAN.
	JOHNSON.	LE SAGE.		
	KIRKE WHITE.	MOLIÈRE.		
ADDISON.	LOCKE.	MONTAIGNE.		FOUQUE.
ALISON.	MILTON.	RACINE.	ALFIERI.	GOETHE.
ANSON.	PARK.	ST. PIERRE.	ARIOSTO.	SCHILLER.
BEATTIE.	POPE.	VOLTAIRE.	DANTE.	WIELAND, &c.
BLAIR.	ROBERTSON.	VERTOT, &c.	MACHIAVELLI.	
BURNS.	SCOTT.		MARCO POLO.	
CHAUCER.	SHAKSPEARE.		PETRARCH, &c.	
COOK.	STERNE.	**SPANISH AND**		**AMERICAN.**
COLLINS.	THOMSON, &c.	**PORTUGUESE.**		
CRABBE.				BRYANT.
DRYDEN.	**FRENCH.**	CAMOENS.	**SWEDISH.**	CHILD.
GOLDSMITH.		CERVANTES.		EMERSON.
GRAY.	BÉRANGER.	LOPE DE VEGA.	BREMER.	IRVING.
IZAAK WALTON.	LA PEROUSE.	QUEVEDO, &c.	CARLEN, &c.	SEDGWICK, &c.

with a varied selection of works from the Greek and Roman Classics and from Oriental writers. The works
chosen from the writers enumerated will be printed from the best texts, and the translation from foreign authors
will be made with accuracy and spirit. Original notes will be added whenever they are considered necessary.

3. *The Excellence of the T*... *ting, and the Paper.*—The work will be printed in a clear readable type, in
double columns, on su*... ...*ressly for this Library.

4. *The Beauty of*... ...*r will contain two or more highly finished engravings; consisting
either of port*... ...*s of scenes forming the subject of the works. The preparation
...*nt artists, among whom may be mentioned Dodgson,

...*r will contain, in addition to the engravings, about
be ONE SHILLING. As, however, it is intended that
lly vary according to the size of the work, but the
octavo pages for one shilling.

Library will be issued which does not contain one
e under no obligation or necessity to continue the
in one number, the works thus embraced, will be
5th of each month, and the subjects specified in
a sufficient number of works on one subject are
e convenience of those who prefer to purchase the
the cost in both cases will be the same.

& CO., 227 STRAND.

Lightning Source UK Ltd.
Milton Keynes UK
UKHW022201270223
417761UK00005B/364